WE'MOON '00

OPEN

GAIA RHYTHMS FOR WOMYN

published by

 Mother Tongue Ink

WE LOVINGLY DEDICATE **WE'MOON '00** TO
MARSHA A. GOMEZ (1951–1998)
(SEE "DEDICATION" P. 188)

Opening
© *Donna Goodwin 1998*

TABLE OF CONTENTS

1. INTRODUCTION

11. MOON CALENDAR*

*Feature writers for the calendar pages of **We'Moon '00**: Astrological predictions by **Gretchen Lawlor**, holy day writing with an herbal focus by **Colette Gardiner**. **Disclaimer:** any herbal or astrological information herein should be used with caution, common sense, and the approval of your health care practitioner, astrologer and/or other sources you trust.

111. APPENDIX

2000

JANUARY

M	T	W	T	F	S	S
					1	2
3	4	5	(6)	7	8	9
10	11	12	13	14	15	16
17	18	19	(20)	21	22	23
24	25	26	27	28	29	30
31						

FEBRUARY

M	T	W	T	F	S	S
	1	2	3	4	(5)	6
7	8	9	10	11	12	13
14	15	16	17	18	(19)	20
21	22	23	24	25	26	27
28	29					

MARCH

M	T	W	T	F	S	S
		1	2	3	4	(5)
6	7	8	9	10	11	12
13	14	15	16	17	18	(19)
20	21	22	23	24	25	26
27	28	29	30	31		

APRIL

M	T	W	T	F	S	S
					1	2
3	(4)	5	6	7	8	9
10	11	12	13	14	15	16
17	(18)	19	20	21	22	23
24	25	26	27	28	29	30

MAY

M	T	W	T	F	S	S
1	2	(3)	4	5	6	7
8	9	10	11	12	13	14
15	16	17	(18)	19	20	21
22	23	24	25	26	27	28
29	30	31				

JUNE

M	T	W	T	F	S	S
			1	(2)	3	4
5	6	7	8	9	10	11
12	13	14	15	(16)	17	18
19	20	21	22	23	24	25
26	27	28	29	30		

JULY

M	T	W	T	F	S	S
					(1)	2
3	4	5	6	7	8	9
10	11	12	13	14	15	(16)
17	18	19	20	21	22	23
24	25	26	27	28	29	(30)
31						

AUGUST

M	T	W	T	F	S	S
	1	2	3	4	5	6
7	8	9	10	11	12	13
(14)	15	16	17	18	19	20
21	22	23	24	25	26	27
28	(29)	30	31			

SEPTEMBER

M	T	W	T	F	S	S
				1	2	3
4	5	6	7	8	9	10
11	12	(13)	14	15	16	17
18	19	20	21	22	23	24
25	26	(27)	28	29	30	

OCTOBER

M	T	W	T	F	S	S
						1
2	3	4	5	6	7	8
9	10	11	12	(13)	14	15
16	17	18	19	20	21	22
23	24	25	26	(27)	28	29
30	31					

NOVEMBER

M	T	W	T	F	S	S
		1	2	3	4	5
6	7	8	9	10	(11)	12
13	14	15	16	17	18	19
20	21	22	23	24	(25)	26
27	28	29	30			

DECEMBER

M	T	W	T	F	S	S
				1	2	3
4	5	6	7	8	9	10
(11)	12	13	14	15	16	17
18	19	20	21	22	23	24
(25)	26	27	28	29	30	31

Fools in Balance

¤ *Martine Palmiter 1998*

◯ = NEW MOON, PST

◯ = FULL MOON, PST

What Is *We'Moon*? A Handbook in Natural Cycles

We'Moon: Gaia Rhythms for Womyn is more than an appointment book, it's a way of life! **We'Moon** is a lunar calendar, a handbook in natural rhythm and comes out of international womyn's culture. Art and writing by we'moon from many lands give a glimpse of the great diversity and uniqueness of a world we create in our own image. **We'Moon** is about *womyn's spirituality* (spirit'reality). We share how we live our truth, what inspires us, how we envision our reality in connection with the whole earth and all our relations.

We'moon means "**women.**" Instead of defining ourselves in relation to men (as in *wo*man or *fe*male), we use the word *we'moon* to define ourselves by our primary relation to the natural sources of cosmic flow ("we of the moon"). Other terms we'moon use are *womyn, wimmin, womon, womb-one*. **We'Moon** is a moon calendar for we'moon. As we'moon, we seek to be whole in ourselves, rather than dividing ourselves in half and hoping that some "other half" will complete the picture. We see the whole range of life's potential embodied by we'moon, and do not divide the universe into sex-role stereotypes according to a heterosexual model. **We'Moon** is sacred space in which to explore and celebrate the diversity of she-ness on earth. The calendar is we'moon's space.

We'moon means "**we of the moon.**" The moon, whose cycles run in our blood, is the original womyn's calendar. Like the moon, we'moon circle the earth. We are drawn to one another. We come in different shapes, colors and sizes. We are continually transforming. With all our different hues and points of view, we are one.

We'moon culture exists in the diversity and the oneness of our experience as we'moon. *We honor both.* We come from many cultures, from very different ways of life. At the same time, we have a culture of our own as we'moon, sharing a common mother root. We are glad when we'moon from many different cultures contribute art and writing. When material is borrowed from cultures other than our own, we ask that it be acknowledged and something given in return. Being conscious of our sources keeps us from engaging in the divisiveness of either *cultural appropriation* (taking what belongs to others) or *cultural fascism* (controlling creative expression). We invite every we'moon to share how the "Mother Tongue" speaks to her, with respect for both cultural integrity and individual freedom.

Casseopeia of the Night Sky
© *Sudie Rakusin 1998*

Gaia Rhythms: We show the natural cycles of the moon, sun, planets and stars as they relate to earth. By recording our own activities side by side with those of other heavenly bodies, we may notice what connection, if any, there is for us. The earth revolves around her axis in one day; the moon orbits around the earth in one month (29$^{1}/_{2}$ days); the earth orbits around the sun in one year. We experience each of these cycles in the alternating rhythms of day and night, waxing and waning, summer and winter. The earth/moon/sun are our inner circle of kin in the universe. We know where we are in relation to them at all times by the dance of light and shadow as they circle around one another.

The Eyes of Heaven: As seen from earth, the moon and the sun are equal in size: "the left and right eye of heaven," according to Hindu (Eastern) astrology. Unlike the solar-dominated calendars of Christian (Western) patriarchy, the **We'Moon** looks at our experience through both eyes at once. The **lunar eye** of heaven is seen each day in the phases of the moon as she is both reflector and shadow, traveling her 29$^{1}/_{2}$-day path through the zodiac. The **solar eye** of heaven is apparent at the turning points in the sun's cycle. The year begins with Winter Solstice (in the Northern Hemisphere), the dark renewal time, and journeys through many seasons and balance points (solstices, equinoxes and the cross-quarter days in-between). The **third eye** of heaven may be seen in the stars. Astrology measures the cycles by relating the sun, moon and all other planets in our universe through the star signs (the zodiac), helping us to tell time in the larger cycles of the universe.

Measuring Time and Space: Imagine a clock with many hands. The earth is the center from which we view our universe. The sun, moon and planets are like the hands of the clock. Each one has its own rate of movement through the cycle. The ecliptic, a band of sky around the earth within which all planets have their orbits, is the outer band of the clock where the numbers are. Stars along the ecliptic are grouped into constellations forming the signs of the zodiac—the twelve star signs are like the twelve numbers of the clock. They mark the movements of the planets through the 360° circle of the sky, the clock of time and space.

Whole Earth Perspective: It is important to note that all natural cycles have a mirror image from a whole earth perspective—seasons occur at opposite times in the Northern and Southern Hemispheres and day and night occur at opposite times on opposite sides of the earth as well. Even the moon plays this game—a waxing crescent moon in Australia faces right (e.g., ☾), while in North America it faces left (e.g., ☽). **We'Moon** has a Northern Hemisphere perspective regarding times, holy days, seasons and lunar phases.

Whole Sky Perspective: It is also important to note that all over the earth, in varied cultures and times, the dome of the sky has been interacted with in countless ways. *The* zodiac we speak of is just one of many ways that hu-moons have pictured and related to the stars. In this calendar, we use the tropical zodiac.   □ *Musawa 1999*

WHAT'S NEW THIS YEAR

We'Moon '00 contains some changes from past years. We are listing them here all in one place for easy reference:
• With the Open theme, each Moon is numbered with Roman numerals (ie., **Moon III**). There are no sub-thematic titles this year (ie., **III. Tides Moon**).
• The names of the days of the week and months are in English with additional foreign language translations included. This year we feature Esperanto, Swahili, German and Hawaiian.
• The pages are now numbered throughout the calendar to facilitate cross referencing. See Table of Contents (p. 3) and Contributor Bylines and Index (pp. 189–198).
• The locations from which eclipses are visible can now be found on the particular date, along with time and type of eclipse.
• We are using only Pacific Time (PST or PDT) for all calendar and astrological events—see World Time Zones (p. 220).
• On the two-page holy day spreads (see all equinoxes, solstices and cross quarter days), we have a new feature which includes holy day descriptions with an herbal focus. This is a marriage of two of our past regular features—the herbal and the holy day writing.   7

How to Use This Book: Key to the *We'Moon*

Below and on the following pages you will find terms and symbols, with explanations, keyed to their uses in **We'Moon**. See "Signs and Symbols at a Glance" (p. 221) for an easy fingertip reference. We think you will find this a very handy guide when using **We'Moon**.

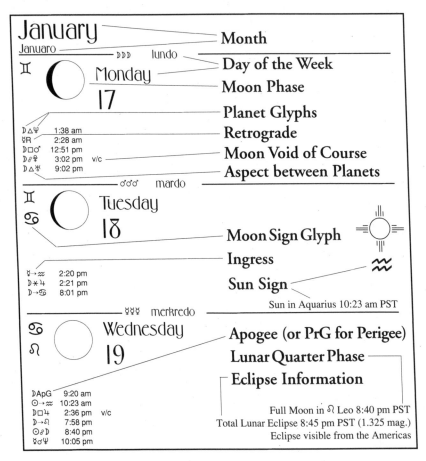

Astrology Basics

Planets: Planets are like chakras in our solar system, allowing for different frequencies or types of energies to be expressed.

Signs: The twelve signs of the zodiac are a mandala in the sky, marking off 30° segments in the 360° circle around the earth. Signs show major shifts in planetary energy through the cycles.

Glyphs: Glyphs are the symbols used to represent planets and signs.

8

Features of the Calendar Pages

Sun Sign: The sun enters a new sign once a month (around the 20th or so), completing the whole cycle of the zodiac in one year. The sun sign reflects qualities of your outward shining self. For a description of sign qualities see "Sun Signs" (pp. 17–19).

Moon Sign: The moon changes signs approximately every $2^1/_2$ days, going through all twelve signs of the zodiac every $29^1/_2$ days (the sidereal month). The moon sign reflects qualities of your core inner self. For descriptions see "Moon Signs and Transits" (pp. 20–21).

Moon Phase: Each calendar day is marked with a graphic representation of the phase that the moon is in. Although the moon is not usually visible in the sky during the new or dark moon, we represent her using miniscule crescent moon graphics for the days immediately before and after the *actual* new moon or conjunction. For more information about the moon see related articles on pp. 22–24.

Lunar Quarter Phase: At the four quarter points of the lunar cycle (new, waxing half, full and waning half) we indicate the phase, sign and exact time for each. These points mark off the "lunar week".

Day of the Week: Each day is associated with a planet whose symbol appears in the line above it (e.g., DDD is for Moon: Moonday, Monday, Luna Day, lundi, lunes). The names of the days of the week are displayed prominently in English with translations appearing in the line above them. The four languages (Esperanto, Swahili, German, Hawaiian) rotate weekly in this order throughout the calendar.

Eclipse: The time of greatest eclipse is given, which is not the exact time of the conjunction or opposition. Locations from where eclipses are visible are also given. For lunar and partial solar eclipses, magnitude is given in decimal form (e.g., 0.881 mag.), denoting the fraction of the moon's diameter obscured by the shadow of Earth. For total and annular solar eclipses, the duration of the eclipse in minutes and seconds is given. For more information see "Eclipses" (p. 25).

Daily Aspectarian

Below are explanations of the various symbols found on each day that indicate a variety of planetary movements and relationships.

Aspects (□△𝄐♂⚹⚻): These show the angle of relation between different planets. An aspect is like an astrological weather forecast for the day, indicating which energies are working together easily and which combinations are more challenging. See "Signs and Symbols at a Glance" (p. 221) for a brief explanation of each kind.

Ingresses (→): Indicate planets moving into new signs.

Moon Void of Course (☽ v/c): The moon is said to be void of course from the last significant lunar aspect in each sign until the moon enters a new sign. This is a good time to ground and center yourself.

Apogee (ApG): This is the point in the orbit of a planet or the Moon that is farthest from Earth. The effects of transits at this time may be less noticeable immediately, but may appear later on.

Perigee (PrG): This is the point in the orbit of a planet or the Moon that is nearest to Earth. Transits with the Moon or other planets when they are at perigee will be more intense.

Direct or Retrograde (D or R): These are times when a planet moves forward (D) or backward (R) through the signs of the zodiac (an optical illusion, as when a moving train passes a slower train which appears to be going backward). When a planet is in direct motion, planetary energies are more straightforward; in retrograde, planetary energies turn back in on themselves, are more involuted.

Other Useful Features of the We'Moon

Moon Pages mark each moon cycle with an art-filled two-page spread near the new moon. They contain the dates of that Moon's solar and lunar events (new and full moon and solar ingresses).

Month and Year at a Glance Calendars can be found on pp. 208–219 and p. 4. Month at a Glance pages include daily lunar phases.

Annual Predictions: For your annual astrological portrait, turn to Gretchen Lawlor's prediction for your sun sign, located around the time of your birthday, on the same page that the sun enters that sign. See also "How to Use the Astrological Predictions" (p. 15).

Holyday/Herb Feature: For descriptions of each of the eight holy days with an herbal focus, turn to Colette Gardiner's writings on pp. 47, 67, 85, 103, 121, 139, 157 and 175.

Time Zones: All aspects are in Pacific Standard/Daylight Time, with the adjustment for GMT and EDT given at the bottom of each page. To calculate for other areas, see "World Time Zones" (p. 220).

Planetary Ephemeris: Exact planetary positions for every day are given on pp. 202–207. These ephemerides show where each planet is in a zodiac sign at noon GMT, measured by degree in longitude.

Asteroid Ephemeris: Exact positions of asteroids for every ten days are given for sixteen asteroids in the zodiac at midnight GMT on p. 201. See "Asteroids" (p. 199) for more information.

Introduction to the Theme: Open

We open this book this year, this century, this millennium, this moment with the theme, *Open*. In our Call for Contributions, we invoked an "open theme" and/or the theme of "open(ing)". The very sound of '00 ("Oh-Oh"), and what happens to your mouth when you say it, introduces our theme, *Open!*

Each year, We'Moon numerology guides us to a Tarot card image for the **We'Moon** theme. '00 evokes the Tarot card numbered zero: The Fool. '0' is a circle with no beginning and no end; '00 is two circles which, when joined together, form the infinity sign. The Fool is the interface in the double helix of the cosmic forces at work (represented by the Major Arcana in Tarot) and the karmic forces of each one's individual lessons (represented by the Minor Arcana in Tarot).

The Cosmic Fool (00) juggles the polarities of life, holding the balance where the two circles join while the earth-bound/karmic fool (0) is tossed around like a ball, up and down with each new experience. In the modern 52-card playing deck, the entire Major Arcana has been reduced to this one wild card, commonly known as the Joker. With only a Joker as our 'spirit guide' in the game of life, is it any wonder that the survival of life on Earth is now poised in the balance? We are no longer playing with a full deck!

The Fool is a character known in many cultures. In Native American traditions, Heyokah is the sacred clown, and Coyote or Raven are tricksters. The Hawaiian mischief-maker is called Kolohe. Baubo is a lusty Greek female clown who made Demeter laugh in her grief. Baubo also appears in ancient Japanese myth. Traditionally the Fool combines the spontaneity and innocence of a child, the power and surprise of a wild animal, the crazy wisdom of a clown. In Tarot, the Fool is an androgynous figure, pictured as a playful child walking on her hands, a disgruntled jester with a dog pulling on the seat of her pants, or a romantic visionary wandering with her head in the clouds about to walk over the edge of a cliff.

The Fool, with her brave and innocent spirit, invites us to leap into the 21st Century and into leap year 2000. Using her guidance, we engage the mystery of life wherever we meet it, to become all of who we are. She asks only that we follow the path of heart and be true to our Spirit selves. This is not an easy task, especially after thousands of years of patriarchial tom-foolery. What she doesn't tell us is that to embark on the Fool's journey, we also risk being fooled, being foolish, being a fool in our unknowing. She plays hide-and-seek with us in the course of our lives, leading us on deeper into the Mystery.

In such a world, we are never sure what is reality and what is illusion. What year is it? Does the new millennium begin now or not? It may sound foolish to ask but really, it depends on the starting point in the calendar you use. What we call the year 2000 in the Christian-based Gregorian calendar is counted as the year 5760 in the Hebrew

© *Katelyn Mariah 1996*

calendar or the year 4637 in the Chinese calendar. Neither the new millennium nor the new year begins now in either of them. Even in the Gregorian calendar, technically speaking, the new millennium does not begin until January 1, 2001, because the current era (CE) began with the year 1 (i.e., there was no year zero between 1 BC and 1 AD) and the passage of 2000 years would therefore bring us to 2001.

And what of Y2K? Even though the designation 2000 CE is arbitrary and meaningless in the grand scheme of things, this demarcation is no simple movement of beads on the abacus. The abacus is now hard-wired into the edifice of contemporary life. Modern society depends on computer networks which may or may not handle this flip of the calendar page gracefully. No one knows how or where the uninstructed computer chips will fall in '00.

The riddle of Y2K is a perfect conundrum for our time. Computer technocrats chose short-run profits over wise planning fifty years ago when they created binary computer dating good only until the end of the century. Consider, by contrast, the wisdom of indigenous cultures where each new change is weighed in light of the people's welfare for seven generations to come.

Earth-loving peoples have always known what Y2K scenarios anticipate: that we and all beings of Gaia, the living earth, are profoundly interconnected. Technology, for all the ways in which it isolates and fragments people, can serve to link us through vast electronic networks, sparking with information, communication and interaction. But technology has tricked us into dependence on and interdependence through machines, endangering our connection with the planet, our selves and one another in the body, here and now. The trick may now be on techno-patriarchy: the man-made webs are fragile indeed, flawed by design, and they may snap—oh oh! Maybe the Joker who brings us the Y2K bug is a Goddess in disguise, trying to shift the consciousness of those who refuse to hear the message in the cries of Mother Earth.

So here we are in a Fool's quandary ourselves as we write this Introduction, not knowing what the year 2000 will bring. When you read this, we will have already gone over the hump—whatever its dimensions—into the '00 year. Luckily, with the Fool as our guide, we get to raise questions; we do not have to know the answers.

By opening a channel for the creative expression of we'moon experience, as always, **We'Moon** invites the living Goddess to speak for Herself. In creating **We'Moon**, we open to what womyn send our way, spin the thematic threads of art and writing and weave them in with natural cycles throughout the year.

The art and writing, along with the movements of heavenly bodies recorded every day, can be viewed as a kind of oracle. What does the image you see today open up for you about your life now? We chose to weave themes loosely through the 13 Moons this year, instead of our customary focus on a sub-theme for each Moon.

The calendar pages open (Moons 0 and I) and close (Moon XIII) with attention to the millennial shift, with strong positive affirmations about global healing and the birth of a new era. In these first Moons, we introduce the Fool's adventures, and we begin to weave the thread of life-cycles, from birth through maturity, to cronehood and death—images of personal and generational change which surface throughout the Moons to follow. Caring for the endangered planet threads through Moons IV and VI, and we see hands-on tending of earth on the Spring and Fall Equinox pages. Love among women enters by Moon V, and the love women give to their work is imaged in

13

Moon IX. We honor Goddess imagery in several Moons, weaving ritual and connection with Spirit into this fabric. Moon X invites us to enter Mystery through gateways and openings, both literal and figurative. At any moment in these Moon pages, or in the course of the year, be prepared to encounter a wild, foolish presence—the surprise of laughter, upside-down reality, the waft of unusual wings.

Whatever the coming year holds for us, there is no fooling about the widespread sense of momentous shifts underway at this time in herstory, whether they have to do with earth changes predicted by ancient and contemporary sources, cybernetic unknowns of the Y2K computer bug, or the cumulative collapse of fundamental structures in society world-wide. The world as we know it is changing drastically. Sheer survival is becoming a dominant issue for endangered species, grade school children, whole peoples, the Earth Herself.

We are all in the position of the Fool facing the unknown, the Mystery. How do people who depend directly or indirectly on technology, the natural world and each other, undertake the challenges of deep transformation and encounter with the unknown? In Eastern and earth-based cultures, the unknown is seen as the sacred source of creation, embodied as a Goddess who is revered. She is known as Innana, Shakti, Kali, Hecate, the Dark Mother, Changing Woman, Spider Woman. Shall we encounter her domain—chaos, the abyss, the void—by opening, by trusting the source of all change and moving to embrace new possibilities? Or will fear and violence shut us down? Destructive events and apocalyptic fantasies abound, as does creative energy for transformation. We are seeing renewed impetus for creating community, restorative ecology, alternative energy, simplicity in lifestyle, wholistic healing, natural building, feminist process, healthier relationships, diversity awareness, opening to spirit. What is the growing edge for you?

May our hearts be open to guidance and to what is asked of us in this year's journey. Let us consciously participate in the Earth's revolution/evolution. This **We'Moon** is an invitation to find our inter-relations through natural means. Let the Moon be our loom through which we weave the web of our spirit connection to one another. Listen to the Motherbeat. As we move with her, we can dance together through the changes to come.

□ *Musawa and Bethroot 1999*

How to Use the Astrological Predictions

Predictions for each sun sign will be found on the We'Moon page where the Sun enters that sign. If you know your rising sign, more specific information may be gathered by reading both sun and rising sign predictions, watching for repeated themes as well as any jangling dissonance. The planetary cycles and shifts provide an excellent symbolic navigational map for your own journey through the year.

© *Hazel Collins 1997*

I include below some recommendations for flower essences that can provide healing or support for challenges we will all encounter in the year 2000.[1]

To nourish jangled nerves due to the Uranian/Aquarian configurations and eclipse aggravations use Aspen for pervading fear without determined cause, Garlic to support depleted immune systems, Indian Pink to attain calm in the midst of social, political and environmental reorganization, Mimulus for anxiety about providing for daily needs of self and family, Pink Yarrow for over-sensitivity to environmental disturbances.

To support participation in the work of reinventing the future use Scotch Broom to serve despite despair, Blackberry to materialize inspirations, Mountain Pride to become a warrior for your beliefs, Tansy to cut through lethargy. To become a vessel of genius: Buttercup to value your unique contribution, Hound's Tongue for integration of right and left brain, Iris to create art beyond cultural limits, Pomegranate to nourish wisdom emerging from womb source, Star Tulip to become conduit for the Divine.

For group work use Quaking Grass to blend individual egos for common purpose, Violet to release fear of losing self in group, Shasta Daisy to weave individual contributions into a greater whole, Sage to create wiser perspective in group decision-making and integrating elder wisdom into the circle. © *Gretchen Lawlor 1999*

[1] These flower essences can be acquired through Centergees Flower Essence Pharmacy 1-800-343-8693 or www.floweressences.com

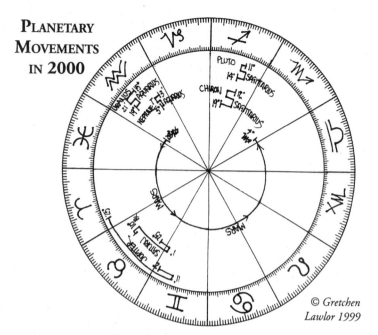

© Gretchen
Lawlor 1999

THE PLANETARY DANCE 2000

What do the skies tell us of this millennial shift? 1999 was a series of political, social, and environmental landmines with changemaker Uranus repeatedly blasting the potent midpoint 15° of Aquarius. Intensified by a series of eclipses, the forces of change cut us free from any habits, old alliances, patterns that no longer served life.

With Uranus moving into the constructive phase of its transit of Aquarius, we will witness more positive innovation during the next 3½ years. Solutions, inventions, new pathways become clear as we reinvent the future, each one of us like tiny electrical storms in the night sky. Pursue rogue impulses, embrace new friends and collaborations. The tribes are reconfiguring in all arenas.

Neptune has joined Uranus in Aquarius in the last few years. Invite imagination and deep compassion through ritual, music or art for a divinely guided, living vision of the future.

Jupiter moves to conjunct Saturn in May 2000. This occurs every 20 years bringing epiphanies of ways to be more involved in our social groupings. Move away from solo, self-gratifying efforts. Watch for opportunities to take on an important social role. Your urges in this new cycle herald a collective move towards a healthier way of being.

© *Gretchen Lawlor 1999*

SUN SIGNS

The zodiac is like a curved measuring tape around the earth, marked off in stars. As the earth whirls and circles in her own rhythm, she sees the constellations turning around her, moving always in the same order. Against their background appear the sun, moon and planets.

Our calendar is based on the tropical zodiac that charts the sun's year-long journey through the signs, beginning with 0° Aries on Spring Equinox in the Northern Hemisphere. As the sun illuminates each sign in turn, we can boldly express the unique genius of that sign. The sun represents vitality, pride, creative energy and the outward expression of self-knowledge. In your natal chart, your sun sign is only one influence among many, but it shows the traits that you strive to develop in order to become most fully yourself. To love your sun sign is to love yourself.

Each sign belongs to a particular element (fire, earth, air or water) and quality (cardinal, mutable or fixed). Within the language of the zodiac, the ancients packed a great deal of esoteric knowledge, and so the signs tell a story about the process of realization. Perhaps their wisest message is that this path is circular, like a spiral staircase that takes you forever higher. All signs both lead and follow each other.

♈ **ARIES** (March 19–April 19): Aries is the essential hero, triumphing over obstacles, shaping herself through action. She is the perennial innocent, always beginning anew. When the sun moves through this cardinal fire sign, you are more spontaneous and independent. Your blood stirs and you're ready to follow it into a new day.

♉ **TAURUS** (April 19–May 20): Taurus moves through the physical world with tranquility and strength, responding to what's real, encouraging us to look honestly at our lives. She builds slowly but for life. When the sun goes through this fixed earth sign, you can put down enduring foundations. Take time also to revel in the sensual pleasures of the moment.

♊ **GEMINI** (May 20–June 20): Gemini is quick and her mind always dancing. She makes lightning connections between one idea and another, between one person and another. Like a cat, closed doors drive her crazy. When the sun goes through this mutable air sign, let your feet and mind roam and check out the interesting people in your neighborhood.

♋ **CANCER** (June 20–July 22): A Cancer womon is both mother and child. She is the gentle care-giver and also the tearful tot gripping her stuffed bear. She is vulnerable and sensitive, so her trust is a precious gift. When the sun is in this cardinal water sign, open yourself up to emotional experiences. Join other womyn who are building caring communities.

♌ **LEO** (July 22–August 22): Brilliant Leo is always the center of attention as she gives everything she is. One minute she's dramatic and the next playful, mesmerizing her audience. Her will is like the magician's wand, a tool for transformation. When the sun moves through this fixed fire sign, celebrate your creative gifts, your passion and joy.

♍ **VIRGO** (August 22–September 22): Virgo, the worker, trains her considerable intellect on the practical realm. She grows plants, heals bodies, fixes broken chairs and draws up intricate plans. When the sun moves through this mutable earth sign, you are very sensitive to details and can handle small, complicated tasks. Your goal is order.

♎ **LIBRA** (September 22–October 22): Libra is the idealist. She is the one who looks out for justice in the world and champions the disenfranchised. Her focus is the shifting energy between two people or ideas. When the sun is in this cardinal air sign, take initiative to promote harmony and balance in relationships and community.

Crow Dancer
◻ *Tracy Harrison 1998*

♏ SCORPIO (October 22–November 21): Scorpio may be quiet and soft-voiced, but she has a definite sense of what's hers. Her emotions run deep—rushing waters filling underground caves. Her strong desires are the source of her power. When the sun goes through this fixed water sign, reach for a friend or lover and explore your own hidden desires.

♐ SAGITTARIUS (November 21–December 21): Sagittarius, the Amazon, is always exploring new territory, racing horseback into the wild unknown. She looks for the spark of inspiration and then fans it into a fire. When the sun goes through this mutable fire sign, you respond to the heat of the moment. You may travel or join others in a noble cause.

♑ CAPRICORN (December 21–January 21): Capricorn, with sustained hard work, reaches the top of the mountain. She feels proud, strong, capable. But then she turns, sees another mountain, and she's off again. When the sun moves through this cardinal earth sign, you are more disciplined and persistent. Whether running for Congress, developing your spiritual practice or building a house, you get it done.

♒ AQUARIUS (January 21–February 19): Valuing truth above everything, Aquarius works to make the world a more enlightened place. She shares everything she has—her wisdom, experience and integrity. When the sun is in this fixed air sign, teach people and learn from them. If you join with other like-minded souls, as Susan B. Anthony said, "failure is impossible."

♓ PISCES (February 19–March 19): Pisces is lyrical and sensitive and endlessly mysterious, even to herself. She absorbs the energy around her, merging, melting, shape-shifting. When the sun's in this mutable water sign, open yourself up to fantasy. Sing, dance and tell the old stories. Watch for the little people as you walk in the woods.

◻ *Jenny Yates 1998*

MOON SIGNS AND TRANSITS

The moon circles the earth quickly, passing through all the signs of the zodiac in 28 days. She is generous with her changes, offering a new zodiacal perspective every 2½ days. When the moon reaches the sign that the sun is in, she becomes invisible, her light vanishing into the sun's brilliance. This is the dark moon, the new moon, a time to seed new beginnings. After this phase, she grows steadily night by night.

When she reaches her fullest form, she is in the opposite sign from the sun. This is a time to express yourself fully, to integrate both the outwardly active sun sign and the inwardly reflective moon sign. The moon urges you to express your inner nature by bringing all truths up to the light. The pressure can be intense leading to bouts of lunacy, but the joy of seeing yourself whole is also intense.

The moon is symbolically connected with emotions, water and the mother. Her changes are reflected deep within us in the ways we nurture ourselves and others. Some signs are more fertile than others, better for planting, creating and conceiving. However, each sign has its gifts for your soul as well as for your garden.

Moon in Aries—As the moon moves into Aries, she raises some basic identity questions. You stand stripped bare of formalities knowing yourself as you truly are. Many new beginnings are hatched now, but the energy is too fiery for safe planting.

Moon in Taurus—In Taurus, the moon brings calm and stability. The buzz subsides and you notice the things that endure: the feel of wood and rock, the smell of your lover's skin, the cycles of the soil. This fertile sign encourages strong, slow growth.

Moon in Gemini—The Gemini moon stimulates your curiosity. Interesting ideas appear constantly, like doors opening up to reveal other doors. Now is the time to make connections, perhaps via e-mail or telephone. Explore your garden, learn from it, but don't plant.

Moon in Cancer—As she moves into Cancer, the moon brings up memories and all the emotions that accompany them. This is a fertile time as tears fall more readily nourishing your roots. All arts are encouraged, especially the alchemy of cooking.

Moon in Leo—When the moon enters Leo, your inner child wants attention, as do your inner clown and your inner prima donna. Turn all the commotion into art and then celebrate your creative power. In the garden, cultivate and admire, but don't plant.

Moon in Virgo—In Virgo, the moon moves towards a simple, useful life. If anything needs mending in body or soul, now is the time to focus your healing powers. In the garden or at home, you can arrange, shape and tend.

Moon in Libra—With the moon in Libra, you need more beauty in your life. Plant flowers, fill your house with them or give them to a woman you love. You are more tender and romantic, conscious of the subtle dances of human connection.

Moon in Scorpio—When the moon passes through Scorpio, feelings are intense and desires powerful. You delve into your deepest self with its shadows and dragons, and you recognize the untapped power there. Anything planted now grows deep and strong.

Moon in Sagittarius—With moon in Sagittarius, feelings range wide as you amble down the road, watch the stars, or read old philosophy books. The search is more important than the finding. Take a break from your garden as your energy is restless now.

Moon in Capricorn—As the moon moves into Capricorn, your inner Wise Woman is very strong. She can show you how to take old fears and sorrows and turn them into resolve, ambition and discipline. Anything you plant now will have strong roots.

Moon in Aquarius—As she moves through Aquarius, the moon brings the liberation of understanding. You can detach yourself from old emotional patterns and see your mother, lover and friends as individuals. Talk to your green friends now, but don't plant new ones.

Moon in Pisces—When the moon's in Pisces, distinctions blur and barriers dissolve. Your rational mind may go hide under a rock while your intuitive mind moves joyfully and unerringly in the cosmic dance. This is a fertile time. Everything yields.

◻ *Jenny Yates 1998*

Lunar Rhythm

Everything that flows moves in rhythm with the moon. She rules the water element on earth. She pulls on the ocean's tides, the weather, female reproductive cycles, and the life fluids in plants, animals and people. She influences the underground currents in earth energy, the mood swings of mind, body, behavior and emotion. The moon is closer to the earth than any other heavenly body. The earth actually has two primary relationships in the universe: one with the moon who circles around her and one with the sun whom she circles around. Both are equal in her eyes. The phases of the moon reflect the dance of all three: the moon, the sun, and the earth, who together weave the web of light and dark into our lives. No wonder so much of our life on earth is intimately connected with the phases of the moon!   ◘ *Musawa 1998*

The Eight Lunar Phases

As above, so below. Look into the sky and observe which phase the moon is in. Then you will know where you are in the growth cycle of each lunar month. The phase that the moon was in when you were born reflects your purpose, personality and preferences.

1. The **new moon** is like a SEED planted in the earth. We cannot see her but she is ready to grow, full of potential and energy for her new journey. We'moon born during the new moon are impulsive, passionate, and intuitive. They are risk takers and pioneers.

2. The **crescent moon** is the SPROUT. The seed has broken through the earth and reaches upward as she ventures from the dark, moist earth she has known. We'moon born during the crescent moon must break from the past, from the culture of their childhood, to create their own destiny. They represent the next generation, the new order that improves on the past.

3. The **first quarter moon** (waxing half moon) is the GROWTH phase. Roots go deeper, the stem shoots up, and leaves form as she creates a new strong body. We'moon born during the first quarter moon live a full life of much activity and excitement as old structures are cleared away to provide room for new developments.

4. The **gibbous moon** is the BUD of the plant, the pulse of life tightly wrapped, wanting to expand. For we'moon born during the gibbous moon, their talents lie in the ability to refine,

organize and purify. They are seekers, utilizing spiritual tools as guides and allies on their journey to self-discovery.

5. She opens and blossoms during the **full moon** into the FLOWER, with the desire to share her beauty with others. We'moon born during the full moon enjoy companionship and partnership and have a desire to merge deeply. Fulfillment, abundance, and illumination are their goals.

6. As we go into the darkening phase of the **disseminating moon,** we get the FRUIT of the plant's life cycle, the fruits of wisdom and experience. For we'moon born during the disseminating moon, life must have meaning and purpose. They enjoy sharing their beliefs and ideas with others and are often teachers.

7. The **last quarter moon** (waning half moon) is the HARVEST phase, when the plant gives her life so that others may continue theirs. We'moon born during the last quarter have a powerful internal life of reflection and transformation. They can assume different roles and wear many masks while balancing their internal and external worlds.

8. The **balsamic moon** is the COMPOST phase, when the nutrients remain in the soil, providing nourishment for the next new seed. We'moon born during the balsamic moon possess the potential to be wise, insightful, understanding and patient. They are prophetic and unique and march to the beat of their own drummer.

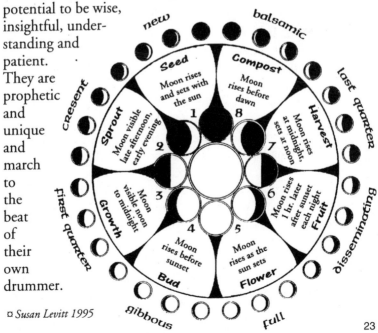

◻ *Susan Levitt 1995*

23

WHERE'S THAT MOON ?

Why is the moon sometimes visible during the day? And why does the moon sometimes rise very late at night? The answers lie in what phase the moon is in, which reflects the angle between the sun and moon as seen from earth. For each of the eight moon phases, the angle between the sun and moon progresses in 45° increments. Each phase lasts approximately 3–4 days of the moon's entire 29^1/$_2$ day cycle.

The **new moon** (or dark moon) rises at sunrise and sets at sunset. Astrologically, the sun and the moon are in *conjunction*. Because the sun's light overpowers the nearby moon in the day, and the moon is on the other side of the earth with the sun at night, she is not visible in the sky at all.

The **crescent moon** (or waxing crescent moon) rises midmorning and sets after sunset. She is the first visible sliver of moon seen in the western sky in the late afternoon and early evening.

The **first quarter moon** (or waxing half moon) rises around noon and sets around midnight. Astrologically, the moon is *square* to the sun. She is visible from the time she rises until she sets.

The **gibbous moon** rises midafternoon and sets before dawn. She is the bulging moon getting ready to be full, visible soon after she rises until she sets.

The **full moon** rises at sunset and sets at sunrise. Astrologically, the sun and moon are in *opposition* (ie., opposite each other in the sky and in opposite signs of the zodiac). She is visible all night long from moonrise to moonset.

The **disseminating moon** is the waning full moon getting visibly smaller. She rises midevening and sets midmorning. She is visible from the time she rises almost until she sets.

The **last quarter moon** (or waning half moon) rises around midnight and sets around noon. Astrologically, the moon is *square* to the sun. She is visible from the time she rises until she sets.

The **balsamic moon** (or waning crescent moon) rises before dawn and sets midafternoon. She is the last sliver of moon seen in the eastern sky in the dawn and the very early morning.

© *Susan Levitt, Musawa and Beth Freewomon 1998*

ECLIPSES

Eclipses demonstrate deep processes of transformation. They crack open doors to our true selves. Eclipses remind us that we are indeed not in control of our lives, and that our choices manifest in our response to external stimuli. We can either recognize our fantastic natures and grow like wild flowers, or react to our external world with fear of change. We can use the alignment of the sun, moon and earth as a great ally in our own process of deep transformation. Since ancient times astrologers have used the eclipse as a means of prediction. To determine the effect of a specific eclipse, check your natal chart and find out in what house the eclipse falls. Each house governs a specific activity or area. The effects of an eclipse are felt whether it's visible or not.

A solar eclipse is a conjunction of the Sun and Moon (new moon) and can be either total, partial or annular. A lunar eclipse is an opposition of the Sun and Moon (full moon) and can be either total, partial or appulse. The dates for the 2000 eclipses are Jan 20, Feb 5, July 1, 16 and 30, and Dec. 25. See these particular dates for eclipse types and places from which they are visible. © *Mari Susan Selby 1998*

RETURN TO SOURCE: MERCURY RETROGRADE ☿ ℞

The cycle of the wing-footed messenger, Mercury, represents our mental and communicative life processes. This companion dancer to the sun (never traveling more than 28° away) inspires mobility and adaptability. Mercury retrogrades three or four times a year, each time in a sign of the same element. During this passage, lasting 20 to 28 days, our attention moves to unfinished business. Since all backward movement symbolizes a return to source, we can use these times to attend to our inner perceptions and reconnect with the spiritual source of our thoughts.

Mercury's Piscean Retrograde in early 2000 (Feb. 21–March 14) finds us recycling our old paradigms. Get in touch with your inner poet to honor the past and rediscover new uses for those old connections. While Summer Solstice shines delightfully on new horizons, use the Cancerian Mercury Retrograde (June 23–July 17) to let "home" happen wherever you go. Embrace the family within, for kin—old and new—may come calling. Mercury's Scorpionic Retrograde (Oct. 18–Nov. 8) allows for penetrating looks to discriminate the decaying from the decadent. It is shakedown time as destiny deals us a new hand. Play with grace. © *Sandra Pastorius 1998*

THE WHEEL OF THE YEAR: HOLY/HOLIDAYS

The seasonal cycle of the year is created by the tilt of the earth's axis, leaning toward or away from the sun, north to south, as the earth orbits the sun. Solstices are the extreme points (like new and full moon in the lunar cycle) when days and nights are longest or shortest. On equinoxes, days and nights are equal (like the light of the half moon). The four cross-quarter days roughly mark the midpoints in between solstices and equinoxes. These natural turning points in the the earth's annual cycle are the holidays we commemorate in We'Moon. We use the dates in the ancient Celtic calendar because it most closely approximates the eight spokes of the wheel of the year. As the wheel of this year turns, **We'Moon** features Colette Gardiner's interpretation of the Celtic holydays (names and dates in bold as follows). The holy/holiday celebrations of many other cultures cluster around these same times with similar universal themes:

Dec. 21: Solstice/Winter: the dwindling and return of the light—Kwanzaa (African-American), Soyal (Hopi), Santa Lucia (Scandanavian), Cassave/Dreaming (Taino), Chanukah (Jewish).

Feb. 2: Imbolc/Mid-Winter: celebrations, prophecy, purification, initiation—Candlemas (Christian), New Years (Tibetan, Chinese, Iroquois), Ground Hog's Day (American).

Mar. 19: Equinox/Spring: rebirth, fertility, eggs, resurrection—Passover (Jewish), Easter (Christian), Festivals of the Goddess: Eostare (German), Astarte (Semite), Persephone (Greek).

May 1: Beltane/Mid-Spring: blossoms, planting, fertility, sexuality—May Day (Euro-American), Root Festival (Yakima), Ching Ming (Chinese), Whitsuntide (Dutch), Tu Bi-Shevat (Jewish).

June 20: Solstice/Summer: sun, fire festivals—Niman Kachina (Hopi), Sundance (Lakota), Goddess festivals: Isis (Egypt), Litha (N. Africa), Yellow Corn Mother (Taino), Ishtar (Babylonian).

Aug. 2: Lammas/Mid-Summer: first harvest, breaking bread, goddesses of abundance: Green Corn Ceremony (Creek), Corn Mother (Hopi), Amaterasu (Japan), Hatshepsut's Day (Egypt).

Sept. 22: Equinox/Fall: gather and store, ripeness, goddesses: Tari Pennu (Bengal), Old Woman Who Never Dies (Mandan), Chicomecoatl (Aztec), Black Bean Mother (Taino).

Oct. 31: Samhain/Mid-Fall: underworld journey, ancestor spirits, Hallowmas/Halloween/Festivals of the Dead around the world, Sukkoth (Jewish harvest/wine festival).   ◻ *Musawa and Nell Stone 1998*

Sources: *The Grandmother of Time* by Zsuzsanna E. Budapest, 1989; *Celestially Auspicious Occasions* by Donna Henes, 1996; and *Songs of Bleeding* by Spider, 1992

2000—The Year of the Dragon

Mighty Dragon flies down from heaven on the new moon of February 5* and everything transforms. Prepare for an exciting, magnificent, but perhaps overwhelming year. 2000 will be a time of power, passion, drive, ambition and daring. Life feels as if all events are magnified tenfold, at maximum volume. Dragon year is an excellent time to start a business, marry, have children and take incredible risks. But unrealistic dreams and fantasies will crash. On a planetary level, expect extreme earth changes, such as earthquakes, volcanic eruptions and tidal waves.

Dragon was the most sacred mystical animal for thousands of years in Chinese history and was associated with imperial majesty. Dragon has magnanimous and spiritual qualities and symbolizes royalty, prosperity and wisdom.

Dragon has magical attributes and can transform herself into any type of creature. Benevolent Dragon is a protector of temples and monasteries. Dragon year occurs every twelve years: 1904, 1916, 1928, 1940, 1952, 1964, 1976, 1988 and 2000. We'moon born in Dragon year are blessed. Their life experiences are very intense because Dragon wears the horns of destiny. There are no casual friendships for a Dragon. Every interaction is a continuation of heavy past life karma that must be resolved now. Therefore, these brave gals have karma to lead and succeed. We'moon Dragons are not afraid to take charge. They are independent thinkers who love freedom and are adamant believers in equal rights. They have powerful personalities, love adventure and want to make a huge impact on the world. But their idealism must be combined with concrete action to make Dragon dreams a reality.

The modern Chinese are trying to remedy the overpopulation problem on our planet by allowing only one child per family. A Dragon son is preferred, so female Dragon babies will be put up for adoption. Most will find homes in

□ *Maya Fulan Yue 1999*

the USA. If you adopt a Dragon daughter, do not expect sugar, spice and everything nice. Instead, plan to meet your teacher. Dragon represents yang chi and corresponds to the Western sign Aries.

□ *Susan Levitt 1998*

*Asian New Year begins the second new moon after Winter Solstice.

THE DEATH AND REBIRTH OF THE GODDESS

Each month the moon unfolds herself as she phases from new to full to dark and then back again to new. The moon's alternation of light and dark phases tells the story of birth, growth, fullness, diminishment, disappearance, with rebirth and growth again. Early peoples noticed that the $29^1/_2$ day cycle of the moon's phases corresponds to the $29^1/_2$ days of a woman's menstrual cycle. They therefore surmised that the moon must be feminine and personified her as divine feminine—The Triple Moon Goddess who birthed, nurtured, destroyed and renewed life. The serpent which sheds its skin and renews itself, like the waxing and waning of the moon, was seen to embody the mysteries of death and renewal and became the symbol of the Goddess' greatest and most secret of mysteries.

If the Goddess is true to her own essential nature she will resonate in attunement to the moon's rhythms of ebb and flow, and, like the moon, will periodically withdraw into the dark phase of her cycle. It is then that she performs her mysteries of renewal and when the mystery of transformation occurs—a process that involves a descent where something old dies in preparation for something new to be born. According to the ancients, this was the time when she was said to be menstruating.

This perception led me to re-examine the feminist belief that ancient matriarchal societies were the victims of centuries of intentional persecution and destruction by violent patriarchal tribes. Instead, I wondered if the disappearance of the Goddess and women of power during the last 5,000 years was a factor that was built into her own cosmology of cyclic renewal. Like the moon cycling from new to full to dark and back to new again, the Goddess herself has had cycles of birth, growth, death and renewal that have transpired over generations of time in the cultural evolution of humanity.

If we look closely at the parallel rhythms of the moon and the Goddess throughout the last 40,000 years, we can see that the development and flowering of the Goddess can be measured by the cycle of waxing and waning phases. The Goddess developed at the dawn of the Upper Paleolithic era in 38,000 B.C.E. and flowered with women's discovery of agriculture around 11,000 B.C.E. That cycle led to the creation of civilizations during the Neolithic era from

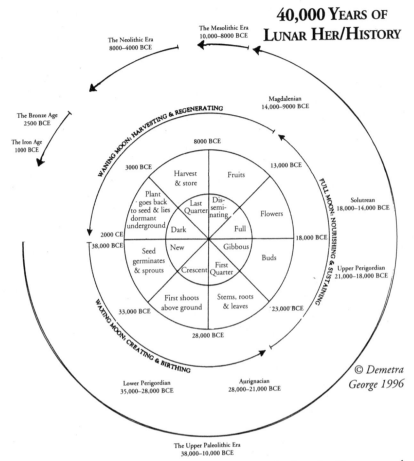

The Neolithic Era
8000–4000 BCE

The Mesolithic Era
10,000–8000 BCE

Magdalenian
14,000–9000 BCE

The Bronze Age
2500 BCE

The Iron Age
1000 BCE

WANING MOON: HARVESTING & REGENERATING

8000 BCE

3000 BCE

13,000 BCE

Harvest & store

Fruits

Plant goes back to seed & lies dormant underground

Last Quarter

Dis-semi-nating

Flowers

Solutrean
18,000–14,000 BCE

FULL MOON: NOURISHING & SUSTAINING

Dark

Full

18,000 BCE

2000 CE

38,000 BCE

Seed germinates & sprouts

New

Gibbous

Buds

Upper Perigordian
21,000–18,000 BCE

Crescent

First Quarter

First shoots above ground

Stems, roots & leaves

23,000 BCE

33,000 BCE

WAXING MOON: CREATING & BIRTHING

28,000 BCE

Lower Perigordian
35,000–28,000 BCE

Aurignacian
28,000–21,000 BCE

© Demetra George 1996

The Upper Paleolithic Era
38,000–10,000 BCE

8000 B.C.E. Her subsequent disappearance during the Bronze and Iron Ages and her current re-emergence complete the cycle. In cyclic process, when the form fulfills the purpose of the cycle, it is then necessary to let go of the old form.

By circa 3000 B.C.E. the Goddess, true to her third dark moon aspect as goddess of death, embodied her mystery teachings that destruction precedes renewal. She retreated into her dark recessive phase in order to actualize her third great mystery—that of regeneration. Having transformed and renewed herself, the Goddess has been recently reborn as has womanspirit arising at the new moon phase of another cycle with the promise and hope that accompanies the rebirth of the light.

© *Demetra George 1996, adapted from*
Mysteries of the Dark Moon *(Harper Collins)*

Thoughts on Y2K

The conversations I have been hearing about Y2K remind me of the 70s when we sat around and talked about the collapse of patriarchy. Some of us grieved the loss of the world-as-we-had-known-it and felt anxiety about the unknown future. Our main response, however, was not to prepare for physical survival, but to joyfully leap into a world of our own making.

Y2K is a wake-up call, a "hundredth monkey" event. But it is not a singularity; it's a piece of a much bigger picture. Paula Gunn Allen sees the Earth's crisis-state (a reality apart from Y2K) as a great planetary initiation. She's becoming someone else. And it is our great honor to attend her passage rites. This transition is "the climacteric, when the beloved planet goes through menopause and takes her place among the wise women planets that dance among the stars." [1]

There is no way to enter the new millennium half way. If Y2K truly heralds a new world, we can't just store up enough food, water, fuel, etc., to get us through and then resume our way of life. Y2K is one element in a planetary transformation affecting every woman, man, child, all creatures, plants, stones, seasons, winds, rains, all waters, the devas, all spirits.

In my neighborhood in the Ozarks, Y2K has sparked great community networking, a coming together of folks from fundamentalists to lesbians. Many people in these hills know how to deal with disaster, how to make do. Some are fixed on apocalyptic predictions but such emphasis on doomsday is a distraction from the current ecological disasters, world hunger and general collapse of the world-as-we-know-it, a reality already.

How can we participate with Earth in this transition? The predicted loss of energy sources and communication networks calls for new sources of energy, new/old ways of communicating, what Sally Gearhart in the 70s called authentic re-sourcing. We need to develop our psychic sense with all the gynergy we can muster. Tap into our psychic information network and experience our connectedness and relatedness with all beings. Trust our intuition, dreams and visions. Simplify and expand our lives and participate in the creation of the universe.

◻ *Linda S. Smith 1999*

[1] "The Woman I Love is a Planet, The Planet I Love is a Tree," Paula Gunn Allen, *Woman of Power*, issue 18, Spring 1991

MOON 0

Moon 0: December 20–January 6

Sun in ♑ Capricorn: Dec. 21; Full Moon in ♋ Cancer: Dec. 22

© Martina Hoffmann 1996

The Coning

December

Decembro

♉
♊
Monday
20

♃ D   6:48 am
☽→♊   9:39 am
☽△♆   2:05 pm
☿⚹♅   2:53 pm

Solstice

I am the breath of Winter
The dark moon of the North
The retreat into the Womb
In my silence all things begin

◻ *Elena I. Rego 1997*

♂♂♂   mardo

♊
Tuesday
21

☽☌♀   3:08 am
☽△♅   8:13 am
☽☌♅   10:03 am
☽△♂   4:57 pm
☉→♑   11:44 pm

Solstice

♑

Sun in Capricorn 11:44 pm PST

☿☿☿   merkredo

♊
♋
Wednesday
22

☽⚹♃   1:03 am   v/c
☽PrG   2:53 am
☽→♋   8:52 am
☉☍☽   9:31 am

♃♃♃   ĵaŭdo

♋
Thursday
23

☽⚹♄   1:38 am
♄⚼☊   3:50 pm
♀☐♂   6:07 pm
☽△♀   6:49 pm

Full Moon in ♋ Cancer 9:31 am PST

♀♀♀   vendredo

♋
♌
Friday
24

☽☐♃   12:31 am   v/c
☽→♌   8:32 am
☽☍♆   1:17 pm

All aspects in Pacific Standard Time; add 3 hours for EDT; add 8 hours for GMT

Walking as Before

Look to each other across chasms of ancient time.
We are moving round a single unchanging point.
Move to the very edge
where the old world ends
and something else begins.

And we have always been walking through this land.
And we have always worn its vision like a skin.
The track is strongly felt, walking as before.
And our footsteps fit, walking as before.
Move to the very edge, where the old world ends
And something else begins, something else begins.

excerpt © Carolyn Hillyer 1997

♌ ───── ♄♄♄   sabato ─────────

Saturday
25

☽□♄	1:49 am
☽△♀	2:51 am
☽☍♅	8:17 am
☽△♉	9:16 pm
☽☍♂	10:50 pm

───── ☉☉☉   dimanĉo ─────────

♌
♍

Sunday
26

☽□♀	12:34 am	
☽△♃	2:07 am	v/c
☽→♍	10:34 am	
♀⚹♃	6:58 pm	
☉△☽	7:03 pm	

December

Desemba

─── ☽☽☽ Jumatatu ───────────

♍

Monday
27

☿⚹♂	1:16 am
☽△♄	4:56 am
☽□♀	6:17 am
☿△♃	6:39 pm

─── ♂♂♂ Jumanne ───────────

♍
♎

Tuesday
28

☽□♅	8:54 am	
☽⚹♀	10:51 am	v/c
♂⚹♃	12:14 pm	
☽→♎	4:14 pm	
☽△♆	9:58 pm	

─── ☿☿☿ Jumatano ───────────

♎

Wednesday
29

☉□☽	6:04 am
☽⚹♀	1:34 pm
☽△♅	7:55 pm

─── ♃♃♃ Alhamisi ─────────── Waning Half Moon in ♎ Libra 6:04 am PST

♎

Thursday
30

♀☌☋	12:51 am	
☽☍♃	4:13 pm	
☽△♂	7:34 pm	v/c
♀→♐	8:54 pm	
☿→♑	10:48 pm	

─── ♀♀♀ Ijumaa ───────────

♎
♏

Friday
31

☽→♏	1:36 am
☽⚹♅	2:01 am
☽□♆	7:50 am
☉⚹☽	9:34 pm
☽☍♄	10:10 pm

All aspects in Pacific Standard Time; add 3 hours for EST; add 8 hours for GMT

Trickster

♏      ♏♏♏ Jumamosi

Saturday

1

⊙△♄   4:37 am
☽□♅   6:59 am

♏
♐   ⊙⊙⊙ Jumapili

Sunday

2

☽□♂   11:28 am   v/c
♀✶♆   1:16 pm
☽→♐   1:32 pm
☽✶♆   8:07 pm
☽☌♀   8:52 pm

MOON 0

A Thousand Years of Healing

With this turning we put a broken age to rest.
We who are alive at such a cusp
now usher in
a thousand years of healing.
From whence my hope, I cannot say,
But it grows in the cells of my skin,
my envelope of mysteries.
In this sheath so akin to the surface of earth
I sense the faint song.
Beneath the wail and dissonance
this singing rises. Winged ones
and four-leggeds,
grasses and mountains and each tree,
all the swimming creatures.
Even we, wary two-leggeds,
hum, and call, and create
the changes. We remake our relations, mend
our minds, convert our minds to the earth.
We practice blending our voices,
living with the vision
of the Great Magic we move within.
We begin
the new habit, getting up glad
for a thousand years of healing.

□ Sue Silvermarie 1998

MOON I

© *Betty LaDuke 1998*

Eritrea: Women Celebrate

January
Januar

———— DDD   Montag ————
♐
Monday
3

D♂♀   12:54 pm
♂→H   7:01 pm
D⚹♅   7:50 pm

© Jill Smith 1995

B-earth

———— ♂♂♂   Dienstag ————
♐
Tuesday
4

DApG   4:22 am
D△♃   5:06 pm   v/c

———— ☿☿☿   Mittwoch ————
♐
♑
Wednesday
5

D→♑   2:24 am
D⚹♂   4:36 am
D♂♅   9:13 pm
D△♄   11:18 pm

———— ♃♃♃   Donnerstag ————
♑
Thursday
6

☉♂D   10:14 am
☿△♄   12:42 pm

———— ♀♀♀   Freitag ————   New Moon in ♑ Capricorn 10:14 am PST
♑
♒
Friday
7

D□♃   6:00 am   v/c
D→♒   2:53 am
D♂♆   9:44 pm

All aspects in Pacific Standard Time; add 3 hours for EST; add 8 hours for GMT

Labor Chant

Opening
I call unto you
All you who have been my mothers
All you who have been my grandmothers
All you who have been my daughters
All who have been my great-grandmothers
Attend me now.

I invoke you
Artemis Ilythia, Brighid of the Bright Flame, Inanna Queen of
   Heaven and Earth
Hecate Tri-via, Krittikas with your keen blade, your obsidian knife
Demeter in your grief, and Baubo with your comedy
Klaedishi, you Trickster and Tonamah, who Weaves the Web
Yemaya of the waves and Coventina of the healing springs
You goddesses who guide and guard and protect me
while I attend to others
Attend me now
in the hour of my birth.

excerpt □ Patricia Worth 1995

ᚻᚻᚻ Samstag —————

≈   ⬤   Saturday
         ♉

♀⚼♄	8:51 am
☽□♄	11:22 am
☽⚹♀	11:39 am
☽⚹☿	2:10 pm
☽☌♅	9:04 pm

————— ☉☉☉ Sonntag —————

≈   ⬤   Sunday
         9

♀☌♀	1:14 pm	
☿ApG	2:19 pm	
☽⚹♃	5:41 pm	v/c

January
'Ianuali

DDD Pō'akahi

Stars
© C. Tall Mountain 1998

♒ ♓

Monday 10

D→♓	1:59 am
♀☌⚷	6:56 am
D☌♂	12:02 pm
D✶♄	9:46 pm

♂♂♂ Pō'alua

♓

Tuesday 11

D□♇	12:38 am	
D□♀	4:19 am	
D✶☿	1:05 pm	
☉✶D	6:23 pm	v/c
♄sD	8:59 pm	

☿☿☿ Pō'akolu

♓ ♈

Wednesday 12

D→♈	10:48 am
♀✶♅	1:32 pm
D✶♆	5:28 pm

♃♃♃ Pō'ahā

♈

Thursday 13

D△♇	8:28 am
D✶♅	2:57 pm
D△♀	5:23 pm

♀♀♀ Pō'alima

♈ ♉

Friday 14

D□☿	3:41 am	
☉□D	5:34 am	
D☌♃	9:47 am	v/c
D→♉	4:38 pm	
D□♆	11:03 pm	

Waxing Half Moon in ♈ Aries 5:34 am PST

All aspects in Pacific Standard Time; add 3 hours for EST; add 8 hours for GMT

Fool's Journey

I break through
the membrane of earth.
Stars greet me
as a piece of light.
I dart exuberant,
a spark of fire.
The depths of space,
of grander dimension
than I had imagined.
Enough room, finally,
for my true size.

Exultant,
I hear stars
singing like whales
in the galactic sea.
This black womb cradles me.
Acupoints
meridian the Milky Way
with starfire.

How can I hold
such luminosity?
I fall back
toward the atmosphere of earth.
Fall fast
back to my disguise.

□ Sue Silvermarie 1998

— ♄♄♄   Pōʻaono —

♉

Saturday
15

☽⚹♂	8:04 am
☽♂♄	10:23 am
☉♂♉	5:19 pm
☽□♅	7:22 pm

— ☉☉☉   Lāpule —

♉
♊

Sunday
16

♉□♃	8:26 am	
☉△☽	12:51 pm	
☽△♉	1:50 pm	v/c
☉□♃	6:51 pm	
☽→♊	7:25 pm	

January

Januaro

♊

Monday
17

☽△♆	1:38 am
♂⚹♄	2:28 am
☽□♂	12:51 pm
☽☍♀	3:02 pm
☽△♅	9:02 pm

♊
♋

Tuesday
18

☽☍♀	7:55 am	
☿→♒	2:20 pm	
☽⚹♃	2:21 pm	v/c
☽→♋	8:01 pm	

♋

Wednesday
19

♂□♀	8:06 am
☽⚹♄	12:32 pm
☽PrG	3:00 pm
☽△♂	3:38 pm

♋
♌

Thursday
20

☉→♒	10:23 am	
☽□♃	2:36 pm	v/c
☽→♌	7:58 pm	
☉☍☽	8:40 pm	
☿♂♆	10:05 pm	

♒

Sun in Aquarius 10:23 am PST
Full Moon in ♌ Leo 8:40 pm PST
Total Lunar Eclipse 8:45 pm PST (1.325 mag.)
Eclipse visible from the Americas

♌

Friday
21

☽☍♆	2:18 am
☽☍♅	2:50 am
☽□♄	12:45 pm
♂□♇	2:36 pm
☽△♀	3:34 pm
♀△♃	8:58 pm
☽☍♅	9:48 pm

All aspects in Pacific Standard Time; add 3 hours for EST; add 8 hours for GMT

Year at a Glance for ♒ AQUARIUS (Jan. 20–Feb. 19)

There is so much going on in Aquarius this year that you may sometimes feel like jumping right out of your skin. Change is upon all of us, and you are manifesting some of the most obvious signs. Experiment, do things differently. You are reinventing yourself; withdraw from the world periodically to do so.

Your ideals and plans for the future are changing. This will be reflected in a change in the people with whom you associate and the groups and movements you identify with. Allow some of the energy that is sparking your system to pass through you to ground. How? Focus upon your domestic life. Carry water, chop wood—it helps. You are building foundations for your newly awakened self and find the rhythms and rituals of daily living useful metaphors for the inner home you are creating.

Land and home are external symbols of your desire for a stable inner life. It is a good time to expand your home or move to a better location that better reflects your new self. The real issue is to honor the deepest feelings and conditions that constitute security for you. You may have to take responsibility for someone in your family. It is appropriate that you weigh the obligations to others with an equally important obligation to yourself.

In 2000 you become acutely aware of a limitation you have inherited from your family of origin. Equally, a gift from this same ancestral lineage will become obvious. Explore your family tree and blood ties to other countries and cultures to help you.

© Gretchen Lawlor 1999

Inward
© Martina Hoffmann 1995

ħħħ   sabato

♌
♍   ○   Saturday
            22

☽△♃   3:53 pm
☽△♀   5:30 pm   v/c
☽→♍   9:07 pm

☉☉☉   dimanĉo

♍   ○   Sunday
            23

☽△ħ   2:48 pm
☽□♀   5:48 pm
☽ℰ♂   11:48 pm   v/c

January
Januari

♍ Monday
24

☉☌♆	10:08 am
♀→♑	11:52 am
♆ApG	4:07 pm
☿□♄	5:18 pm

———— ♂♂♂ Jumanne ————————————————

♍
♎ Tuesday
25

☽→♎	1:09 am
☽□♀	2:30 am
☽△♆	8:33 am
☉△☽	10:20 am
☿⚹♀	5:55 pm
☽⚹♀	11:27 pm

———— ☿☿☿ Jumatano ————————————————

♎ Wednesday
26

☽△☿	12:17 am
☽△♅	6:48 am
☿⚹♆	10:36 pm

———— ♃♃♃ Alhamisi ————————————————

♎
♏ Thursday
27

☽☍♃	3:59 am	v/c
☽→♏	9:01 am	
☽⚹♀	4:36 pm	
☽□♆	5:06 pm	
☉□☽	11:57 pm	

———— ♀♀♀ Ijumaa ———— Waning Half Moon in ♏ Scorpio 11:57 pm PST

♏ Friday
28

☿☌♅	1:55 am	
☽☍♄	5:31 am	
☽□♅	4:56 pm	
☽□☿	7:23 pm	
☽△♂	11:11 pm	v/c

All aspects in Pacific Standard Time; add 3 hours for EST; add 8 hours for GMT

© *Willow Fox 1998*

evolution

I dream of a time when blackberries grow back over crumbling concrete, when grass, animals and trees move in and the infrastructure is local . . . when I pick and skip my way across the land by foot, horse or bicycle over abandoned cars and strip malls by moonlight, traveling between villages slowly and camping out with birds in old bank buildings . . . meeting fellow travelers in the wild world beyond and within this one, when progress ends and a more conscious evolution begins, has begun . . .

¤ *Brenna Jael Nies 1998*

───────── ♄♄♄ Jumamosi ─────────

♏
♐   Saturday
        29

☽→♐   8:17 pm

───────── ☉☉☉ Jumapili ─────────

♐   Sunday
        30

☽✶♆   4:55 am
☉✶☽   5:28 pm
☉□♄   9:15 pm
☽♂♀   9:17 pm

January
Januar

♐

Monday
31

☽✳⛢ 5:39 am
☽□♂ 3:58 pm
☽ApG 5:15 pm
☽✳♀ 6:22 pm

Flying High an' Four Days Overdue
© *Prinny Alavi 1996*

♐
♑

Tuesday
1

☽△♃ 5:08 am v/c
☽→♑ 9:10 am
☉✳♀ 3:00 pm

February

♑

Wednesday
2

♀△♄ 5:07 am
☽△♄ 6:52 am
☽♂♀ 7:04 am

Imbolc/Candlemas

♑
♒

Thursday
3

☽✳♂ 8:48 am
☽□♃ 6:16 pm v/c
☽→♒ 9:31 pm

♒

Friday
4

☿✳♃ 1:31 am
☉✳⛢ 4:59 am
☽♂♆ 6:22 pm
☽□♄ 6:52 pm
☽✳♀ 10:06 pm

All aspects in Pacific Standard Time; add 3 hours for EST; add 8 hours for GMT

Mother cradles her belly,
bleached white cardamom pod
enclosing seeds that are spice
and medicine and aromatic
sweet of flesh.
excerpt © Sabrina Vourvoulias 1997

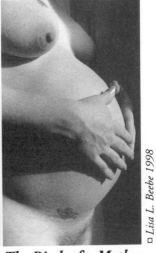

□ *Lilinda 1997*

□ *Lisa L. Beebe 1998*

Darlingtonia   **The Birth of a Mother**

Imbolc

Imbolc is a holiday celebrating quickening. The water in healing wells may boil and rise. Our projects and visions conceived or birthed at solstice are rising up out of the well of our creativity, starting to take shape. They are moving upwards with the sap, like children starting to reach out to the world. The flame of inspiration burns bright. It's time to initiate our reborn selves into the community.

Our challenge physically is to help our bodies adapt to the slightly quickened pulse of budding spring. Spring tonics are traditional in many cultures. Greens such as Chickweed and Bitter Cress (actually spicy not bitter) nourish the blood, are mildly laxative and help us move with the flow of the seasons. Using spring greens and new shoots in salads and teas helps us release winter sluggishness and take in the earth's vital force.

Our emotional and spiritual challenge is to start to put our ideas into reality, to move out of inner contemplation and into healing and regeneration, to speak our truth with passion and move forward. Use Violet flowers to help our hearts move out from under winter's examination of self. Add them to salads or eat them fresh. Coltsfoot blooms in late winter before the leaves appear, showing an indomitable spirit. Place the flowers on your altar or dry and use as incense.

© Colette Gardiner 1999

Ma-Lekma: Bright Edges

Quickening

I feel her essence
waking
quickening
in me
in a million women

Like a new babe
a waxing moon
eyelids of a 1,000 souls
opening to moonlight

An influx of understanding
reality expanding
and the milk from
a million prayers
can finally be summoned

For her presence
is awakening
like a new babe
a waxing moon

We feel her quickening

▢ Kathleen Sweeney 1998

ħħħ   Samstag

♒ Saturday
5

♉→♓   12:08 am
☉☌☽   5:03 am
☽☌♅   6:28 am
☉☌♅   11:14 pm

Lunar Imbolc
Partial Solar Eclipse 4:50 am PST (0.580 mag.)
New Moon in ♒ Aquarius 5:03 am PST
Eclipse visible from Antarctica

☉☉☉   Sonntag

♒
♓ Sunday
6

☽⚹♃   5:34 am   v/c
☽→♓   8:02 am
☽☌♉   12:52 pm
♅ApG   8:42 pm

---

laugh

laugh
when there is nothing left
grief has eaten you
laugh.

fill the belly and the lung
with air the healer and the cleanser.
sing throat songs bird songs
smile: tooth grin and air roaring.
laugh to remember
what moves all moves you.

if you close your gateway of mouth
bitterness will linger, will
coat your mouth and organs with
long decaying staying.
movement reprieves us, relates us,
reminds us:

belly dances nose singing
mouth chortle   laugh.

□ *Marna 1995*

MOON II

Moon II: February 5–March 4

New Moon in ♒ Aquarius: Feb. 5;
Sun in ♓ Pisces: Feb. 19;
Full Moon in ♍ Virgo: Feb. 19

Village Crone, Thailand
© *Angie Coffin 1998*

February
Pepeluali

In the Yoruba religion of Ifa there is a saying, *Esu ni ba ko*, which means "the Divine Messenger is a Trickster."

excerpt □ Joey Garcia 1998

———— ⅅⅅⅅ   Pō'akahi ————

♓︎

Monday
7

☽✶♄	4:47 am
☽☐♀	7:47 am
☽✶♀	5:05 pm

———— ♂♂♂   Pō'alua ————

♓︎
♈︎

Tuesday
8

| ☽♂♂ | 11:46 am | v/c |
| ☽→♈︎ | 4:17 pm | |

———— ☿☿☿   Pō'akolu ————

♈︎

Wednesday
9

☽✶♆	12:48 am
☽△♀	3:11 pm
☽✶♅	11:14 am

———— ♃♃♃   Pō'ahā ————

♈︎
♉︎

Thursday
10

☽☐♀	5:37 am	
☉✶☽	6:39 am	
☽♂♃	9:19 pm	v/c
☽→♉︎	10:21 pm	

———— ♀♀♀   Pō'alima ————

♉︎

Friday
11

☽☐♆	6:40 am
☽✶♅	4:18 pm
♂→♈︎	5:04 pm
☽♂♄	5:56 pm

Maggie of the Street

You can see her on the street
A toothless smile, big boots on her feet
A dirty overcoat
Over another coat
She says she's gonna have a baby
Although she's sixty-five, people say that she's crazy
Maggie of the street   Maggie of the street

Maggie of the street
Is looking for a sign
To release the child divine
Conceived with God inside her mind

In the photo is Ann Marie
She was taken away from Maggie
Shortly after she came
They said Maggie was insane
They put her in an institution
Her stolen child, they never made restitution
To Maggie of the street   To Maggie of the street

Maggie of the street
Is looking for a sign
To release the child divine
Conceived with God inside her mind
Maggie of the street   Maggie of the street   Maggie of the street

song excerpt ¤ Barb Ryman 1994

ℏℏℏ Pōʻaono

♉ **Saturday**
12

☽□♅ 4:20 am
☿⚹♄ 10:28 am
☉□☽ 3:21 pm
☽△♀ 3:22 pm v/c

Waxing Half Moon in ♉ Taurus 3:21 pm PST

☉☉☉ Lāpule

♉
♊ **Sunday**
13

☽→♊ 2:23 am
☽⚹♂ 4:17 am
☽△♆ 10:33 am
☿□♀ 3:23 pm
☽☍♀ 11:46 pm

February
Februaro

♊

Monday
14

☽□♀ 12:28 am
☽△♅ 7:34 am
♃→♉ 1:39 pm
☉△☽ 9:51 pm v/c

♊
♋

Tuesday
15

☽→♋ 4:45 am
☽⚹♃ 4:55 am
☽□♂ 9:24 am
☽⚹♄ 11:37 pm

♋

Wednesday
16

☽△♀ 5:46 am
☽PrG 6:21 pm

♋
♌

Thursday
17

☽☍♀ 4:51 am v/c
☽→♌ 6:11 am
☽□♃ 6:56 am
☿□♎ 9:37 am
☽△♂ 1:31 pm
☽☍♆ 2:21 pm
♀→♒ 8:43 pm

♌

Friday
18

☽□♄ 1:12 am
☽△♀ 3:07 am
♂⚹♆ 6:07 am
♀□♃ 9:04 am
☽☍♅ 11:05 am v/c

All aspects in Pacific Standard Time; add 3 hours for EST; add 8 hours for GMT

Year at a Glance for ♓ PISCES (Feb. 19–March 19)

Pisces began a major cycle of growth in 1998. An increased sense of self-confidence and adventure led you to test your skills in the marketplace. In 1999 managing the material world helped you understand yourself better. You struggled with communication issues with painful realizations about how your own negative thinking contributed to failures you encountered.

In 2000 you will continue to struggle with communication problems but will benefit greatly from acquiring new skills in this area. It is a great time to organize your ideas, to become more focused in an area of study or to offer your knowledge through writing or teaching. You may not see where all this is leading but trust your intuition. Pisces needs, more than ever, to leave space for spirit to be part of your life. Find a place and time for contemplation, even prayer, in your daily routines.

Pluto conjuncts Chiron in your solar 10th house this year so you may be dealing with power issues associated with career and public image. You are likely to be actively involved in Millennial projects related to the transformation of education, politics or the media. With Uranus still in your solar 12th house, you continue to experience instability from factors over which you have little control. In the second half of 2000 you will benefit from therapy to clear up old family issues. Take advantage of this opportunity to discover and eliminate some powerful self-limiting belief, particularly anything that stems from an early relationship between you and your mother.

Dolphins Making Love
© Musawa 1998

© *Gretchen Lawlor 1999*

ħħħ   sabato

♌
♍   ◯   Saturday
19

☉→♓	12:33 am
☽→♍	7:53 am
☉☌☽	8:27 am
☽△♃	9:15 am
☉⚹♃	9:57 pm

♓

Sun in Pisces 12:33 am PST
Full Moon in ♍ Virgo 8:27 am PST

☉☉☉   dimanĉo

♍   ◯   Sunday
20

☽△ħ	3:39 am	
☽□♀	5:26 am	
☽☍♅	12:59 pm	v/c

February
Februari

────── ☽☽☽ Jumatatu ──────

♍︎
♎︎ ○ Monday
21

♀sR	4:46 am
☽→♎︎	11:21 am
☽△♀	8:02 pm
☽△♆	8:24 pm

When all formulas
known to science fail us,
there is still the ancient magic
of a spring thaw.
Crocus pocus,
crocus pocus.

excerpt ☐ Veronica M. Murphy 1998

────── ♂♂♂ Jumanne ──────

♎︎ ◐ Tuesday
22

♀♂♆	12:06 am	
☽☌♂	1:19 am	
☽✶♀	10:09 am	
☽△♅	7:15 pm	v/c

────── ☿☿☿ Jumatano ──────

♎︎
♏︎ ◑ Wednesday
23

| ☽→♏︎ | 5:58 pm |
| ☽☌♃ | 8:59 pm |

────── ♃♃♃ Alhamisi ──────

♏︎ ◑ Thursday
24

☉△☽	3:45 am
☽□♆	3:46 am
☿□☋	7:34 am
☽□♀	9:15 am
☽☌♄	4:52 pm

────── ♀♀♀ Ijumaa ──────

♏︎ ◑ Friday
25

| ☽△☿ | 12:33 am | |
| ☽□♅ | 4:18 am | v/c |

All aspects in Pacific Standard Time; add 3 hours for EST; add 8 hours for GMT

Awaiting the Change
© *Marsha A. Gomez 1996*

Stone Woman

She has no shape or colour
she merges with everything
absorbs the unremarkable
sinks into clay
part of the ordinary
unobserved day.

She waits
like the grainy hollow in the stone
for rain
and holds it
till the work of creation
ferments in her body
© *Cora Greenhill 1997*

ちちち Jumamosi

♏︎
♐︎

Saturday
26

☽→♐︎	4:10 am
☽✶♆	2:41 pm
☉□☽	7:53 pm

Waning Half Moon in ♐︎ Sagittarius 7:53 pm PST

☉☉☉ Jumapili

♐︎

Sunday
27

☽✶♀	3:06 am	
☽△♂	3:39 am	
☽☌♀	5:54 am	
☽□♅	8:43 am	
♀✶♂	3:29 pm	
☽✶♅	4:28 pm	v/c
♀□♄	6:57 pm	

February
Februar

leap and the net will appear
love is there behind our fear
© Singing Tree 1998

☽☽☽ Montag

♐
♑

Monday
28

♀✶♇ 6:06 am
☽ApG 12:52 pm
♂△♇ 3:35 pm
☽→♑ 4:45 pm
☿□♇ 8:07 pm
☽△♃ 9:53 pm

♂♂♂ Dienstag

♑

Tuesday
29

☿✶♄ 7:06 am
☉✶☽ 2:21 pm
☽✶☿ 5:01 pm
☽△♄ 5:56 pm
☽□♂ 8:38 pm v/c

☿☿☿ Mittwoch

♑

Wednesday
1

March

☉☌☿ 7:10 am

♃♃♃ Donnerstag

♑
♒

Thursday
2

☽→♒ 5:14 am
♀✶⚷ 9:31 am
☽□♃ 11:13 am
☉✶♄ 12:19 pm
☽☌♆ 3:59 pm
☉□♇ 7:25 pm

♀♀♀ Freitag

♒

Friday
3

☽□♄ 6:06 am
☽✶♇ 6:34 am
☽✶♂ 12:08 pm
♀☌♅ 4:39 pm
☽☌♅ 5:09 pm
☽☌♀ 5:12 pm v/c

All aspects in Pacific Standard Time; add 3 hours for EST; add 8 hours for GMT

□ *Zella Bardsley 1998*

Flight

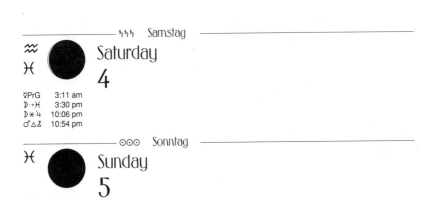

♒
♓

Saturday
4

☿PrG	3:11 am
☽→♓	3:30 pm
☽⚹♃	10:06 pm
♂△⚷	10:54 pm

♓

Sunday
5

☽♂♅	5:19 am	
☽⚹♄	3:32 pm	
☽□♀	3:37 pm	
⊙♂☽	9:17 pm	v/c

New Moon in ♓ Pisces 9:17 pm PST

Healing

The life of a dreamer is not easy.
The dreams keep you awake.

Essie Parrish, *Pomo Indian Healer*

Dream your hands
like twin suns rise
to flower in the heat,
each hand, a perfect
five-petalled blossom.

Dream your hands
emerge from wounded earth
like animal teeth or trees
cut for timber. You will
itch to reforest city lot.

Dream your fast hands swat flies
Your cool hands kill fever
Your piano hands kiss tusk
Your angry hands slap back
Your thieving hands steal time
Your dragon hands melt doubt
Your blind hands see
for the first time
the aura above my skin—
And in the single motion of the flock
your hands swoop down to release me
from my cage of worry—
flowing cloud hands
spilling over the whole thirsting Earth—

Imagine what will be
when our fluttering, drumming,
smoking, laboring, twitching,
snapping, scarred, bitten, broken, pale,
dark horse hands
thick with clay
shape dawn—

Yes, dream
Imitate your dreams
until you become them.

□ *Ann Megisikwe 1998*

MOON III

Moon III: March 5–April 4

New Moon in ♓ Pisces: March 5; Full Moon in ♍ Virgo: March 19; Sun in ♈ Aries: March 19

© Lilian de Mello 1998

March
Malaki

—))) Pōʻakahi —

♓
♈

Monday
6

♄⊼♀	3:56 am
☉□♇	7:48 pm
))→♈	10:54 pm

this will be no silent spring
her chant her stare her secret from
the void will blaze a brilliance
a wildness a wail so total

the Goddess trembles

excerpt © Nell Stone 1981

♈

— ♂♂♂ Pōʻalua —

Tuesday
7

♂⚹♅	5:06 am
))⚹♆	8:55 am
))△♀	9:56 pm

♈

— ☿☿☿ Pōʻakolu —

Wednesday
8

))⚹♅	7:58 am
))♂♂	9:25 am
))⚹♀	6:34 pm v/c

♈
♉

— ♃♃♃ Pōʻahā —

Thursday
9

☿⚹♃	3:05 am
))→♉	4:01 am
))⚹☿	11:13 am
))♂♃	11:41 am
))□♆	1:49 pm

♉

— ♀♀♀ Pōʻalima —

Friday
10

))♂♄	2:58 am
))□♅	12:20 pm
☉⚹))	3:50 pm

Ratna Dakini

© Jennet Inglis 1991

Dakinis, found in all ancient and modern cultures, are female nature spirits which express powerful forces of nature as well as our own range of primal emotions—from fear and rage to creative energy and grace. Dakini, translated from Tibetan means sky-goer—one who travels through many dimensions and has the power of transformation. By invoking the Dakinis, we see how we can either be trapped by our patterns and beliefs or be freed from them. By reclaiming the Dakini inside ourselves, we are affirming the quirks and chaos of nature as part of our own nature.

excerpt © Mari Susan Selby 1998

♄♄♄ Pōʻaono

♉
♊

Saturday
11

☽□♀	3:31 am	v/c
☽→♊	7:46 am	
☽□♉	1:18 pm	
☽△♆	5:31 pm	

☉☉☉ Lāpule

♊

Sunday
12

☽☍♀	5:47 am	
☽△♅	3:48 pm	
☽⚹♂	10:34 pm	
☉□☽	10:59 pm	v/c

Waxing Half Moon in ♊ Gemini 10:59 pm PST

March
Marto

♊
♋

Monday
13

♀→♓	3:36 am
☽→♋	10:51 am
☽△♀	11:33 am
☽△♅	3:38 pm
☽⚹♃	7:50 pm

♋

Tuesday
14

☽⚹♄	10:01 am
☿sD	12:39 pm
☽PrG	3:35 pm

♋
♌

Wednesday
15

♀sR	3:49 am	
☽□♂	4:16 am	
☉△☽	5:43 am	v/c
☿♂♀	10:23 am	
☽→♌	1:43 pm	
☽□♃	11:28 pm	
☽☍♆	11:36 pm	

♌

Thursday
16

♃□♆	9:15 am
☽△♀	11:37 am
☽□♄	1:16 pm
☽☍♅	10:00 pm

♌
♍

Friday
17

☽△♂	10:07 am	v/c
☽→♍	4:48 pm	
☽☍♀	10:32 pm	

Year at a Glance for ♈ ARIES (March 19–April 19)

Aries bloomed in 1999. You were filled with contagious passion for an exciting territory you had recently discovered. It brought about an ongoing commitment to a faith or social/political issue, and required either travel or further education. In 2000, insights into your early life experiences catapult you into an even more zealous pursuit of this new world. Travel in January 2000 gives you fresh horizons that will continue to inspire you for the next twelve years.

This year you are inspired/driven to live out new values. Though life's practicalities demand attention, adjust your material world to better reflect transformed, deeper values. Work opportunities will appear but may not yet truly reflect your dreams for the future. A long-term plan to achieve these dreams calms your restlessness.

Immerse yourself in the company of like-minded individuals. With their support, you experience the emergence of your unique and spiritual elements, though they are likely to meet resistance from established corners of your life. You may feel conflicts as you attempt to find balance between your old and new lives. Watch the missionary zeal. Your ideas are meant to inspire—not turn others off.

Windows of opportunity in work are well worth pursuing but take small steps at a time. Your wonderful vital essence is best expressed in a very personal setting. Restrain spending.

© *Gretchen Lawlor 1999*

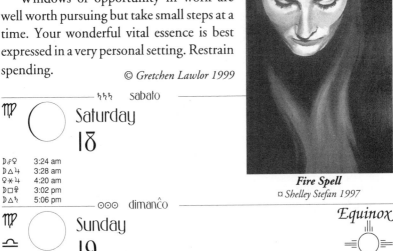

Fire Spell
◻ *Shelley Stefan 1997*

♍ ☽ — ♄♄♄ sabato —

Saturday

18

☽☌♀	3:24 am
☽△♃	3:28 am
♀✱♃	4:20 am
☽□♀	3:02 pm
☽△♄	5:06 pm

--- ☉☉☉ dimanĉo ---

♍ ☽
♎

Sunday

19

☉☌☽	8:44 pm	v/c
☽→♎	8:57 pm	
☉→♈	11:35 pm	

Equinox

♈

Full Moon in ♍ Virgo 8:44 pm PST
Sun in Aries 11:35 pm PST

What to Do on Spring Equinox

Compost this poem:
take out all the words that remind you of winter,
words that slip frozen into the heart,
bare limbs of words that stick into the sky and shake.
Prune out dead wood;
rough ragged never gonna fruit,
done is done.
Pay attention to what is here,
not what isn't.
Send your roots into another row or field or bed.
Mow. Rake up all the grass.
Layer, as if you're expecting hail or a deep frost;
the end of winter is always unpredictable.
Add manure, plenty of manure
and call in the flies, the dung beetles, the worms.
Soon, they'll be heat. Steam.
The pile will soften, break down, give in, let go.
Compost winter into spring,
take off those old clothes you've been wearing,
the despair like a hat on your head,
dig into the pile,
into the heat and the heart of what matters.
Plant your garden and remember, each year,
everything will be different,
compost what you can.

□ *Amy Schutzer 1998*

© *Keely Meagan 1996*

Spring Equinox

Spring Equinox is a time of promise, potential and rapid change. Equal day, equal night. It's a time for celebrating new life. Flowers open. Old patterns fall away and our ideas and projects start to show new life and possibilities. Excitement is in the air. The earth is alive, renewed and full of activity.

Our challenge physically is to stay adaptable as the weather fluctuates in the changing of the season. Using herbs to support lungs, kidneys and liver can keep us healthy now and later in the year. Mullein leaf helps relax the lungs, dries up excess mucus and soothes inflamed membranes. Use in tea as a daily tonic or in tincture form, 1–2 droppers several times a day for spring colds. Nettle leaf is an energy booster, a kidney and blood tonic and can help prevent pollen allergies when taken regularly. Use tea of fresh leaves or dry pre-flowering leaves.

Our emotional and spiritual challenge is to become fully aware of our potential—balancing our inner and outer selves. We begin to use our will in pursuit of learning and knowledge. The yellow flowers of Cowslip help us engage our will and look at life with youthful vigor. Use in the bath or on the altar. © *Colette Gardiner 1999*

March
Machi

♎︎ Monday

20

ⅅ△♆   7:29 am
ⅅ⚹♀   7:58 pm

σσσ — Jumanne

♎︎ Tuesday

21

ⅅ△♅   7:25 am

☿☿☿ — Jumatano

♎︎
♏︎ Wednesday

22

ⅅ☍σ   2:26 am   v/c
ⅅ→♏︎   3:17 am
ⅅ△♅   1:54 pm
ⅅ□♆   2:30 pm
ⅅ☍♃   4:45 pm
σ→♉︎   5:25 pm

♃♃♃ — Alhamisi

♏︎ Thursday

23

ⅅ△♀   2:26 am
ⅅ☍♄   6:47 am
♀□♀   1:52 pm
ⅅ□♅   3:53 pm   v/c

♀♀♀ — Ijumaa

♏︎
♐︎ Friday

24

ⅅ→♐︎   12:43 pm
☉△ⅅ   10:24 pm

All aspects in Pacific Standard Time; add 3 hours for EST; add 8 hours for GMT

Persephone
© Selina di Girolamo 1998

♐ **Saturday**
25

☽✳Ψ	12:40 am	
♀✳♄	2:31 am	
☽□♅	3:45 am	
☿✳♃	8:34 am	
☽♂♀	2:16 pm	
☽□♀	7:52 pm	

⊙⊙⊙ Jumapili

♐ **Sunday**
26

⊙✳Ψ	2:38 am	
☽✳♅	3:26 am	v/c

March
März

♐
♑ ## Monday
27

☽→♑	12:51 am
♀□♂	2:38 am
☽△♂	7:41 am
☽ApG	9:25 am
☉□☽	4:21 am
☽△♃	5:42 am
♂sR	8:29 pm
☽⚹♂	9:16 pm

© *Maya Fulan Yue 1999*

Waning Half Moon in ♑ Capricorn 4:21 pm PST

♑ ## Tuesday
28

☽△♄	7:34 am
☽⚹♀	3:43 pm v/c

♑
♒ ## Wednesday
29

☽→♒	1:34 pm

♒ ## Thursday
30

☽□♂	12:13 am
☽☌♆	1:51 am
☽□♃	7:13 am
☉⚹☽	10:07 am
☿□♀	2:25 pm
☽⚹♀	3:02 pm
☽□♄	8:04 pm

♒ ## Friday
31

♂□♆	4:11 am
☽☌♅	4:19 am v/c

All aspects in Pacific Standard Time; add 3 hours for EST; add 8 hours for GMT

Playing Goddess
© *Anna Oneglia 1994*

The Fool

do I appear ridiculous
turning handsprings and somersaults
leaping into things, the way I do?

but smell the breeze
feel the rain on your face
laugh at the wrong time
or at nothing at all
unravel the lines on your palms
do everything backwards

any minute now,
it will all become clear

¤ *Michèle A. Belluomini 1998*

— ♄♄♄ Samstag
≈
ⓧ Saturday
♓
1

☽→♓	12:12 am
☽✶♂	1:46 pm
☽✶♃	5:54 pm
☉△♀	10:18 pm

— ☉☉☉ Sonntag
♓
Sunday
2

☽□♀	12:12 am
☿✶♄	3:19 am
☽✶♄	6:28 am
☽♂♉	6:45 am

April

Daylight Savings Time begins 2:00 am PST

Intergenerations–Intertribal

We are a sisterhood rising up with one huge shout and we proclaim: IT IS NOT ALL RIGHT WITH US THAT THE BEAUTY OF THE WORLD IS BEING DESTROYED AND THE VALUE OF LIFE DISREGARDED! IT IS NOT ALL RIGHT THAT WE ARE BECOMING ACCUSTOMED TO THE LONG, SLOW DEATH OF EVERYTHING! WE CLAIM THE EARTH TO GROW OLD IN HER BOSOM. WE CLAIM THE EARTH TO BEQUEATH TO OUR CHILDREN'S CHILDREN'S CHILDREN. STEP WITH US, OR STEP ASIDE!

excerpt □ Christina Baldwin 1998

MOON IV

Moon IV: April 4–May 3

New Moon in ♈ Aries: April 4;
Full Moon in ♎ Libra: April 18;
Sun in ♉ Taurus: April 19

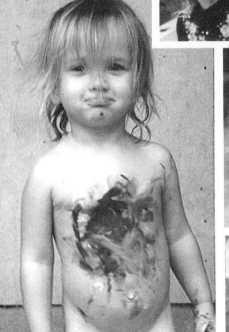

Clockwise from top left: *Ché Tonantzín* ¤ *Amber Fires 1998; Angela, Rita and Barbara—Homeless Children, Missoula, MT* © *Angie Coffin 1998; We Were All Children Once* © *Erin Kenny 1998; Tree Hug* © *Ghermaine Knight 1998; Ring in the New* © *Erin Kenny 1998;*

April
'Apelila

Sanctuary
© Jodi Reeb-Myers 1996

))) Pō'akahi

♓
♈

Monday
3

) ☌ ♀	12:44 am	v/c
) → ♈	8:22 am	
♀ □ ♄	10:00 am	
) ✳ ♆	7:26 pm	

♂♂♂ Pō'alua

♈

Tuesday
4

) △ ♀	6:53 am	
☉ ☌)	11:12 am	
) ✳ ♅	7:03 pm	v/c

☿☿☿ Pō'akolu

♈
♉

Wednesday
5

New Moon in ♈ Aries 11:12 am PDT

) → ♉	12:29 pm	
) □ ♆	11:09 pm	
♂ ☌ ♃	11:41 pm	

♃♃♃ Pō'ahā

♉

Thursday
6

) ☌ ♃	6:09 am	
) ☌ ♂	6:23 am	
☉ △ ♄	9:17 am	
♀ → ♈	11:37 am	
) ☌ ♄	3:50 pm	
) □ ♅	10:04 pm	

♀♀♀ Pō'alima

♉
♊

Friday
7

) ✳ ♅	1:24 am	v/c
) → ♊	2:58 pm	
) ✳ ♀	5:33 pm	

All aspects in Pacific Daylight Time; add 3 hours for EDT; add 7 hours for GMT

Full

Moon
I implore you:
take this child
this blood
these bones
Pull these tides from me.
There is nothing to be
Pregnant
about.
There is barely food for One
these days
and there is only one,
not two,
not ten,
not thousands
who will hold me.
Moon,
Mother,
Goddess,
I ask again:
Let me bleed.

□ Greta Undersun 1998

───── ↳↳↳ Pōʻaono ─────────────

♊ Saturday

♉

☽△♆ 1:33 am
☽☍♀ 12:17 pm
☽PrG 3:12 pm

───── ☉☉☉ Lāpule ─────────────

♊ Sunday
♋
9

☉⚹☽ 12:00 am
☽△♅ 12:25 am
♂⚻♀ 5:52 am
☉⚹♅ 6:09 am
☽□♅ 9:01 am   v/c
☽→♋ 5:16 pm

April
Aprilo

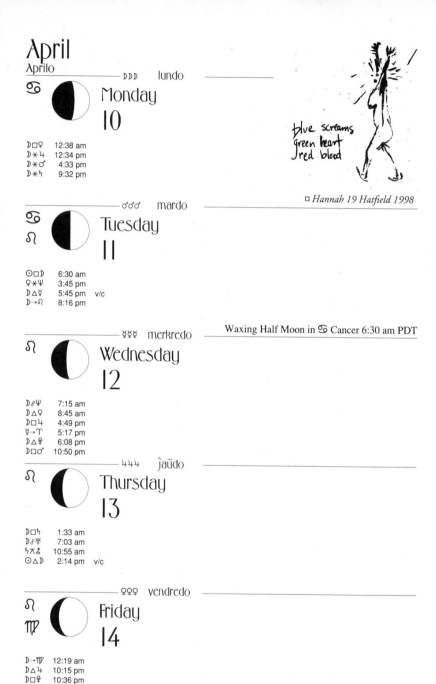

─────))) lundo ─────

♋ **Monday**
10

)□♀ 12:38 am
)⚹♃ 12:34 pm
)⚹♂ 4:33 pm
)⚹♄ 9:32 pm

blue screams
green heart
red blood

□ *Hannah 19 Hatfield 1998*

───── ♂♂♂ mardo ─────

♋
♌ **Tuesday**
11

☉□) 6:30 am
♀⚹♆ 3:45 pm
)△♅ 5:45 pm v/c
)→♌ 8:16 pm

Waxing Half Moon in ♋ Cancer 6:30 am PDT

───── ☿☿☿ merkredo ─────

♌ **Wednesday**
12

)☍♆ 7:15 am
)△♀ 8:45 am
)□♃ 4:49 pm
♅→♈ 5:17 pm
)△♀ 6:08 pm
)□♂ 10:50 pm

───── ♃♃♃ ĵaŭdo ─────

♌ **Thursday**
13

)□♄ 1:33 am
)☍♅ 7:03 am
♄⚼♃ 10:55 am
☉△) 2:14 pm v/c

───── ♀♀♀ vendredo ─────

♌
♍ **Friday**
14

)→♍ 12:19 am
)△♃ 10:15 pm
)□♀ 10:36 pm

───────────────────

All aspects in Pacific Daylight Time; add 3 hours for EDT; add 7 hours for GMT

Woman's Shame

Shame of liking sex too much
Shame of not liking it enough

Shame of having too many children
Having none, or too many abortions

Shame of bleeding
Shame of not bleeding anymore

Shame of a mother who works a job
Shame of one who stays at home

Shame of being a married possession
Shame of being an ugly duckling

Shame of being full-breasted
Shame of being flat-chested

Shame of being too submissive
Shame of being too aggressive

Madonna or Whore
is a too tight shoe to wear
And shame is a blame game
that I'm not playing

◻ *Colleen Redman 1998*

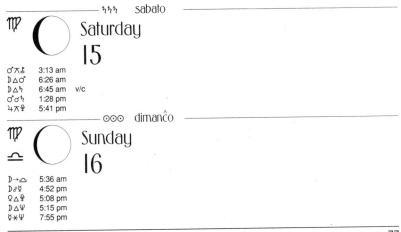

ħħħ   sabato

♍ Saturday

15

♂⊼⚷   3:13 am
☽△♂   6:26 am
☽△♄   6:45 am   v/c
♂☌♄   1:28 pm
♃⊼♀   5:41 pm

⊙⊙⊙   dimanĉo

♍ ♎ Sunday

16

☽→♎   5:36 am
☽☍♅   4:52 pm
♀△♀   5:08 pm
☽△♆   5:15 pm
♅⚹♆   7:55 pm

April
Aprili

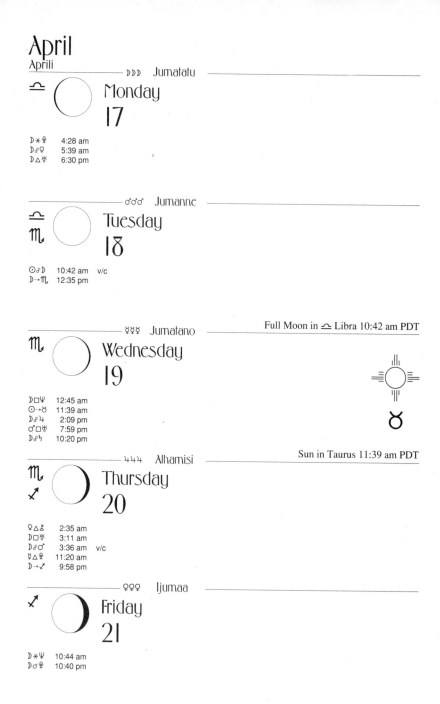

Monday
17

D ⚹ ♀ 4:28 am
D ☍ ♀ 5:39 am
D △ ♅ 6:30 pm

Tuesday
18

☉ ☍ D 10:42 am v/c
D → ♏ 12:35 pm

Wednesday
19

Full Moon in ♎ Libra 10:42 am PDT

D □ ♆ 12:45 am
☉ → ♉ 11:39 am
D ☍ ♃ 2:09 pm
♂ □ ♅ 7:59 pm
D ☍ ♄ 10:20 pm

♉

Thursday
20

Sun in Taurus 11:39 am PDT

♀ △ ♇ 2:35 am
D □ ♅ 3:11 am
D ☍ ♂ 3:36 am v/c
☿ △ ♀ 11:20 am
D → ♐ 9:58 pm

Friday
21

D ⚹ ♆ 10:44 am
D ☌ ♀ 10:40 pm

All aspects in Pacific Daylight Time; add 3 hours for EDT; add 7 hours for GMT

Year at a Glance for ♉ TAURUS (April 19–May 20)

For the last three years, you have been restless and dissatisfied. You passionately want to be an agent of change, but Uranus (the Awakener) in your house of work/right livelihood scatters your focus, keeps you experimenting and changing your job. Taurus is usually steadier with more determination and greater consistency than other signs but you've had opportunities flying at you from the most unexpected quarters. If you've been flexible enough to respond, you've experienced some fabulous moments. You have truly unique gifts and they have been witnessed. But then that moment disappears, leaving you in limbo until the next opportunity beckons.

You will find the greatest satisfaction in the service fields, improving the circumstances of those less advantaged. Saturn (discipline) moves into Taurus in February and hones your resourcefulness, adds determination and enables you to take on more responsibilities. You will need much more sleep than usual. Jupiter (expansion) joins Saturn from February through June, bringing a burst of enthusiasm. Expect breakthroughs. You command respect for your talents and will travel with your work.

An important fifteen-year cycle ended in 1999. You are just beginning to create a new self-image but will struggle with bouts of obscurity this year. You are recombining the scattered pieces of your old self into a new one. Use a wise friend or therapist to provide support during this time of restructuring. © *Gretchen Lawlor 1999*

Rocks-In-formations
© *Jodi Reeb-Myers 1995*

––––––– ♄♄♄ Jumamosi –––––––

♐ ◐ **Saturday**
22

☽△♉	4:45 am	
☽△♀	1:14 pm	
☽⚹♅	2:25 pm	v/c
☿△♃	7:54 pm	

––––––– ☉☉☉ Jumapili –––––––

♐ ◐ **Sunday**
♈ **23**

♀⚹♅	12:54 am	
☽→♈	9:47 am	
☉△☽	6:14 pm	

April
April

As a child of the universe,
think of the size of your playground.

excerpt © Helen C. Castonguay 1998

─────))) Montag ─────

♑

Monday
24

ⅅApG	5:26 am
ⅅ△♃	3:43 pm
☿⚹♅	9:29 pm
ⅅ△♄	11:16 pm

───── ♂♂♂ Dienstag ─────

♑
≈

Tuesday
25

ⅅ□♉	4:26 am
ⅅ□♀	9:07 am
ⅅ△♂	11:12 am v/c
ⅅ→≈	10:42 pm

───── ☿☿☿ Mittwoch ─────

≈

Wednesday
26

☉□♆	4:35 am
ⅅ☌♆	11:52 am
☉□ⅅ	12:30 pm
ⅅ⚹♀	11:38 pm

───── ♃♃♃ Donnerstag ───── Waning Half Moon in ≈ Aquarius 12:30 pm PDT

≈

Thursday
27

ⅅ□♃	5:26 am
ⅅ□♄	12:12 pm
ⅅ☌♅	3:39 pm

───── ♀♀♀ Freitag ─────

≈
♓

Friday
28

ⅅ□♂	2:44 am
ⅅ⚹♉	3:33 am
ⅅ⚹♀	3:44 am v/c
☿☌♀	6:27 am
ⅅ→♓	10:06 am

All aspects in Pacific Daylight Time; add 3 hours for EDT; add 7 hours for GMT

As joy
—powerfully—
strengthened my back,

as joy
—tremendously—
took off the pressure,

as joy
—gloriously—
warmed my heart,

I raised
like a bird
from my shackles

and flew peacefully
over the sea
of my troubles
© *Ingrid Kiehl-Krau 1988*

Isis
© *Sudie Rakusin 1998*

ᔋᔋᔋ Samstag
♓ ## Saturday
29

☉⚹☽	4:05 am
☽□♀	9:37 am
☽⚹♃	4:14 pm
☿→♉	8:53 pm
☽⚹♄	10:03 pm

⊙⊙⊙ Sonntag
♓ ## Sunday
♈ ### 30

☽⚹♂	2:13 pm	v/c
☽→♈	5:54 pm	
♀→♉	7:49 pm	

MOON IV

Ritual

The perfume of its skin intoxicates.

Having made the labyrinth
she placed the fruit carefully in its centre
not realizing
she was giving it back to herself.

She has breathed dust and sharp dry grasses.
She has sore knees and hands
from crawling
breasts hanging to dry earth
along the winding path.

She has taken a bulb
between her teeth
from the dust,
felt its hard promise,
dropped it at the centre,
delivered.

Now teeth
break a different membrane
split wax red taut resistant skin.
Sweet as honey, lime sharp juice
spurts from buttery flesh

and she
is swallowed whole by the apple,
rolled in pleasure's mouth
drunk on her back
ravenous.

On the outward journey
she finds the rattling firesticks
that call up power,
hold spells,
speak from the bones

and takes them to her place in the circle.

© *Cora Greenhill 1998*

MOON V

□ *Mimi and Dolfin 1998*

Birthing Self

Spiritual centering is not the practice of perfection: it is the practice of return. Returning again and again to claim our relationship with Spirit. This is the private core of a spirit-based life: little moments when we stand heart-naked, head bowed and say to Spirit, "Well . . . okay, then . . . I'm back." The resonance begins to hum again within the cells of our bodies, and we are not alone.

excerpt □ Christina Baldwin 1998

May
Mei

Honour friends and lovers
that we might cradle
each other in kindness
excerpt © Helen C. Castonguay 1998

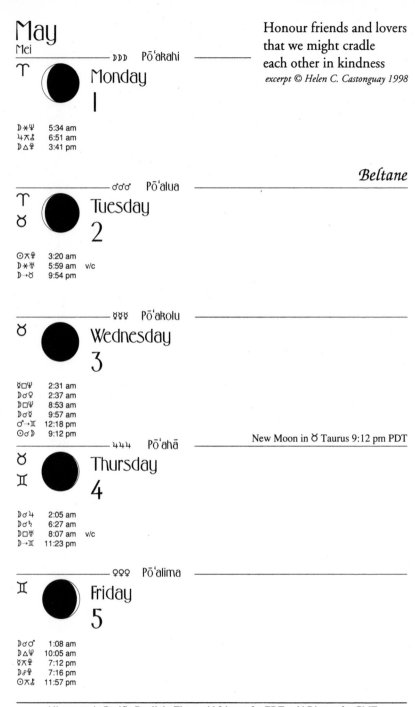

☽☽☽ Pō'akahi

♈

Monday 1

☽⚹♆ 5:34 am
♃⚻⚷ 6:51 am
☽△♇ 3:41 pm

Beltane

♂♂♂ Pō'alua

♈
♉

Tuesday 2

☉⚻♇ 3:20 am
☽⚹♅ 5:59 am v/c
☽→♉ 9:54 pm

☿☿☿ Pō'akolu

♉

Wednesday 3

☿□♆ 2:31 am
☽☌♀ 2:37 am
☽□♆ 8:53 am
☽☌☿ 9:57 am
♂→♊ 12:18 pm
☉☌☽ 9:12 pm

New Moon in ♉ Taurus 9:12 pm PDT

♃♃♃ Pō'ahā

♉
♊

Thursday 4

☽☌♃ 2:05 am
☽☌♄ 6:27 am
☽□♅ 8:07 am v/c
☽→♊ 11:23 pm

♀♀♀ Pō'alima

♊

Friday 5

☽☌♂ 1:08 am
☽△♆ 10:05 am
☿⚻♇ 7:12 pm
☽☍♇ 7:16 pm
☉⚻⚷ 11:57 pm

□ submitted by Marlene Permar 1999, photographer unknown

Beltane

Beltane marks the full emergence into the upper half of the wheel of the year. It is a celebration of the earth's fertility and life force, and a time to honor our sexuality and the erotic nature of the earth around us. Our sexuality is celebrated to ensure a fruitful harvest, to recognize the role it plays in the earth's survival and to bring us joy. Beltane is a time to celebrate our openness in order to learn and make wise choices.

Our challenge physically is to make sure our bodies are strong and solid for increased summer activity. Calendula petals can be used in salads or teas as a mild anti-infective. Oil made from the flowers soothes the skin and muscles. The leaves appear to have a beneficial effect on the immune system. Use the leaves sparingly in soups as a tonic. Use Red Clover flowers in tea for nerve and blood support.

Our emotional and spiritual challenge is to be strong enough to take risks and to explore options. Hawthorn berry helps us to feel nurtured and safe. Use 15–30 drops of tincture. Use Meadowsweet as incense to draw the interest of others. Use Ladies Mantle to help unfold our strength and beauty.

© *Colette Gardiner 1999*

Artichoke on a First Date

First;
look at her from the corner of your eye
the way she catches the leaves
between her tongue and teeth
letting them slip in and then out.
Second;
listen as her lips linger
slow as they circle the leaves
pulling, pulling on the artichoke's flesh.
Third;
smell garlic and basil, butter and lemon
on her fingers
as they unravel the leaves
carefully from the stem.
Fourth;
taste dusk, purple and dark and briny,
as it falls through the window
and over her hands uprooting the thistle
with one fast tug.
Fifth;
feel your bones shift
and your pulse sweeten
as she offers you
a bite of the heart.

¤ Amy Schutzer 1998

The River

□ Lisa de St. Croix 1995

Longing

There is a river
I long for like a lover,
to swim in its pools
and know it from the inside
where I can taste its memory
in a single drink,
where I can feel its kiss
against my trembling skin.

excerpt □ Laura Weaver 1998

—————— ♄♄♄ Pōʻaono ——————

♊

Saturday
6

☽PrG	2:02 am	
♀□Ψ	3:57 am	
☽△♅	9:01 am	v/c
☿ApG	10:29 pm	

—————— ☉☉☉ Lāpule ——————

♊
♋

Sunday
7

☽→♋	12:14 am	
☿⊼♃	1:03 pm	
☽⚹♀	1:52 pm	
☉♂♃	9:08 pm	

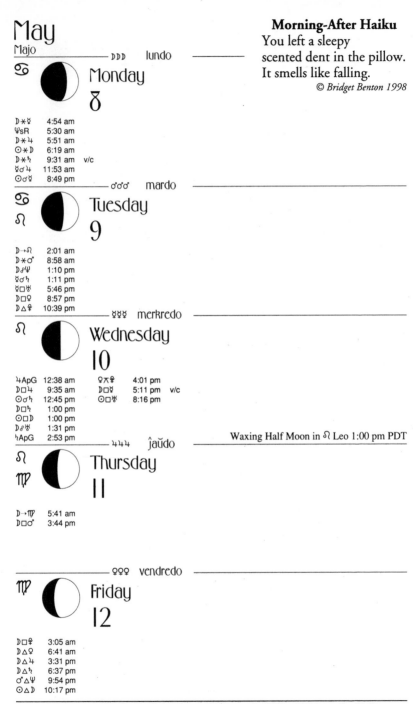

May
Majo

Morning-After Haiku
You left a sleepy
scented dent in the pillow.
It smells like falling.
© Bridget Benton 1998

☽☽☽ lundo

♋

Monday 8

☽✶☿	4:54 am	
♆sR	5:30 am	
☽✶♃	5:51 am	
☉✶☽	6:19 am	
☽✶♄	9:31 am	v/c
☿☌♃	11:53 am	
☉☌☿	8:49 pm	

♂♂♂ mardo

♋ ♌

Tuesday 9

☽→♌	2:01 am
☽✶♂	8:58 am
☽☍♆	1:10 pm
☿☌♄	1:11 pm
☿□♅	5:46 pm
☽□♀	8:57 pm
☽△♇	10:39 pm

☿☿☿ merkredo

♌

Wednesday 10

♃ApG	12:38 am	
☽□♃	9:35 am	
☉☌♄	12:45 pm	
☽□♄	1:00 pm	
☉□☽	1:00 pm	
☽☍♅	1:31 pm	
♄ApG	2:53 pm	
♀⚻♇	4:01 pm	
☽□☿	5:11 pm	v/c
☉□♅	8:16 pm	

Waxing Half Moon in ♌ Leo 1:00 pm PDT

♃♃♃ ĵaŭdo

♌ ♍

Thursday 11

☽→♍	5:41 am
☽□♂	3:44 pm

♀♀♀ vendredo

♍

Friday 12

☽□♇	3:05 am
☽△♀	6:41 am
☽△♃	3:31 pm
☽△♄	6:37 pm
♂△♆	9:54 pm
☉△☽	10:17 pm

Journal Excerpt—Morning Musings

I wondered again this morning, have the birds always sung so sweetly? Or am I learning to listen in a new way? Senses open, I imagine taking the morning into me, a holy communion. Letting it slide down my throat and into my belly like rich red wine, strengthening my blood, my bones and my passion for the day. The breath of morning air upon my skin, the touch of wind against my face, and the lingering aroma of honeysuckle warmed by the sun feed my morning hunger and nourish me for the day to come.

excerpt © Diane Goldsmith 1998

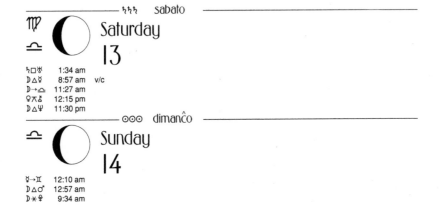

ħħħ sabato

♍ Saturday
♎ 13

ħ□♅	1:34 am	
☽△♉	8:57 am	v/c
☽→♎	11:27 am	
♀⊼♃	12:15 pm	
☽△♆	11:30 pm	

☉☉☉ dimanĉo

♎ Sunday
14

♉→♊	12:10 am	
☽△♂	12:57 am	
☽✶♀	9:34 am	

May
Mei

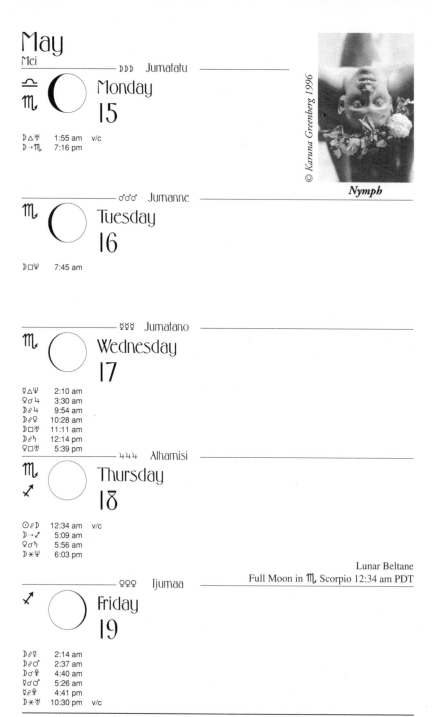

───── ☽☽☽ Jumatatu ─────

♎︎ ♏︎ Monday
15

☽△♅   1:55 am   v/c
☽→♏︎   7:16 pm

© *Karuna Greenberg 1996*

Nymph

───── ♂︎♂︎♂︎ Jumanne ─────

♏︎ Tuesday
16

☽□♆   7:45 am

───── ☿☿☿ Jumatano ─────

♏︎ Wednesday
17

☿△♆   2:10 am
♀︎♂♃   3:30 am
☽☍♃   9:54 am
☽☍♀   10:28 am
☽□♅   11:11 am
☽☍♄   12:14 pm
♀︎□♅   5:39 pm

───── ♃♃♃ Alhamisi ─────

♏︎ ♐︎ Thursday
18

☉☍☽   12:34 am   v/c
☽→♐︎   5:09 am
♀︎♂♄   5:56 am
☽⚹♆   6:03 pm

Lunar Beltane
Full Moon in ♏︎ Scorpio 12:34 am PDT

───── ♀︎♀︎♀︎ Ijumaa ─────

♐︎ Friday
19

☽☍♅   2:14 am
☽☍♂   2:37 am
☽♂♀   4:40 am
☿♂♂   5:26 am
☿☍♀   4:41 pm
☽⚹♅   10:30 pm   v/c

All aspects in Pacific Daylight Time; add 3 hours for EDT; add 7 hours for GMT

Year at a Glance for ♊ GEMINI (May 20–June 20)

By mid-year 2000, you complete an important fifteen-year cycle and a very different life will begin to emerge for you. Your energy has been focused outwards, into the world, into others or into your children.

Tie up loose ends; it's time for whatever you have been pouring yourself into to stand independently of you. Clean out your closets, rid yourself of old baggage—figuratively and literally—and make space in your life for the goddess to inspire you. Expect resistance from those close to you. You need to reevaluate your contacts. A profound interaction with someone acts as a catalyst, breaking you open to a new level of interplay with the world.

The world is hungry for the creations of your original mind. You are on the lookout for the right container or customer. Be adventurous in July (travel is electrifying). As Saturn enters your sign in August (where it will stay until June 2003), disciplined effort will pay off. Find a tangible form for your originality but keep your efforts small and personal. Use the language of the arts.

Be true to yourself. What you used to do, how you used to do it and what others have expected you to do, will no longer work. You are shedding a self-image that you learned from others. Gemini thrives on duality and has a gift for integrating diverse fields. Let your work be inspired by foreign cultures, use technology and be theatrical in your presentations. © *Gretchen Lawlor 1999*

PrettyYoungMaidens
◻ *Fay Leta 1998*

♄♄♄ Jumamosi

♐
♑ ◐ **Saturday**
20

♃□♅	6:16 am
☉→♊	10:49 am
♂☍♀	1:24 pm
☽→♑	5:01 pm

♊

Sun in Gemini 10:49 am PDT

☉☉☉ Jumapili

♑ ◐ **Sunday**
21

♉☍♄	7:53 am
☽ApG	8:54 pm

May
Mai

♑ **Monday**
22

☽△♃ 12:24 pm
☽△♄ 1:42 pm

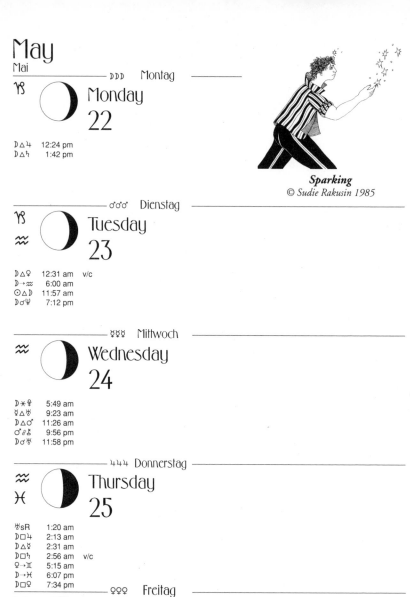

Sparking
© *Sudie Rakusin 1985*

♑
♒ **Tuesday**
23

☽△♀ 12:31 am v/c
☽→♒ 6:00 am
☉△☽ 11:57 am
☽☌♆ 7:12 pm

♒ **Wednesday**
24

☽✱♀ 5:49 am
☿△♅ 9:23 am
☽△♂ 11:26 am
♂♊♂ 9:56 pm
☽☌♅ 11:58 pm

♒
♓ **Thursday**
25

♅sR 1:20 am
☽□♃ 2:13 am
☽△♅ 2:31 am
☽□♄ 2:56 am v/c
♀→♊ 5:15 am
☽→♓ 6:07 pm
☽□♀ 7:34 pm

♓ **Friday**
26

☉□☽ 4:55 am
☽□♀ 4:49 pm

Waning Half Moon in ♓ Pisces 4:55 am PDT

All aspects in Pacific Daylight Time; add 3 hours for EDT; add 7 hours for GMT

like sleep

she speaks and eloquent but i can't quite make out the meaning.
something neptunian in this, some strand of sleeptime is in her
mouth and it wafts out with the words. i am shrouded in her
meaning. it diffuses in. but it is not like cutting the hair with scissors.
it is not like a flashlight. it is not like punching. more like tickling.
more like piano played with two hands. more like cloud color at
sunset. less like carburators. less like licorice strands. more like leaf
veins. more like wind in the tree. more like sap rising. more like
eucalyptus bark. less like embroidery. less like hems. more like
jellyfish. more like warm rivers running over rock. less like pencils
and more like crayon done without looking at the paper. yes she lives
her dream like, like drawing without looking at the paper. she lives
her life without looking down. at the pencil of her feet, where she is
scribbling with her body. she is not a pencil looking down at the page
of the ground. she is not a ballpoint pen. she is the sunset minstrel
lyre and harp, many brushes painted without looking down. she
doesn't speak the language but she is eloquent. many brushes
passionately moving without looking down. that is why she is like
flying. more like wings. less like harpoons.

excerpt ¤ Marna 1997

♓   ♄♄♄   Samstag

Saturday
27

☽□♂	1:39 am
☉△♆	4:38 am
☽✶♃	1:19 pm
☽✶♄	1:29 pm
☽□♅	9:17 pm v/c

♓   ☉☉☉   Sonntag
♈

Sunday
28

☽→♈	3:08 am
♃♂♄	9:04 am
☽✶♀	10:19 am
☽✶♆	2:52 pm
☉✶☽	5:33 pm

Becoming a Living Forest

We are bowing mothers
cradling wounded deer,
removing hooks
from the mouths of ancient fish,
setting the broken wings of birds,
and lifting them again to fly.

We gather flocks of children
in our skirts,
collect wood for the fire,
feeding bits of ourselves
to sustain the ever burning flame
in the center of the earth.

We are stroking hair,
chanting the words
that have been given
from mother to mother,
the words children hear
in wind, trees, and dreams.

We come from the trunks of women
whose roots are twisted and gnarled,
whose branches are heavy and broken
from the despair of forced silence.

We look out
from this place of mute rage
into the madness of infinity,
howling at the chill spaces
between us.

We carry our hearts
to the altar of our hope,
and embrace this struggle
of becoming a living forest
breathing and giving life.

◻ *Laura Weaver 1997*

MOON VI

Moon VI: June 2–July 1

New Moon in ♊ Gemini: June 2; Full Moon in ♐ Sagittarius: June 16; Sun in ♋ Cancer: June 20

Second Birth

May
Mei

☽☽☽ Pōʻakahi

♈

Monday
29

☽△♇ 12:07 am
☽✶♂ 11:18 am
☽✶♅ 4:15 pm v/c
⚷PrG 6:15 pm
☿→♋ 9:27 pm

The Eco-feminist

For the love of a tree,
  she went out on a limb.
For the love of the sea,
  she rocked the boat.
For the love of the earth,
  she dug deeper.

excerpt © C. Tall Mountain 1998

♂♂♂ Pōʻalua

♈ ♉

Tuesday
30

☽→♉ 8:02 am
☽✶☿ 9:18 am
♀△♆ 11:04 am
☽□♆ 6:54 pm

☿☿☿ Pōʻakolu

♉

Wednesday
31

☽□♅ 6:39 pm
♇PrG 10:10 pm
☽☌♄ 10:30 pm
☽☌♃ 11:08 pm v/c

♃♃♃ Pōʻahā

June

♉ ♊

Thursday
1

☽→♊ 9:34 am
☉☍♇ 11:17 am
☽△♆ 7:53 pm

♀♀♀ Pōʻalima

♊

Friday
2

☽☌♀ 1:01 am
☽☍♇ 4:03 am
☉☌☽ 5:14 am
♂△♅ 2:35 pm
☽△♅ 6:50 pm
☽☌♂ 7:03 pm v/c

New Moon in ♊ Gemini 5:14 am PDT

All aspects in Pacific Daylight Time; add 3 hours for EDT; add 7 hours for GMT

Many Moons in a Tree! Is She Insane?

Self Portrait
□ Julia Butterfly Hill 1999

Just as I was finishing my third term of General Psychology 203 at Portland Community College, I ran across an article in *Time* magazine about a young woman, Julia Hill, who has perched herself in the top of a giant Redwood next to the Eel River in northern California. Julia calls herself, Butterfly.

Butterfly is sitting in a tree that is at least a thousand years old. She believes it deserves to live and that to kill it to produce wall paneling is not a good exchange. I agree! She believes the tree spoke to her during a storm to calm her fears of falling off in the high winds. Butterfly says the tree spoke to her in a beautiful, very powerful female voice and said, "Julia, think of the trees . . . Think of how the trees allow their branches to blow in the wind. I'll do everything to save you." *(Time)*

Sane or insane? I say let's follow the fools who hug trees in their madness because they lead us to a better world.

excerpted from Spirited Women *(July–August 1998)* © *Amethyst Crow 1998*

For further information and to get involved write PO Box 388, Garberville, CA 95542; www.lunatree.org; or call the hotline: 415-337-4302

———————— ♄♄♄   Pōʻaono ————————

♊
♋

Saturday
3

☽PrG	6:20 am
☽→♋	9:30 am
♉⊼♆	9:59 am
♀☍♀	1:30 pm
☽♂♉	8:36 pm

———————— ☉☉☉   Lāpule ————————

♋

Sunday
4

☉☍♇	4:17 am
☽⚹♄	11:27 pm

June
Junio

♋
♌   Monday

5

☽✶♃	12:48 am	v/c
☽→♌	9:45 am	
♀☍♂	3:17 pm	
☽☍♆	8:12 pm	

♌   Tuesday

6

☽△♀	4:33 am
☽✶♀	10:34 am
☉✶☽	12:52 pm
☽☍♅	8:13 pm

♌
♍   Wednesday

7

☽✶♂	1:23 am	
☽□♄	1:35 am	
☽□♃	3:22 am	v/c
☽→♍	11:57 am	
☿⚻♀	3:22 pm	

♍   Thursday

8

☽□♀	7:40 am
☽✶♅	9:03 am
☽□♀	7:16 pm
☉□☽	8:29 pm

Waxing Half Moon in ♍ Virgo 8:29 pm PDT

♍
♎   Friday

9

☽△♄	6:29 am	
☽□♂	8:36 am	
☽△♃	8:48 am	v/c
☽→♎	4:58 pm	

All aspects in Pacific Daylight Time; add 3 hours for EDT; add 7 hours for GMT

Everyday Things

Sometimes I feel old like the hill
For I am so undisturbed by everyday things.
I like reading.
Disappearing.
Being still.
I could be scared of trees
Scared to stop.
But then I would lose all I have loved.
Stillness protects me.
Trees resurrect me.
I know life could end, so I stop to fix it.
To mend it.
To keep it.
To tend the sub-conscious ruins.
Sew up the tattered curtains
For they hold my days.
Inhale with me.
Be still . . .
As I needle the silk again
As I create seam from what was broken
I feel old—like the silk
For I am so gently torn by everyday things.

© Sioux Patullo 1998

ħħħ   sabato

  Saturday
10

☿⚹♄	12:20 am
☽△♆	4:28 am
☽⚹♀	1:43 pm
☽□☿	7:33 pm

⊙⊙⊙   dimanĉo

Sunday
11

♀ApG	12:30 am	⊙△☽	7:48 am
⊙△♅	1:12 am	☽△♀	7:54 am
♀△♅	1:43 am	☽△♂	7:14 pm v/c
⊙☌♀	3:31 am		
☽△♅	7:18 am		

June
Juni

━━━ ⊅⊅⊅ Jumatatu ━━━━━━━━━━━━━━━━━━━

♎︎
♏︎

Monday
12

⊅→♏︎   12:55 am
⊅□♆   12:54 pm

━━━ ♂♂♂ Jumanne ━━━━━━━━━━━━━━━━━━━

♏︎

Tuesday
13

⊅△☿   8:40 am
⊅□♅   4:55 pm

━━━ ☿☿☿ Jumatano ━━━━━━━━━━━━━━━━━━━

♏︎
♐︎

Wednesday
14

⊅☍♄   12:58 am
⊅☍♃   4:31 am   v/c
⊅→♐︎   11:18 am
⊅✶♆   11:37 pm

━━━ ♃♃♃ Alhamisi ━━━━━━━━━━━━━━━━━━━

♐︎

Thursday
15

⊅♂♀   9:31 am

━━━ ♀♀♀ Ijumaa ━━━━━━━━━━━━━━━━━━━

♐︎
♑︎

Friday
16

⊅✶♅   4:31 am
♂→♋︎   5:30 am
☉☍⊅   3:27 pm
⊅☍♀   6:50 pm   v/c
⊅→♑︎   11:26 pm

Full Moon in ♐︎ Sagittarius 3:27 pm PDT

All aspects in Pacific Daylight Time; add 3 hours for EDT; add 7 hours for GMT

© *Mara Friedman 1999*

Gaia's Daughter

♑

Saturday
17

☽☌♂︎ 12:31 am

♑

Sunday
18

☽ApG 5:57 am
☽☍♅ 2:28 pm
♀→♋ 3:15 pm

Golden Grace

I shall paint my fingers and toes gold
like Cleopatra like Nefertiti
like my ancestral sisters who
wove their gold
wore their gold
in rows, encircled, entwined
I shall paint my fingers and toes gold
for I have only riches that cannot be
mined, stolen, sold
my treasures are simple
a triangular face
bequeathed to me by the Mantis God
eyes
that have seen the boomerang rebound
there is music in my body
and strength in my loins
the legacy of a dance with the earth
I have sturdy thighs and high hips
and caramel/chocolate milky/deep dark
skin
this skin houses the riches that will always be
my wealth within
Yes, I shall paint my fingers and toes gold
and adorn the wilderness

¤ *Viviane Gordon Voa 1998*

Sunflower Field
© *Tamara Leibfarth 1997*

Summer Solstice

Summer Solstice is the longest day and the top of the wheel of the year. It celebrates the peak of summer and the richness of life and is a time of expanded awareness and vitality. It is the time when plants shift from growth phase to reproduction. Solstice symbolizes the point we reach when we have grown and explored as much as we can and need to direct our lives.

Our physical challenge is to make use of warm weather and fresh food to make ourselves as strong as possible, knowing that our work now will pay off in increased winter health. Use Arnica flowers steeped in oil externally to soothe summer injuries that can become winter aches. Lavender flower tea is calming and centering in the midst of summer's stimulation. Use the tea as a wash for sunburn.

Our emotional and spiritual challenge is to learn to commit, direct and protect ourselves. Use Lavender in any form to help you define life purpose. Place Baby's Breath on altars for appreciation of the sweetness and briefness of life. Hang Fennel in doorways for protection.

© *Colette Gardiner 1999*

June
Juni

♑
♒

Monday
19

☽△♄ 2:59 am
☽△♃ 7:46 am   v/c
☽→♒ 12:26 pm

———— ♂♂♂ Dienstag ————

♒

Tuesday
20

☽☌♆ 12:51 am
☽⚹♀ 10:49 am
☉→♋ 6:48 pm

Solstice

♋

Sun in Cancer 6:48 pm PDT

———— ☿☿☿ Mittwoch ————

♒

Wednesday
21

☽☌♅ 5:58 am
♀☌♂ 12:27 pm
☽□♄ 4:12 pm
☽□♃ 9:25 pm   v/c

———— ♃♃♃ Donnerstag ————

♒
♓

Thursday
22

☽→♓ 12:52 am
☉△☽ 3:26 am
☽△♂ 9:00 am
☽△♀ 10:03 am
☽□♆ 10:28 pm

———— ♀♀♀ Freitag ————

♓

Friday
23

♅sR 1:32 am
♀⚹♆ 1:12 pm
☽△♅ 3:50 pm

All aspects in Pacific Daylight Time; add 3 hours for EDT; add 7 hours for GMT

Year at a Glance for ♋ CANCER (June 20–July 22)

In 1999 a new direction in life opened up for Cancer. It came through a call to explore new ways of creating safe space for yourself and others in your life. You began to develop new abilities, a better sense of yourself and a new circle of companions. You began to discover how much more could be accomplished in collaboration. In 2000 you may decide to leave behind old commitments to pursue more of this new way of being. If so, your circumstances could change swiftly and profoundly.

Or, you may decide to pursue every opportunity to expand your current options and build new structures into your life. Change is inevitable. It's your own choice how to accommodate the old with the new.

Life is nudging you in a definite direction. You may feel your fate is being determined by circumstances beyond your control. Disturbances in the lives of family members or mates require that you adjust your own plans. Exchanges with people—financial, sexual or emotional—ask you to be responsive to what they need and value. You may have to set your own needs aside for a while to tend to someone you love. Be very honest in joint endeavors and discriminating about whom you put your faith in.

Patterns of behavior that once kept you safe have become towers of isolation. You are ready to move on. Get inspiration from therapy or a spiritual practice. Friendships provide encouragement and support.

© *Gretchen Lawlor 1999*

Whale's Eye
© *Marja de Vries 1994*

ℏℏℏ　Samstag

♓
♈　　**Saturday**
　　24

☽✶♄	3:14 am	
☽✶♃	8:40 am	v/c
☽→♈	10:55 am	
☉□☽	6:00 pm	
☽□♂	9:45 pm	
☽✶♆	10:08 pm	

☉☉☉　Sonntag

Waning Half Moon in ♈ Aries 6:00 pm PDT

♈　　**Sunday**
　　25

☽□♀	1:38 am
♂⊼♆	4:56 am
☽△♀	7:10 am
☽□♅	10:59 pm

June
Iune

───))) Pō'akahi ───

♈
♉

Monday
26

☽⚹♅ 12:23 am v/c
☽→♉ 5:19 pm

─── ♂♂♂ Pō'alua ───

♉

Tuesday
27

☉⚻♆ 12:48 am
☽□♆ 3:39 am
☉⚹☽ 3:52 am
☽⚹♂ 6:04 am
♀⚻♀ 11:27 am
☽⚹♀ 12:06 pm

─── ☿☿☿ Pō'akolu ───

♉
♊

Wednesday
28

☽⚹♅ 1:51 am
☽□♅ 4:04 am
☽♂♄ 2:06 pm
♀⚻♄ 7:13 pm
☽♂♃ 7:34 pm v/c
☽→♊ 7:59 pm

─── ♃♃♃ Pō'ahā ───

♊

Thursday
29

☽△♆ 5:37 am
☽☍♀ 1:33 pm

─── ♀♀♀ Pō'alima ───

♊
♋

Friday
30

♃→♊ 12:34 am
☽△♅ 4:47 am v/c
☽→♋ 8:09 pm

All aspects in Pacific Daylight Time; add 3 hours for EDT; add 7 hours for GMT

Rainforest

Womb
Inside
Womb
Inside
Womb
Inside
Womb
I drip like rain trees.
I drip seed to the forest floor.
Life forms in the darkness.

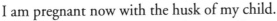

□ Shiloh McCloud 1998

I am pregnant now with the husk of my child.
Sediment gathers at the base of my womb.
Child drips from the canopy of forest leaves.
Inside
Womb
I surround my child's tiny womb.
Forest is womb for each drop of rain.
Mother's cave womb surrounds me.
Generations of womb surround us all by time and death.
Forest is reflected in every drop.
All inside my own womb.
Inside   Womb   Inside   Womb.

© Sioux Patullo 1997

ℏℏℏ   Pō'aono

♋ **Saturday**
1

☉♂♂	8:50 am
☽♂♂	12:16 pm
☉♂☽	12:20 pm
☽PrG	3:29 pm
☽♂♀	9:56 pm
☽♂♅	11:23 pm

July

New Moon in ♋ Cancer 12:20 pm PST
Partial Solar Eclipse 12:33 pm PST (0.477 mag.)
Eclipse visible from southern Argentina and Chile

☉☉☉   Lāpule

♋
♌ **Sunday**
2

☉☌♀	1:30 am	
♂☌♀	8:35 am	
☿♂♀	10:39 am	
☽✶ℏ	2:36 pm	v/c
☽→♌	7:38 pm	
☽✶♃	8:34 pm	

Heaven is hers!
Earth is hers!
She is a warrior,
She is a falcon,
She is a great white cow.
She fought the dragon, and slew it.
She seduced the scorpion, and tamed it.
The golden lion slept at her side.
She is the singer,
She is desire.
She is the mountain of silver, gold and lapis.
On her hips tall trees grow, and grasses.
From Her womb waters spout, and savory grains.
Her lap is holy,
Her lips are honey,
Her hand is law.
Her breast pours heavenly rain.
She is the healer,
She is life-giver,
She is the terror, the anger, the hunger.
Fierce winds blow from her heart.
Hers is the thunder, the lightning, the glory.
She is the morning,
She is the evening,
She is the star.
She wears the gown of mystery.
Heaven is hers!
Earth is hers!
Who can argue?

MOON VII

Moon VII: July 1–July 30

New Moon in ♋ Cancer: July 1; Full Moon in ♑ Capricorn: July 16; Sun in ♌ Leo: July 22

© Sandra Stanton 1998

Mawu

July
Julio

♌

───── ☽☽☽   lundo ─────

Monday
3

☽☌♆	4:55 am
☽△♀	12:48 pm
☉⊼♂	2:12 pm
☿PrG	5:12 pm

───── ♂♂♂   mardo ─────

♌
♍

Tuesday
4

☽☌♅	4:11 am	
♂⊼♂	11:58 am	
☽□♄	3:26 pm	v/c
☽→♍	8:19 pm	
☽□♃	10:00 pm	

───── ☿☿☿   merkredo ─────

♍

Wednesday
5

♀⊼♅	1:25 am
☽□♀	2:15 pm
☽⚹♂	6:12 pm
☉⚹☽	8:34 pm
☽⚹♅	9:25 pm

───── ♃♃♃   ĵaŭdo ─────

♍
♎

Thursday
6

☉☌♅	4:35 am	
☽⚹♀	9:25 am	
☽△♄	6:57 pm	v/c
☽→♎	11:47 pm	

───── ♀♀♀   vendredo ─────

♎

Friday
7

☽△♃	2:21 am
☿☌♂	7:08 am
☽△♆	9:59 am
☽⚹♀	6:52 pm

All aspects in Pacific Daylight Time; add 3 hours for EDT; add 7 hours for GMT

Jungle Mama

© Elizabeth Rosefield 1998

Mother Dance

Small toes bruise my knees
Tangled together we sleep
Seed and husk.
Until star fish fists climb my hair
And monkey grasp pinches the back of my hand.
Love bites my fingers with two new teeth.

I am here for you to push against,
Sometimes shattering as you grow
Breaking my shell
Excavating dawn
To the tune of wonder hatching.

© *Selina di Girolamo 1998*

ħħħ   sabato

♎ Saturday
                        8

☽□♉	12:15 am
☽□♂	1:59 am
☉□☽	5:53 am
☽△♅	12:13 pm
☽□♀	9:10 pm v/c

Waxing Half Moon in ♎ Libra 5:53 am PDT

☉☉☉   dimanĉo

♎
♏ Sunday
                       9

☽→♏	6:48 am
☽□♆	5:34 pm

July
Julai

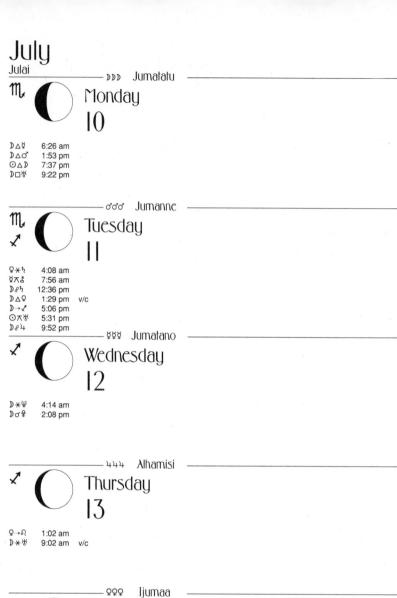

♏ ☽ **Monday**
10

☽△♅	6:26 am
☽△♂	1:53 pm
☉△☽	7:37 pm
☽□♅	9:22 pm

♏
♐ ☽ **Tuesday**
11

♀✶♄	4:08 am
☿⊼♇	7:56 am
☽☍♄	12:36 pm
☽△♀	1:29 pm	v/c
☽→♐	5:06 pm
☉⊼♅	5:31 pm
☽☍♃	9:52 pm

♐ ☽ **Wednesday**
12

| ☽✶♆ | 4:14 am |
| ☽☌♀ | 2:08 pm |

♐ ☽ **Thursday**
13

| ♀→♌ | 1:02 am |
| ☽✶♅ | 9:02 am | v/c |

♐
♑ ☽ **Friday**
14

| ☽→♑ | 5:27 am |

All aspects in Pacific Daylight Time; add 3 hours for EDT; add 7 hours for GMT

Moon Dancer

© *Schar Cbear Freeman 1998*

Full Moon

She makes the water look like cellophane or salmon skin.
She makes the waves look like lace.
She cuts my face into velvet ribbons.
Turns my shadow to mosaic.
She braids my hair into lizard scales.
And turns my blood to wine.
Pouring milk into my womb of glass.
And serpent up my spine.

© *Sioux Patullo 1997*

───── ♄♄♄ Jumamosi ─────

♑

Saturday

15

☽☍♉	2:59 am
☽ApG	8:31 am
♀✶♃	1:33 pm
☿⊼♀	6:33 pm
☽☍♂	9:27 pm

───── ☉☉☉ Jumapili ─────

♑
≈≈

Sunday

16

♂⊼♅	3:29 am	
☉☍☽	6:55 am	
☽△♄	2:48 pm	v/c
☽→≈	6:27 pm	

Full Moon in ♑ Capricorn 6:55 am PDT
Total Lunar Eclipse 6:57 am PDT (1.768 mag.)
Eclipse visible from Australia, Indonesia, Malaysia, Japan and the Philippines

July
Juli

♒ ## Monday
17

☽△♃	1:18 am
☽☍♀	4:48 am
☽♂♆	5:30 am
⚵sD	6:20 am
♀☍♆	11:30 am
☽⚹⚷	3:35 pm

♒ ## Tuesday
18

| ⚵⊼⚷ | 8:15 am |
| ☽♂♅ | 10:17 am |

♒
♓ ## Wednesday
19

☽□♄	3:37 am	v/c
☽→♓	6:44 am	
☽□♃	2:22 pm	

♓ ## Thursday
20

☽□♀	3:16 am
☽△⚵	3:59 am
☉⚹♄	5:38 pm
♂ApG	10:16 pm

♓
♈ ## Friday
21

☽△♂	3:57 am	
♀△⚷	11:50 am	
☽⚹♄	2:34 pm	
☉△☽	4:08 pm	v/c
☽→♈	5:09 pm	
⚵⊼⚸	10:38 pm	

All aspects in Pacific Daylight Time; add 3 hours for EDT; add 7 hours for GMT

Year at a Glance for ♌ LEO (July 22–August 22)

The year 2000 will be a high profile year for Leo. Your natural radiance will shine, and it is a good time to put your abilities on trial. Your dedication to work in the last few years is paying off. You will receive prestige or authority as you demonstrate your gifts and talents. Your attitude is critical and will be the true scale on which your efforts will be judged. Your greatest potential is being tested, and you may experience significant challenges from those closest to you. Be willing to adapt to circumstances and change your strategies in personal and official partnerships. Old fears of loss, failure or abandonment may haunt your efforts.

From February through June, any effort you make should result in considerable progress. Do travel for work or undertake advanced training. Be alert for a tendency to be overbearing. It may provoke others to sabotage your efforts. If you are in a relationship, you already know you have to be open to making changes in your agreements. You are being asked to make your relationship more spiritually significant. If you aren't presently involved, you are likely to meet someone through friends, especially from June onwards. People you meet now will help you move away from old partnership models. Don't expect things to be placid. If you have children, they will want more autonomy. Don't try to live through them or force them to your will—they will resent you. You need your own outlets for self-expression though you may be expressing something from the collective unconscious which others will find compelling.

© Gretchen Lawlor 1999

Zenobia
© Sudie Rakusin 1998

ħħħ Samstag

♈ **Saturday**
22

☽✶♃	1:18 am
☽✶♆	3:15 am
☉→♌	5:43 am
♀△♅	7:28 am
☽△♀	12:44 pm
☽□♅	3:16 pm
☽△♀	3:24 pm

Sun in Leo 5:43 am PDT

☉☉☉ Sonntag

♈ **Sunday**
23

☽✶♅	5:47 am	
☽□♂	3:11 pm	v/c

July
Iulai

♈
♉

Monday
24

D→♉   12:44 am
⊙□D   4:02 am
D□♆   10:09 am

© Hazel Collins 1997

Waning Half Moon in ♉ Taurus 4:02 am PDT

♉

Tuesday
25

D⚹♉   12:09 am
D□♀   3:02 am
D□♅   11:04 am
D⚹♂   10:36 pm

♉
♊

Wednesday
26

D♂♄   3:20 am   v/c
D→♊   5:01 am
⊙⚹D   11:52 am
D♂♃   1:35 pm
D△♆   1:47 pm
D☍♀   10:18 pm

♊

Thursday
27

♃△♆   4:23 am
♆PrG   9:50 am
D⚹♀   10:29 am
D△♅   1:18 pm   v/c
⊙☍♆   3:49 pm
⊙⚹♃   6:41 pm

♊
♋

Friday
28

D→♋   6:30 am
♀☍♅   7:00 pm

The Bath

The photo that always bothered me the most
was little, tiny me—a small baby a couple weeks old.
A bath scene.
I am bright red, screaming in fear.
My father is holding my head up by two fingers,
the rest of me unsupported, totally terrified.
My mother says now—
"Those baths! It always looked like we were boiling you in oil."
This morning my baby daughter and I took a bath together.
I didn't want her to be afraid,
so I held her close, naked against me,
warm and slippery like after her birth.
I cradled her in my lap, her head on my thigh,
her whole body supported, enveloped, by me and by warm water.
She was calm.
She smiled up at me.
And I cried for her—precious, vulnerable child.
And I wept for me—
it didn't HAVE to be that way.
If I screamed so every time,
Why not CHANGE how you bathed me, how you held me?
No, I say, clinging to my baby in our shared towel,
this time it will be different. You have a chance not to fear.
And I hug her tight.

© beth milander 1996

ħħħ   Pōʻaono

♋

Saturday
29

☽♂♉   10:19 am

☉☉☉   Lāpule

♋
♌

Sunday
30

☽PrG	12:38 am	♂⚹ħ	6:21 pm
☽♂♂	4:47 am	☉♂☽	7:25 pm
☽⚹ħ	5:18 am v/c	☽△♀	10:43 pm
☽→♌	6:23 am		
☽☍♅	2:30 pm		
☽⚹♃	3:34 pm		

Partial Solar Eclipse 7:14 pm PDT (0.603 mag.)
New Moon in ♌ Leo 7:25 pm PDT
Eclipse visible from northern Asia and Greenland and northwestern N. America

The Fool and the Fire

My heart pumps hot blood faster as
we drum and rattle under August stars.
The guide has readied us well.
I watch the others one by one
walk the fire without harm.
Red coals wink and beckon,
This heated bed makes eyes at me!

Onto a new plane I move resolutely.
The crunch under my bare feet,
licks and steams, how on earth
can it feel cold as old popcorn?
Seven steps I walk as ten companions chant.
I part the curtain of fear. The world
changes. At the end of the bed

I step laughing to my lover's arms.
She and I take hands to make the return.
I want to slow those moments down, sear
them into my heart. No challenge can
undo me now. What belief cannot be changed?
The curtain melts away. Expecting safety
I need no longer pursue it.

□ *Sue Silvermarie 1998*

MOON VIII

Moon VIII: July 30–August 29

New Moon in ♌ Leo: July 30; Full Moon in ♒ Aquarius: Aug. 14; Sun in ♍ Virgo: Aug. 22

© Pamela Moore 1997

Tempered

July
Julio

Acorn Woman

 ♌

ⅅⅅⅅ   lundo

Monday
31

☿⚹♅	12:11 am	
☽☍♅	1:06 pm	
♂→♌	6:21 pm	
☽♂♀	7:14 pm	

♌
♍

♂♂♂   mardo

Tuesday
1

August

☽□♄	5:34 am	v/c
☽→♍	6:27 am	
☽□♃	4:25 pm	
☉△♀	10:53 pm	
☽□♀	11:14 pm	

♍

☿☿☿   merkredo

Wednesday
2

Lammas

☉△♗	8:54 pm
☽⚹☿	9:03 pm

♍
♎

♃♃♃   ĵaŭdo

Thursday
3

☽△♄	7:50 am	v/c
☽→♎	8:31 am	
☽⚹♂	11:33 am	
☽△♆	5:09 pm	
☽△♃	7:41 pm	

♎

♀♀♀   vendredo

Friday
4

☽⚹♀	2:20 am
☉⚹☽	6:16 am
☽△♅	6:08 pm

All aspects in Pacific Daylight Time; add 3 hours for EDT; add 7 hours for GMT

Lammas

Lammas is the celebration of the harvest of grain and first fruits, a time to offer the first loaf o f bread or the last stalks of grain harvested to the earth. The harvest isn't complete, but our efforts are starting to pay off. It is time to acknowledge our bounty and celebrate as we start to reap the benefits of our labors and our commitments in our gardens and lives. Careful steering and tending is still needed if we are to have a successful harvest.

Our physical challenge is to assess our physical strengths and to continue to build on them. The pigments in berries are especially high in bioflavinoids that can help support many body functions, especially circulation. Blueberries, Raspberries and Hawthorn berries are all high in nutrients that help us nurture all parts of our body.

Our emotional and spiritual challenge is to acknowledge our abilities and resources, to be patient while we wait for results, and to acknowledge the efforts of others. Use Rosemary as tea or incense for clarity. Use Hollyhock flower tea to soften and soothe the throat, allowing us to speak with grace and tact.

***Surrendering
to the Fool***

© *Hope Harris 1998*

nectarine
i woke with such a hunger
for ripe fruit
and orgasm
stumbled into the kitchen
groping
for the first bite
still blind with sleep
i carried it back to my bed
sat on my white sheets
at three in the morning
alone and i
didn't care about the stains
of summer's juices
running down my chin
dripping onto my belly
sweaty from the hot night
so sweet
like singing
like coming under the tongues
of angels   ¤ *Shae Irving 1995*

hot flash

awake at midnight
images erupt in a flash of heat
coursing through my body
words flow like
molten lava
from the core of me
spew themselves across the page
volcanic poems
rising from
the fire in me

so this is menopause
this is the heat
of my body
growing older
flaming sweaty
jewel of the night!

so this is the steamy
hot wisdom
of my womb
boiling over
dripping words
gushing stories
wildly
all over me!

© *Diane Goldsmith 1998*

ħħħ   sabato

♎︎
♏︎

Saturday
5

☽□♉	9:03 am	
☽⚹♀	11:56 am	v/c
☽→♏︎	2:04 pm	
☽□♂	8:10 pm	
☽□♇	11:15 pm	

☉☉☉   dimanĉo

♏︎

Sunday
6

♀□ħ	6:25 am
♀→♍	10:32 am
☉□☽	6:02 pm
☿⚹ħ	8:20 pm
☿→♌	10:42 pm

Waxing Half Moon in ♏︎ Scorpio 6:02 pm PDT

August
Agosti

DDD Jumatatu

♏ ☾ **Monday**
♐
7

D□♅ 2:02 am
D☌♄ 11:17 pm v/c
D→♐ 11:30 pm

Strength
© *Jodi Reeb-Myers 1993*

♂♂♂ Jumanne

♐ ☾ **Tuesday**
8

D□♀ 3:40 am
D△♅ 3:51 am
♂☍♆ 7:04 am
D⚹♆ 9:07 am
D△♂ 9:15 am
D☍♃ 1:41 pm
D☌♀ 7:44 pm

☿☿☿ Jumatano

♐ ☾ **Wednesday**
9

☉△D 10:13 am
D⚹♅ 1:15 pm v/c
☿☍♆ 1:33 pm
♄→♊ 7:25 pm

♃♃♃ Alhamisi

♐ ☾ **Thursday**
♑
10

♅PrG 12:32 am
☿☌♂ 5:37 am
♀⚻♆ 8:27 am
D→♑ 11:44 am
☉☍♅ 10:20 pm
☿⚹♃ 10:44 pm
D△♀ 11:02 pm v/c

♀♀♀ Ijumaa

♑ ☾ **Friday**
11

DApG 3:27 pm

All aspects in Pacific Daylight Time; add 3 hours for EDT; add 7 hours for GMT

Strength

© *Angie Làzaro 1997*

♑

Saturday
12

⚷sD	12:14 am
☿△♀	7:14 am
♀□♃	5:50 pm
☿△⚸	5:51 pm
♂⚹♃	6:50 pm

♑
♒

Sunday
13

☽→♒	12:43 am
☽△♄	1:04 am
☽☌♆	10:16 am
☽△♃	4:37 pm
☽☍♂	5:35 pm
☽⚹♀	9:12 pm

August

August

────────── ☽☽☽ Montag ──────────

♒

Monday
14

☽☍♅ 4:53 am
☽♂♅ 2:17 pm
♀□♀ 4:55 pm
☉☍☽ 10:13 pm v/c

Lunar Lammas
Full Moon in ♒ Aquarius 10:13 pm PDT

────────── ♂♂♂ Dienstag ──────────

♒
♓

Tuesday
15

♀□♋ 10:28 am
☽→♓ 12:41 pm
☽□♄ 1:17 pm

────────── ☿☿☿ Mittwoch ──────────

♐

Wednesday
16

☽□♃ 4:47 am
☽□♀ 8:34 am
☿☍♅ 11:43 am
♂△♀ 12:34 pm
☽☍♀ 12:58 pm v/c

────────── ♃♃♃ Donnerstag ──────────

♓
♈

Thursday
17

☽→♈ 10:44 pm
♂△♋ 11:02 pm
☽✶♄ 11:31 pm

────────── ♀♀♀ Freitag ──────────

♈

Friday
18

☽✶♆ 7:27 am
☽✶♃ 2:48 pm
☽△♀ 5:52 pm
☽△♂ 8:41 pm

All aspects in Pacific Daylight Time; add 3 hours for EDT; add 7 hours for GMT

She had a desert temperament
    hot, dry, raw, dusty
    unforgiving
With bursts of
    spectacular color
    impossible vistas
A mosaic of unexpected life-forms
    woven into
      the dirt
Unadorned, she was,
    a welcome change from
    the dripping cloying
    moodiness
Of those seeking comfort
    but not ready for the
    briskness
Of a wide open
    summer
    sky . . .

© Patricia Dines 1998

♄♄♄   Samstag

♈ **Saturday**
19

☽✶♅   9:26 am
☽△♀   10:31 pm

☉☉☉   Sonntag

♈
♉ **Sunday**
20

☉△☽   2:14 am   v/c
☽→♉   6:31 am
☽□♆   2:46 pm
♀sD   3:41 pm

August
'Aukake

☽☽☽ Pō'akahi

¤ *Becky Bee 1999*

♉

Monday 21

☽□♂ 6:17 am
♀⚻♅ 10:28 am
☽□♅ 3:35 pm
☽△♀ 4:07 pm
☉☌☿ 6:05 pm

♂♂♂ Pō'alua

♉ ♊

Tuesday 22

☿→♍ 3:11 am
☿□♄ 10:23 am
☉□☽ 11:51 am v/c
☽→♊ 11:55 am
☉→♍ 12:48 pm
☽☌♄ 12:57 pm
☽□☿ 1:22 pm
☽△♆ 7:43 pm

♍

Waning Half Moon in ♉ Taurus 11:51 am PDT
Sun in Virgo 12:48 pm PDT

☿☿☿ Pō'akolu

♊

Wednesday 23

☽☌♃ 3:33 am
☉□♄ 4:16 am
☽☍♇ 5:27 am
☽✶♂ 1:08 pm
☽△♅ 7:23 pm

♃♃♃ Pō'ahā

♊ ♋

Thursday 24

☽□♀ 12:57 am v/c
☿⚻♆ 9:46 am
☽→♋ 2:59 pm
☉✶☽ 6:35 pm

♀♀♀ Pō'alima

♋

Friday 25

☽✶☿ 12:22 am

Year at a Glance for ♍ VIRGO (Aug. 22–Sept. 22)

Hard work towards your ambitions begins to pay off, especially if you are involved with advanced education, publishing or foreign cultures. In 1999 you were learning the rules of the game, in 2000 you play it with determination. You are looking for a simple, effective container into which you can pour your insights and make them accessible to the world. Travel for specific training or for professional development is quite likely.

Uranus and Neptune are both influencing your work, particularly with changing tools and techniques, perhaps an unsettled work environment. Your work may require you to integrate spiritual or occult techniques, or to work with people in spiritual crisis. The most fulfilling work involves caring for others or creative and artistic work.

Virgo is deeply committed to service. Further education or exploration of new horizons will bear fruit. You have been restless, frustrated or rebelling against expectations at work. You need to express your own style and originality. You have exciting insights into the mind-body link. Your relationship to your own body is changing, reflecting energetic changes in your make-up. You benefit from alternative healing techniques, which seek out the subtle causes of ill health and use gentle means to rebalance the system. Your body needs health regimes that incorporate new diets and exercise practices with a mystical or artistic component. Pluto conjunct Chiron continues to provide breakthroughs.

© *Gretchen Lawlor 1999*

Bean Womyn
© *Angie Làzaro 1998*

------------------ ♄♄♄ Pōʻaono ------------------

♋
♌

Saturday
26

☽⚹♀	7:10 am	v/c
☽→♌	4:17 pm	
☽⚹♄	5:28 pm	
☽☍♆	11:25 pm	

------------------ ☉☉☉ Lāpule ------------------

♌

Sunday
27

♀□♃	12:31 am	♀□♀	9:23 am	
☉⚻♆	2:14 am	♀ApG	12:41 pm	
☽PrG	7:00 am	☽♂♂	8:28 pm	
☽⚹♃	7:41 am	☽☍♅	9:44 pm	v/c
☽△♀	8:45 am	♀□♅	11:12 pm	

Cave Walls

© *Sierra Lonepine Briano 1998*

Her Story

My Body tells a story
I look at my hands,
They are also the hands of my ancestors.
I turn them, palms facing me,
Like a book, I begin to read the story again.
□ *Claire Serpell 1998*

MOON IX

Moon IX: August 29–September 27

New Moon in ♍ Virgo: Aug. 29; Full Moon in ♓ Pisces: Sept. 13; Sun in ♎ Libra: Sept. 22

© *Angie Coffin 1998*

Village Elder, Thailand

August
Aŭgusto

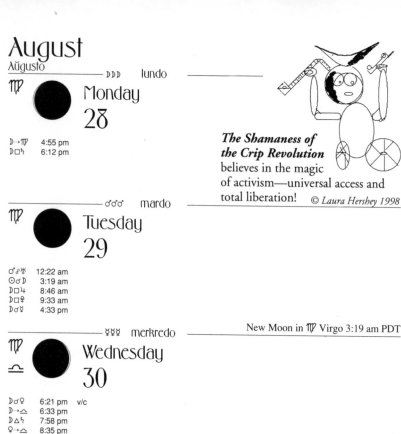

The Shamaness of the Crip Revolution believes in the magic of activism—universal access and total liberation! © *Laura Hershey 1998*

♍ ☽☽☽ lundo

Monday
28

☽→♍ 4:55 pm
☽□♄ 6:12 pm

♍ ♂♂♂ mardo

Tuesday
29

♂☍♅ 12:22 am
☉☌☽ 3:19 am
☽□♃ 8:46 am
☽□♀ 9:33 am
☽☌♅ 4:33 pm

♍ ☿☿☿ merkredo

Wednesday
30

♍
♎

☽☌♀ 6:21 pm v/c
☽→♎ 6:33 pm
☽△♄ 7:58 pm
♀→♎ 8:35 pm

New Moon in ♍ Virgo 3:19 am PDT

♎ ♃♃♃ ĵaŭdo

Thursday
31

☽△♆ 1:52 am
☽△♃ 11:27 am
☽⚹♀ 11:56 am
♀△♄ 1:21 pm
☿⚻♅ 4:24 pm

♎ ♀♀♀ vendredo
♏

Friday
1

☽△♅ 1:36 am
☽⚹♂ 5:23 am v/c
☉□♃ 9:46 am
☽→♏ 10:55 pm

September

© *Keely Meagan 1997*

Women Build Houses

♏ Saturday

2

☉□♀ 2:01 am
☽□♆ 6:40 am
☉⚹☽ 6:50 pm

♏ Sunday

3

♀△♆ 7:36 am
☽□♅ 8:04 am
☉□♇ 8:41 am
☽□♂ 3:13 pm
☽⚹♅ 6:34 pm   v/c

September
Septemba

□ *Nancy Bareis 1998*

DDD Jumatatu ─────────

♏︎
♐︎ Monday

4

♃ ⚹ ♀	3:53 am
D → ♐︎	7:08 am
D ☍ ♄	8:56 am
D ⚹ ♆	3:21 pm
D ⚹ ♀	6:56 pm

♂♂♂ Jumanne ─────────

♐︎ Tuesday

5

D ☌ ♀	3:09 am
D ☍ ♃	3:17 am
☉ □ D	9:27 am
D ⚹ ♅	6:21 pm

☿☿☿ Jumatano ─────────

Waxing Half Moon in ♐︎ Sagittarius 9:27 am PDT

♐︎
♑︎ Wednesday

6

D △ ♂	5:22 am
D □ ♅	3:26 pm v/c
D → ♑︎	6:47 pm

♃♃♃ Alhamisi ─────────

♑︎ Thursday

7

D □ ♀	2:02 pm
☿ → ♎︎	3:22 pm

♀♀♀ Ijumaa ─────────

♑︎ Friday

8

☉ △ D	3:27 am v/c
♀ ⚹ ♀	5:04 am
☿ △ ♄	5:27 am
D ApG	5:36 am
♀ △ ♃	10:29 am

All aspects in Pacific Daylight Time; add 3 hours for EDT; add 7 hours for GMT

glassblowing

and i ask her
    maybe you'd like to be a vase today
    to be filled with flowers on a sunny windowsill?

and she will oblige
    if i touch her sweetly
    and dance with her gracefully
    and keep her hot and flowing like honey.

my breath gives her life
    by gently expanding her to the size i want
    while gravity helps me stretch her long.

my fingers constantly turn the blowpipe
    to keep her centered on the end
        so i can touch her evenly.

wood and paper are my allies
    to cool her down where she needs it.
and metal tools carefully used
    will leave no scars.

but my best friend is her mother—Heat
    in the fiery glory hole she goes
    warmed until i can touch and dance
        and flow with her some more.

and i let her speak to me
    and i learn
as my fingers turn and turn and turn.

◻ Joell Lanfrank 1998

---- ⊁⊁⊁ Jumamosi ----

♈ ☽ **Saturday**
♒ **9**

☽→♒ 7:44 am
♀✶♇ 8:51 am
☽△♄ 9:42 am
☽△♅ 2:10 pm
☽☌♆ 4:05 pm
☉⊼♅ 8:19 pm

---- ⊙⊙⊙ Jumapili ----

♒ ☽ **Sunday**
10

♅△♆ 4:09 am
☽✶♀ 4:26 am
☽△♃ 5:11 am
☽△♀ 9:47 am
☽☌♅ 7:17 pm

September

September

———— ☽☽☽ Montag ————————————

♒
♓ 🌒 Monday
11

☽☌♂ 1:09 pm v/c
☽→♓ 7:34 pm
☽□♄ 9:29 pm

———— ♂♂♂ Dienstag ————————————

♓ 🌕 Tuesday
12

♄sR 4:34 am
☽□♀ 3:34 pm
☽□♃ 4:30 pm

———— ☿☿☿ Mittwoch ————————————

♓ 🌕 Wednesday
13

☉☍☽ 12:37 pm v/c

———— ♃♃♃ Donnerstag ———————————— Full Moon in ♓ Pisces 12:37 pm PDT

♓
♈ 🌖 Thursday
14

☿⚹♀ 3:18 am
♀△♅ 4:53 am
☽→♈ 5:00 am
☽⚹♄ 6:50 am
☿△♃ 12:03 pm
☽⚹♆ 12:33 pm

———— ♀♀♀ Freitag ————————————

♈ 🌖 Friday
15

☽△♀ 12:12 am
☽⚹♃ 1:16 am
☽☍♅ 2:57 am
☿⚹♇ 5:01 am
☽⚹♅ 1:28 pm
☽☍♀ 4:54 pm

———————————————————————————

All aspects in Pacific Daylight Time; add 3 hours for EDT; add 7 hours for GMT

The Advocate

© *Jude Woods 1998*

I made this painting, *The Advocate*, when I was coping with emerging childhood abuse memories. I created a character and discovered the wise fool within who would take care of me. She knows the truth and she is always fair and kind. It would be no understatement to say that this painting saved my life.

© *Jude Woods 1998*

—————— ♄♄♄ Samstag ——————

♈
♉

Saturday

16

☽△♂ 11:50 am v/c
☽→♉ 12:05 pm
♂→♍ 5:19 pm
☽□♆ 7:18 pm

—————— ☉☉☉ Sonntag ——————

♉

Sunday

17

☽□♅ 7:19 pm

Her Giveaway Dance

How does she know each perfect
moment to release her hold? So clean,
no questions, her twigs unsnap.

In Spring she was Maiden, surprised
and proud with new beauty.
White dream at the edge of the green,
she trusted her bud into bloom.
One day she was transparent
with love, the whole tree
quivered in ecstasy, the blossoms
were mating with bees. Her petals
snowed down upon me all day long.

Now this miracle: flower to fruit. Such
a production to offer so casually. When an apple
strikes and rolls from the roof, her rhythm
of deliverance slaps the edge of a djembe.
When one thuds to the earth: bass
from the drum's center. Her Giveaway Dance
goes on for weeks. We gather red bounty
every day. We eat apples for breakfast,
for dessert. In fever we eat them to become
summer. Still she dances apples down.
Each gesture, a cupped breast. Again
and again until her mothering's done.

□ *Sue Silvermarie 1998*

© Mara Friedman 1998

Fall Equinox

The Fall Equinox is a celebration of balance and harvest. Equal day, equal night. In spring we celebrated potential. In fall enough of our work has come to fruition that we can judge our harvest. The careful tending phase is over—we harvest what we've sown. It's time to celebrate and assess what we've accomplished.

Our challenge physically is to identify weaknesses that still need tending to. Look at this year's gain and remember last winter's difficulties and weigh the balance. Essential fatty acids support many immune and anti-inflammatory responses and are often overlooked as a factor in general health. Find them in uncooked seeds, avocados and olive oil. Reishii and Shiitake mushrooms are warming immune tonics. Some types can be grown at home or purchased from local growers. Reishiis are woody and should be simmered and used as tea periodically. Shiitakes can be used in food.

Our emotional and spiritual challenge is to accept the consequences of our actions, and to find the wisdom to reflect, balance and discern. Use Garden Sage tea as a wash or use the oil to anoint yourself when you wish to find and celebrate your personal wisdom.

© Colette Gardiner 1999

September
Kepakemapa

□ *Becky Bee 1999*

〇〇〇 Pō'akahi

♉
♊ **Monday**
18

♂□♄	5:18 am
☉△☽	10:31 am v/c
☽→♊	5:22 pm
☽♂♄	7:01 pm
☽□♂	7:41 pm
☿△♅	10:38 pm

♂♂♂ Pō'alua

♊ **Tuesday**
19

☽△♆	12:19 am
☽☍♀	11:30 am
☽♂♃	12:40 pm
☽△♅	11:39 pm

☿☿☿ Pō'akolu

♊
♋ **Wednesday**
20

☽△♉	2:34 am
☽△♀	1:19 pm
☉□☽	6:28 pm v/c
☽→♋	9:16 pm

♃♃♃ Pō'ahā   Waning Half Moon in ♊ Gemini 6:28 pm PDT

♋ **Thursday**
21

☽✶♂	1:57 am

♀♀♀ Pō'alima

♋ **Friday**
22

Equinox

☉→♎	10:28 am
☽□♉	11:15 am
☽□♀	8:58 pm v/c
♂⚹♆	10:49 pm

Sun in Libra 10:28 am PDT

All aspects in Pacific Daylight Time; add 3 hours for EDT; add 7 hours for GMT

Year at a Glance for ♎ LIBRA (Sept. 22–Oct. 22)

The Millennium is a good time to be an air sign. Air signs (Gemini, Libra and Aquarius) are future-oriented and exist in the world of ideas. This often leaves them uncomfortably ahead of their time. At this point in history, however, the ideas of air signs are needed to show us the way to a very different world.

With both Uranus (Awakener) and Neptune (Dissolver/ Dreamer) in Aquarius in your house of creativity, Libra finds a passion for creative experimentation in matters of love and self-expression. This is a great year to be flamboyantly unconventional. It is also good for creative attempts at social reform, particularly those that incorporate the arts or spiritual techniques.

Jupiter and Saturn, contradictory energies of expansion and constriction, occupy Taurus and your house of transformation. Positively, these two planets work together to provide opportunities for significant growth through patient effort. Negatively, they pull at each other creating restlessness and impatience. To improve your life, you may need to cut loose from something dragging you down. Other Librans may decide to stick it out for some long-term aspiration. If in doubt, wait until July for insight.

Sociable Libra benefits from solitude to explore profound subjects. As you confront your own limits, use affirmations and mental discipline to communicate more efficiently. July onwards, take advantage of opportunities for advanced training. Expect to be teaching or writing about your insights within the next year.

© Gretchen Lawlor 1999

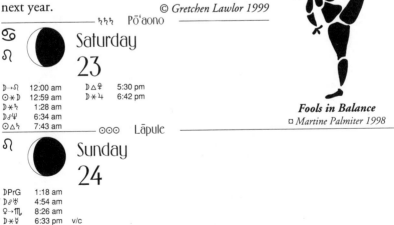

Fools in Balance
□ Martine Palmiter 1998

ħħħ   Pōʻaono

♋
♌

Saturday
23

☽→♌	12:00 am	☽△♀	5:30 pm
☉✶☽	12:59 am	☽✶♃	6:42 pm
☽✶ħ	1:28 am		
☽♂Ψ	6:34 am		
☉△ħ	7:43 am		

⊙⊙⊙   Lāpule

♌

Sunday
24

☽PrG	1:18 am	
☽♂♅	4:54 am	
♀→♏	8:26 am	
☽✶♉	6:33 pm	v/c

MOON X

Moon X:
September 27–October 27

New Moon in ♎ Libra: Sept. 27;
Full Moon in ♈ Aries: Oct. 13;
Sun in ♏ Scorpio: Oct. 22

Gateway

Gateway, I know you so well.
I have circled around you
and looked at you from every angle.
I have sat in silence before you,
contemplating how you got here,
why you sit before me
and I sit before you,
staring at each other.

And here you are again,
right in front of me.
Did you move? Did I move?
How did I get here?

excerpt ¤ Tracy Harrison 1998

From Top, left to right:
Chaco Canyon Ruins, New Mexico © *Ellen Jaffe 1990;* **The Opening** © *Keely Meagan 1998;* **Going Under** © *Suzanne Harding 1990;* **Goddess Entrance** ¤ *Sara-Lou Klein 1997;* **Journey** © *Bridget Benton 1996;* **Gateway at Temple of Aphrodite** ¤ *DebRA Sawers 1998;* **Holy Well on Agnes Isle** ¤ *Raggy Chris L. 1994*

September

Septembro

♌
♍

Monday
25

♀⊼♄	12:45 am	
☽→♍	2:02 am	
☽□♄	3:24 am	
☽⚹♀	3:40 am	
☽☌♂	11:13 am	
☽□♀	7:33 pm	
☽□♃	8:44 pm	v/c

the sickle moon shows
a crack in the sky
where the breath
of the Goddess
blows through

excerpt © Erin Dragonsong 1998

♍

Tuesday
26

☉△♆	9:40 am

♍
♎

Wednesday
27

☽→♎	4:22 am
☽△♄	5:41 am
☽△♆	10:58 am
♀□♆	12:34 pm
☉☌☽	12:53 pm
☽⚹♀	10:25 pm
☽△♃	11:35 pm

♎

Thursday
28

☿→♏	6:28 am	
☽△♅	9:57 am	v/c
☿⊼♄	8:39 pm	

New Moon in ♎ Libra 12:53 pm PDT

♎
♏

Friday
29

♃sR	5:52 am
☽→♏	8:30 am
☽☌♅	11:07 am
☽□♆	3:24 pm
☽☌♀	8:35 pm
☽⚹♂	11:31 pm

All aspects in Pacific Daylight Time; add 3 hours for EDT; add 7 hours for GMT

Bush Spirit

♏︎ — ♄♄♄ — sabato

Saturday
30

☽□♅ 3:42 pm v/c

♏︎ — ☉☉☉ — dimanĉo
♐︎

Sunday
1

October

☿□♆ 11:27 am
☽→♐︎ 3:50 pm
☽☍♄ 5:03 pm
☽✳︎♆ 11:11 pm

October
Oktoba

☽☽☽ Jumatatu

♐

Monday 2

☉✶☽ 10:46 am
♀✶♂ 10:50 am
☽□♂ 10:54 am
☽☌♇ 12:22 pm
☽☍♃ 1:28 pm

♂♂♂ Jumanne

♐

Tuesday 3

☽✶♅ 1:03 am v/c
☉✶♇ 7:12 am
♀⚻♃ 12:38 pm
♂□♇ 4:55 pm
☉△♃ 8:08 pm

☿☿☿ Jumatano

♐
♑

Wednesday 4

☽→♑ 2:42 am
♂□♃ 12:28 pm
☽✶☿ 5:40 pm

♃♃♃ Alhamisi

♑

Thursday 5

☽△♂ 2:02 am
☉□☽ 3:59 am
☽✶♀ 5:34 am v/c
☉✶⚷ 11:21 pm
☽ApG 11:58 pm

♀♀♀ Ijumaa

Waxing Half Moon in ♑ Capricorn 3:59 am PDT

♑
♒

Friday 6

☽→♒ 3:33 pm
☽△♄ 4:28 pm
☽☌♆ 11:17 pm

All aspects in Pacific Daylight Time; add 3 hours for EDT; add 7 hours for GMT

© Nell Stone 1992

Walking Through

The rock calls me from my purposeful walk,
its shape and color compelling me to stop.

And in a quick magnificence,
I perceive my madness and inhale,
ancient and rugged with the sudden gift.

Rocks are doorways.

I resume my walk.

¤ *Avrilyn Margaea 1998*

♄♄♄ Jumamosi

♒ ◖ **Saturday 7**

☽□☿ 12:02 pm
☽✶♀ 1:21 pm
☽△♃ 2:03 pm
☉△☽ 10:19 pm

☉☉☉ Jumapili

♒ ◖ **Sunday 8**

☽□♀ 1:18 am
☽☌♅ 1:55 am v/c
♂□⚷ 4:23 am
♀□♅ 7:19 am
☿⚻♃ 2:23 pm

October
Oktober

☽☽☽ Montag

♒ ♓

Monday 9

☽→♓ 3:36 am
☽□♄ 4:16 am
☉△♅ 5:28 pm

¤ *Shiloh McCloud 1998*

♂♂♂ Dienstag

♓

Tuesday 10

☽□♇ 12:39 am
☽□♃ 1:02 am
☽△☿ 3:32 am
☽☍♂ 8:18 am
☽△♀ 6:09 pm v/c

☿☿☿ Mittwoch

♓ ♈

Wednesday 11

☽→♈ 12:51 pm
☽✶♄ 1:16 pm
☽✶♆ 7:52 pm

♃♃♃ Donnerstag

♈

Thursday 12

☽△♇ 8:52 am
☽✶♃ 8:57 am
☽✶♅ 7:52 pm

♀♀♀ Freitag

♈ ♉

Friday 13

♃☍♇ 1:24 am
☉☍☽ 1:53 am v/c
♂⊼♅ 6:20 pm
☽→♉ 7:06 pm

Full Moon in ♈ Aries 1:53 am PDT

All aspects in Pacific Daylight Time; add 3 hours for EDT; add 7 hours for GMT

Dancing in the Womb of Papaya

© Mara Friedman 1994

♉

Saturday
14

☽□♆   1:47 am
☽☌♉   9:36 pm

♉
♊

Sunday
15

☽□♅   12:46 am
☽△♂   2:14 am
♆ѕD   7:12 am
☽☌♀   4:26 pm
ħ→♉   5:46 pm
☽☌ħ   11:17 pm   v/c
☽→♊   11:19 pm

October
'Okakopa

DDD   Pō'akahi

♊

Monday
16

D △ Ψ   5:50 am
D ♂ 4   5:42 pm
D ☍ ♀   6:13 pm

It's well-known that we are all born.
Each day to rise, unzip sleeping
bag of dreams, ask to be born
blink blink, today exists. Here I am.
excerpt ◻ J. Davis Wilson 1998

♂♂♂   Pō'alua

♊

Tuesday
17

D △ ♅   4:19 am
D □ ♂   8:11 am
☉ △ D   6:01 pm   v/c

☿☿☿   Pō'akolu

♊
♋

Wednesday
18

D → ♋   2:37 am
☿sR   6:41 am
♀ ☍ ♄   7:46 pm
♀ → ♐   11:18 pm

---
4 4 4   Pō'ahā

♋

Thursday
19

D △ ♉   5:25 am
D ✶ ♂   1:39 pm
D PrG   2:50 pm

♀♀♀   Pō'alima

♋
♌

Friday
20

☉ □ D   12:59 am
D ✶ ♄   5:15 am   v/c
D → ♌   5:42 am
D △ ♀   8:34 am
D ☍ Ψ   12:10 pm
D ✶ 4   11:30 pm

Waning Half Moon in ♋ Cancer 12:59 am PDT

All aspects in Pacific Daylight Time; add 3 hours for EDT; add 7 hours for GMT

Year at a Glance for ♏ SCORPIO (Oct. 22–Nov. 21)

For Scorpions, 1999 was a challenging year for relationships. People close to you wanted more from you, pushing for clarification of roles or clearer commitments. You may have taken on a business partner (and wondered at times if it was worth the effort). 2000 is an excellent year for testing your new skills and ideas in the public arena. Feedback, good and bad, needs to be seriously considered, and your efforts need to be adjusted if you wish your schemes to fly.

Keep things simple. Some relationships will clearly not work so be willing to end them. Home circumstances may continue to be in flux with people coming and going and you may have difficulty settling anywhere. An old base of operations is eroding, throwing you out of comfortable habits. You were ready, though you may not acknowledge it right now. Watch your dreams, give yourself the permission to float around, to try out possible scenarios without pressure of committing immediately. You will be more open to accepting changes after June.

Watch for an invitation this year to participate in someone's business scheme. They may have a better sense of your gifts than you. Get professional help to clarify legal agreements. This will protect you.

Scorpions like to be in control, and yet it is crisis that always calls the very best from you. 2000 will be a challenging year for everyone. You have a resourcefulness that really shines in adversity. Your efforts open doors that are not currently visible.

© *Gretchen Lawlor 1999*

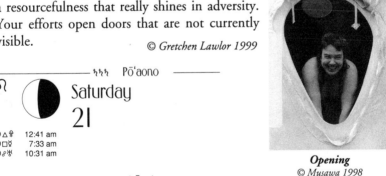

Opening
© *Musawa 1998*

♌ ☽ ‐‐‐‐‐‐ ♄♄♄ Pōʻaono ‐‐‐‐‐‐

Saturday
21

☽△♀   12:41 am
☽□♅   7:33 am
☽♂♅   10:31 am

♌ ♍ ☽ ‐‐‐‐‐‐ ☉☉☉ Lāpule ‐‐‐‐‐‐

Sunday
22

♀⚹♆   2:31 am
☉⚹☽   8:02 am
☽□♄   8:12 am   v/c
☽→♍   8:52 am
☉⚻♄   10:05 am
☽□♀   4:36 pm
☉→♏   7:47 pm

♏

Sun in Scorpio 7:47 pm PDT

October
Oktobro

☽☽☽ lundo

♍

Monday
23

☽□♃ 2:30 am
☽□♇ 4:05 am
☽⚹☿ 8:51 am

Owl Goddess
© *Singing Tree 1997*

♂♂♂ mardo

♍
♎

Tuesday
24

☽☌♂ 12:59 am
☽△♄ 11:34 am v/c
☽→♎ 12:30 pm
☽△♆ 7:08 pm

☿☿☿ merkredo

♎

Wednesday
25

☽⚹♀ 1:21 am
☽△♃ 6:08 am
☽⚹♇ 8:10 am
☽△♅ 6:03 pm v/c

♃♃♃ ĵaŭdo

♎
♏

Thursday
26

♅sD 8:24 am
☉□♆ 3:54 pm
☽→♏ 5:23 pm

♀♀♀ vendredo

♏

Friday
27

☽□♆ 12:17 am
☉☌☽ 12:58 am
♀☍♃ 4:17 am
☿⚻♃ 10:54 am
☽☌☿ 11:20 am

Lunar Samhain
New Moon in ♏ Scorpio 12:58 am PDT

All aspects in Pacific Daylight Time; add 3 hours for EDT; add 7 hours for GMT

Wild Womb/Universe

There are women
Loud spoken, soft spoken,
who touch the sky with their tongues
dig into the cool, coarse landscape
ungloved with trowel and toes.

There are women
with triumphant undulating bellies
and wicked wanton thighs
women grown into their curves,
grown like agrarian creatures
into their own spoken language,
in their own creative countries,
in their own undomesticated territories.

There are women
four-footed,
clay-skinned
Earth Mothers
who are reinvented,
reawakened,
reborn into the primal
wild womb
wild universe.

excerpt © Christine Fox 1997

ħħħ   sabato

♏︎   Saturday
       28

☽□♅	12:10 am	
♀☌♀	8:32 am	
☿PrG	3:03 pm	
☽⚹♂	5:37 pm	
☽☍ħ	11:04 pm	v/c

☉☉☉   dimanĉo

♏︎
♐︎   Sunday
       29

☽→♐	12:40 am	
☽⚹♆	6:59 am	
☉☌♉	6:09 pm	
☽☍♃	6:13 pm	
☽☌♀	9:32 pm	

Daylight Savings Time ends 2:00 am PDT

Buffalo Jump

Some cliffs beg to be spring-boards
this garbage dives to its death
on generations of buffalo bones

there she sits, on her haunches
peering across the coulee
she's guarding the bones
guarding the garbage
and she breathes a veil of smoke
around her wind-shredded grocery-bag hair

I go to her, kneel before her

where shall I place my offering
Goddess of the Garbage, Lady of the Refuse
can you open your cloak wide enough
for all my mistakes?

and she takes a buffalo's shin bone
turned to stone, strung with tin cans
and she drums on a water heater
drums in the thunder
her long breasts sway
in the wind before the storm

and I dance and I dance till the rain comes in

she smudges me with an exhale of her smoky breath
Go, she whispers. Everything is for always.

◻ *Soma 1998*

MOON XI

Moon XI: October 27–November 25

New Moon in ♏ Scorpio: Oct 27; Full Moon in ♉ Taurus: Nov. 11; Sun in ♐ Sagittarius: Nov. 21

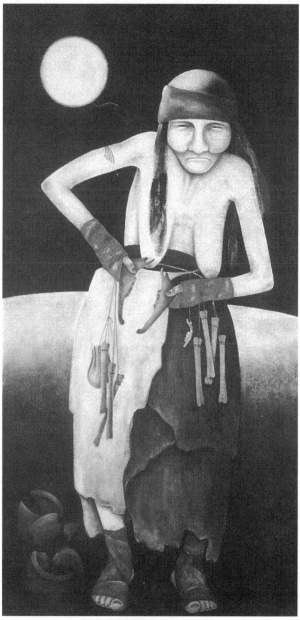

© Carolyn Hillyer 1997

Grave Hag

October
Oktoba

—— ☽☽☽　Jumatatu ——————————————

♐

Monday
30

☽☌♀　1:33 am
☽⚹♅　8:11 am

—— ♂♂♂　Jumanne ——————————————

Samhain/Hallowmas

♐
♑

Tuesday
31

☽□♂　5:43 am　v/c
☽→♑　10:01 am
☽⚹♅　6:53 pm
♀☌♇　8:42 pm

—————————— ☿☿☿　Jumatano ——————

♑

Wednesday
1

November

☉⚹☽　4:53 am
☉⚻♃　6:10 am
♅□♆　6:29 am
♀⚹♅　9:25 pm
♂△♄　9:41 pm

—————————— ♃♃♃　Alhamisi ——————

♑
♒

Thursday
2

☽ApG　7:22 pm
☽△♄　8:13 pm
☽△♂　9:37 pm　v/c
☽→♒　10:41 pm

—————————— ♀♀♀　Ijumaa ——————

♒

Friday
3

☽□♅　2:46 am
☽☌♆　6:36 am
☽△♃　5:24 pm
♂→♎　6:00 pm
☽⚹♀　10:16 pm
☉□☽　11:27 pm

Waxing Half Moon in ♒ Aquarius 11:27 pm PST

All aspects in Pacific Standard Time; add 3 hours for EST; add 8 hours for GMT

□ Rosa Davis 1998

Samhain

Samhain is year's ending and year's beginning, marking earth's entry into the darkest part of the wheel of the year. It is a time to go inward, honor the dark, to release and let go. In earth-based societies it made sense to end the year with the end of the earth's active phase. At this time the veil between the worlds is thinnest and we can honor and receive guidance from those who have passed over. It is a time to descend and prepare for the still time of winter's sleep.

Our challenge physically is to shift our focus to the active prevention of illness. Occasionally, use Astragalus root in teas or simmer a piece in soups. The root is a warming tonic that supports deep level immunity. Use Skullcap tincture if needed to support the nervous system, as it works hard to absorb information while the veil is thin. Use 30–60 drops of tincture before bed.

Our challenge emotionally and spiritually is to learn to let go of what is no longer needed in preparation for the next round on the spiral—to embrace the darkness and to understand the need to go within. Sitting with Cedar or Cypress trees can help us connect to and work with grief and loss issues from our past. Burn Rosemary to release them. Mugwort as incense increases intuitive awareness.

© Colette Gardiner 1999

Shauna

How should we best
Say goodbye to you
How best deal with your bones?
By earth, by air, by water
Or fire?

To bury you deep in wet earth
Damp with tears and worms turning
In a casket of wood   With brass handles,
Dig a hole and sink you under
Lay you down like bed   And we were lovers watching?

Or spread you out high   On a trestle or rock,
Letting your meat dry a little
Edges shrivel and you begin to stink?
Then shall we watch you call
All the monarch and ministers of the wing,
Their sharp beak and talons   To make you clean
So your white bones
Will sing with wind whistle?

Or shall we fling you
Shrouded and weighted with stone
Into some far unfathomable pond
And hope some hand   Empty of sword will offer
Final security and caress,   Seeing only water bubble
And imagining who knows what?

No, only the fire will do.
Wrap you in the newsprint
Of our first acquaintance,
Let us burn you bright   As you burnt live
As you set us alight.
Candle, beacon and open door   You were,
We owe you
One last chance to rise in fire.
Eyes no longer blue,
Staring, hair on end,   Rictus aflame,
Terrible and wonderful
We see you passing,
Burnt into our memory.

Ancient Growth

© *Tracey Schavone 1995*

Many creatures still live and exist in complex ecosystems in the ancient ruins and temples of the Goddess as they did 3,000 years ago, infiltrating the walls, absorbing the memory, keeping the stories. Imagine what they might have to say . . . to teach . . .

excerpt ¤ DebRA Sawers 1998

─────────── ♄♄♄ Jumamosi ───────────

♒ Saturday
4

☽☌♅ 9:03 am
☽✶♀ 3:44 pm

─────────── ☉☉☉ Jumapili ───────────

♒
♓ Sunday
5

☽□♄ 8:26 am v/c
☽→♓ 11:13 am
☽△♅ 12:04 pm

November

November

──────── ☽☽☽ Montag ────────

♓ Monday
6

☽□♃	4:47 am
☽□♀	10:10 am
☉△☽	4:22 pm
☿→♎	10:46 pm

──────── ♂♂♂ Dienstag ────────

♓
♈ Tuesday
7

☽□♀	8:51 am	
☽⚹♄	6:04 pm	v/c
☿sD	6:28 pm	
☽→♈	9:02 pm	

──────── ☿☿☿ Mittwoch ────────

♈ Wednesday
8

☽☍♂	2:00 am
☽⚹♆	4:23 am
☽⚹♃	1:02 pm
☿→♏	3:57 pm
☉□♅	5:57 pm
☽△♀	6:43 pm

──────── ♃♃♃ Donnerstag ────────

♈ Thursday
9

| ☽⚹♅ | 4:07 am | |
| ☽△♀ | 9:07 pm | v/c |

──────── ♀♀♀ Freitag ────────

♈
♉ Friday
10

☽→♉	3:12 am
☽☍♉	3:59 am
♂△♆	5:14 am
☽□♆	10:08 am

All aspects in Pacific Standard Time; add 3 hours for EST; add 8 hours for GMT

Reflections #2

© Anna Oneglia 1997

Blackbird

My shadow is a blackbird,
she eats silver fishes and steals time.
She twists chronology
into ellipses that open like windows.
Blackbird flies through windows
dressed up in poems.

excerpt © Julie Weber 1997

ħħħ   Samstag

♉

Saturday

11

♀⊼ħ   5:01 am
☽□♅   8:31 am
☉☍☽   1:15 pm

⊙⊙⊙   Sonntag

Full Moon in ♉ Taurus 1:15 pm PST

♉
♊

Sunday

12

☽☌ħ   3:12 am   v/c
☽→♊   6:27 am
☽△♆   1:10 pm
☽△♂   3:37 pm
♀→♑   6:14 pm
☽☌♃   8:03 pm

November

Nowemapa

Make room in your heart for yourself.
You are the path.

excerpt © Eleanor Carolan 1996

─────))) Pō'akahi ─────

♊ 🌙 Monday
13

☽☍♀	2:22 am	
☽△♅	10:51 am	v/c
♅✶♇	5:43 pm	

───── ♂♂♂ Pō'alua ─────

♊
♋ 🌙 Tuesday
14

☽→♋	8:21 am	
☽☍♀	11:47 am	
☽△☿	2:25 pm	
☽PrG	3:12 pm	
☽□♂	7:38 pm	
☿□♆	11:58 pm	

───── ☿☿☿ Pō'akolu ─────

♋ 🌙 Wednesday
15

───── ♃♃♃ Pō'ahā ─────

♋
♌ 🌙 Thursday
16

☉△☽	12:46 am	
☽✶♄	6:30 am	v/c
♂△♃	6:38 am	
☽→♌	10:19 am	
☽☍♆	5:11 pm	
☽□☿	8:33 pm	
☽✶♃	11:07 pm	

───── ♀♀♀ Pō'alima ─────

♌ 🌙 Friday
17

☽✶♂	12:00 am	
☽△♀	6:41 am	
☽☍♅	3:12 pm	

All aspects in Pacific Standard Time; add 3 hours for EST; add 8 hours for GMT

Pain

My pain is a wild
    Telegraph
        that parallels my growth.

Twinges, ripples, bumps and
    sharp-shooting Spasms travel
        up and down my body's varied ways
Knocking away, filing down, wiping away all traces:

Mapa-mundi of ancient lives, old architecture
    veiling Our Lady of Scars;

Peeling back the layers
    to the naked,
        damp
            Quick.

My pain is a telegraph:
    And on my journey,

My road to Freedom.

      ¤ *Carol Sawyer 1995*

© Marsha A. Gomez 1998

Prayer to the Moon

───── ♄♄♄ Pōʻaono ─────

♌
♍ **Saturday**
18

☿⊼♃	12:14 am	
⊙□♃	7:24 am	
☽□♄	9:03 am	v/c
☽→♍	1:15 pm	
♀⊼♃	9:33 pm	

Waning Half Moon in ♌ Leo 7:24 am PST

───── ⊙⊙⊙ Lāpule ─────

♍ **Sunday**
19

☽□♃	1:54 am
☽△♀	2:21 am
♄PrG	2:34 am
⊙♂♄	4:41 am
☽⚹☿	4:45 am
☽□♀	10:18 am

November

Novembro ———— ☽☽☽ lundo ————

♍︎
♎︎

Monday
20

☽△♄ 12:57 pm
☉✳☽ 3:45 pm v/c
☽→♎︎ 5:35 pm

———— ♂♂♂ mardo ————

♎︎

Tuesday
21

☽△♆ 12:58 am
☽△♃ 6:05 am
☽□♀ 12:12 pm
☽☌♂ 1:00 pm
☽✳☿ 3:24 pm
☉→♐ 4:19 pm

♐

Sun in Sagittarius 4:19 pm PST

———— ☿☿☿ merkredo ————

♎︎
♏︎

Wednesday
22

☽△♅ 12:18 am v/c
♀□♂ 5:43 am
☽→♏︎ 11:33 pm

———— ♃♃♃ ĵaŭdo ————

♏︎

Thursday
23

☽□♆ 7:17 am
♂✳♀ 9:03 pm

———— ♀♀♀ vendredo ————

♏︎

Friday
24

☽✳♀ 12:23 am
☽☌☿ 5:00 am
☽□♅ 7:28 am

All aspects in Pacific Standard Time; add 3 hours for EST; add 8 hours for GMT

Year at a Glance for ♐ SAGITTARIUS (Nov. 21–Dec. 21)

Life is full of change for Sagittarius in 2000, as Pluto, planet of transformation, and Chiron, planet of the healing gift, activate your sign. Those of you born in the first week of December will be most influenced, sensing a compelling call to a specific political, social or spiritual action.

If you are experiencing blockages or disruptive changes coming at you from the world around you, you may be resisting the need for an internal shift. Old ways of asserting your power and presenting yourself to the world will not work again the way they once did. It may be helpful to spend time on a meditative or creative autobiography. It's a good time for cleansing, discovery and renewal. Honor the past and move forward.

Your healing gifts and talents are being developed. Because of the challenges you have faced in the last few years, you have a special understanding of other people whose lives are touched by crisis. You will be asked to take on significant responsibilities without much recognition. Don't worry, the skills you are developing will prove extremely valuable in the future. Pay particular attention to simple techniques with a deep or enduring impact. Do not ignore the limitations of your own health, share with others whatever you use for personal regeneration.

Short trips spark inspired thinking and dramatically improve your ability to express yourself. Opportunities to create new and stimulating community abound close by. Make sure everyone is on the same wavelength before committing to any big dreams.

© *Gretchen Lawlor 1999*

Pony Earth Goddess
¤ *Candida Sea Blyth 1996*

──── ♄♄♄　sabato ────

♏
♐

Saturday
25

☽☍♄	1:52 am	v/c	☽☍♃	7:50 pm
♀□♅	3:02 am		☉✶♆	9:38 pm
☽→♐	7:33 am			
☉☌☽	3:11 pm			
☽✶♆	3:42 pm			

──── ☉☉☉　dimanĉo ────

New Moon in ♐ Sagittarius 3:11 pm PST

♐

Sunday
26

♃PrG	7:02 am	
☽☌♀	7:27 am	
☽✶♂	10:17 am	
☽✶♅	4:57 pm	v/c

They Are (The Ancestors)

They are like glass
        or water
the shimmer.

They are like heat
        or wind
the current.

They are like animals
        or dust
the river.

They are like moons
        or walking
the promise.

They are like wanting
        or fear
the insistence.

They are like ocean or
        mist
the deliverance.

They are like broom or
        bowl
the dailiness.

They are like fever or
        flower
the exception.

They are like pattern
        or song
the artistry.

They are like babe
        or cane
inevitable.

They are like stones
        or mouths
our ancestors.

□ *Patricia Worth 1998*

MOON XII

Moon XII: November 25–December 24

New Moon in ♐ Sagittarius: Nov. 25; Full Moon in ♊ Gemini: Dec. 11; Sun in ♑ Capricorn: Dec. 21

© *Diana Bryer 1997*

Ancient Ways

November
Novemba

© Monica Sjöö 1997

Archaic Goddess

DDD Jumatatu

♐
♑

Monday
27

D→♑   5:57 pm
☉⚹♄   6:12 pm

♂♂♂ Jumanne

♑

Tuesday
28

☿☿☿ Jumatano

♑

Wednesday
29

D□♂   12:57 am
D♂♀   9:49 am
D⚹☿   6:47 pm
D△♄   11:34 pm   v/c

♃♃♃ Alhamisi

♑
♒

Thursday
30

D→♒   6:26 am
D♂♆   3:22 pm
DApG   3:44 pm
D△♃   6:08 pm

♀♀♀ Ijumaa

♒

Friday
1

December

☉⚹D   1:50 am
☿⚹♄   6:07 am
D⚹♀   8:10 am
D△♂   5:16 pm
D♂♅   6:00 pm

All aspects in Pacific Standard Time; add 3 hours for EST; add 8 hours for GMT

Spin-Cycle

"How long will I live?" I ask in journey-trance, right breast gone to cancer, moon-times and hair gone to chemo—good sense gone for the moment, too.

"Oh, the thread of your life has already been spun, measured and cut!" my spirit-allies gleefully reply. "Cut?!" I gasp. "Oh, yes! See?" River-Woman caresses a slender cord. "It doesn't look very long, does it?" She smiles, holds the short strand full length, hand to hand, then flings the thread up, catches and twirls it.

"Spun! Measured! AND CUT!" my other allies chant, stomping the ground. She tosses the flimsy thing to Deer, where it dangles from an antler. "No, not very long at all!" he chortles.

"And she's about *here* right now, isn't she?" says Eagle, gesturing with her wing as I groan, near tears. "Aw, look, she's upset about the length... Let's stretch it for her!" Deer and Eagle begin a tug-of-war. Terrified, I brace for a terminal snap.

"Yes, you're about *here*." Grandmother plucks the taut fiber. "But which end is which?" she asks. She swishes the thread through the air, drawing spirals, infinity figure-eights. "Are we measuring from *this* end? Or the other?

"Indeed," she answers my thoughts, "the way we move your life *can* make you dizzy. But this is a good, sturdy cord and we plan to keep it in motion for some time to come."

"Ooh, how *much* time?" one mimics. "*Wild* motion," assures another.

When I leave, they're playing cat's cradle, still laughing.

© Renna Shesso 1997

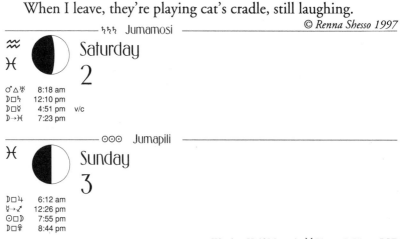

──────── ꜩꜩꜩ Jumamosi ────────

♒︎
♓︎   **Saturday**
    2

♂△♅   8:18 am
☽□♄   12:10 pm
☽□♅   4:51 pm   v/c
☽→♓︎   7:23 pm

──────── ☉☉☉ Jumapili ────────

♓︎   **Sunday**
    3

☽□♃   6:12 am
☿→♐︎   12:26 pm
☉□☽   7:55 pm
☽□♀   8:44 pm

Waxing Half Moon in ♓︎ Pisces 7:55 pm PST

December
Dezember

ⅅⅅⅅ Montag

♓

Monday
4

☉☌♀ 6:03 am
♀△♄ 7:54 pm
♀ApG 8:59 pm
☽✶♄ 11:05 pm
☽✶♀ 11:26 pm v/c

Today's rain in the trees
and down my neck
sounds like a million
delicate spiders
walking in the same
direction.

© Selka D. Kind 1998

♂♂♂ Dienstag

♓
♈

Tuesday
5

☽→♈ 6:17 am
☽△♅ 12:07 pm
☽✶♆ 2:50 pm
☽✶♃ 3:55 pm
♂✶⚷ 7:05 pm

☿☿☿ Mittwoch

♈

Wednesday
6

☽△♀ 6:21 am
☉△☽ 10:16 am
☿✶♆ 10:49 am
☽✶♅ 3:09 pm
☿☍♃ 5:10 pm
☽☍♂ 7:50 pm

♃♃♃ Donnerstag

♈
♉

Thursday
7

☽□♀ 12:22 pm v/c
☽→♉ 1:27 pm
☽□♆ 9:30 pm

♀♀♀ Freitag

♉

Friday
8

♀→♒ 12:48 am
☽□♅ 8:08 pm

All aspects in Pacific Standard Time; add 3 hours for EST; add 8 hours for GMT

do not walk
with head down
shoulders scrunched
hands stuffed deep
in pockets

accept the rain.

realize
it is simply
falling
and you
are simply walking
in its path

¤ *Ann Marie Mitchell 1990*

¤ *May Trillium 1998*

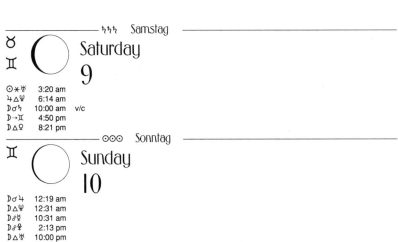

ħħħ Samstag

♉
♊

Saturday
9

⊙✶♅ 3:20 am
♃△♆ 6:14 am
☽♂♄ 10:00 am   v/c
☽→♊ 4:50 pm
☽△♀ 8:21 pm

⊙⊙⊙ Sonntag

♊

Sunday
10

☽♂♃ 12:19 am
☽△♆ 12:31 am
☽♂♉ 10:31 am
☽♂♀ 2:13 pm
☽△♅ 10:00 pm

December

Kēkēmapa ——))) Pōʻakahi ——————————————

♊︎
♋︎ ◐ Monday
11

☉☍☽	1:03 am	
☽△♂	6:15 am	v/c
☉☌♅	3:18 pm	
♀△♃	5:16 pm	
☽→♋︎	5:48 pm	
♅☌♀	10:11 pm	

—————— ♂♂♂ Pōʻalua ——————————————

Full Moon in ♊︎ Gemini 1:03 am PST

♋︎ ◐ Tuesday
12

♀☌♆	1:24 am
☽PrG	2:33 pm

—————— ☿☿☿ Pōʻakolu ——————————————

♋︎
♌︎ ◑ Wednesday
13

☽□♂	8:36 am	
☽⚹♄	11:03 am	v/c
☽→♌︎	6:09 pm	

—————— ♃♃♃ Pōʻahā ——————————————

♌︎ ◑ Thursday
14

☽⚹♃	12:39 am
☽☍♆	1:51 am
☽☍♀	5:53 am
☽△♀	3:33 pm
☽△♅	11:10 pm
☽☍♅	11:24 pm

—————— ♀♀♀ Pōʻalima ——————————————

♌︎
♍︎ ◑ Friday
15

☿⚹♅	1:24 am	
☉△☽	9:35 am	
☽⚹♂	11:45 am	
☽□♄	11:57 am	v/c
♂⚼♍︎	3:54 pm	
☽→♍︎	7:30 pm	

All aspects in Pacific Standard Time; add 3 hours for EST; add 8 hours for GMT

Ancient Mother
☐ *Lavonne Marie 1987*

What will I do with the rest of my life that I'll be able at the end to call real living? Simple being, blissful simplicity, every second. Peace and quiet and *knowing* . . . meditate on the wonder and impossibility of life and the illusion of everything but Nature . . . to live among trees in the woods.

I want to ask old, old Nature. She might show me how to part with myself. Like a mother.

© *Moon 1997*

♄♄♄   Pōʻaono

♍   **Saturday 16**

☽□♃	1:49 am
☉⊼♄	5:18 pm
☽□♀	5:53 pm
♀♂♇	10:27 pm

☉☉☉   Lāpule

♍ ☊   **Sunday 17**

☽□☿	8:07 am	
☽△♄	2:51 pm	
☉□☽	4:41 pm	v/c
☽→☊	11:01 pm	

Waning Half Moon in ♍ Virgo 4:41 pm PST

Priestess Rising   © Lynn Dewart 1995

Winter Solstice

I stand alone, this bottom of the year,
the sands of time running out towards the end.
This time, this end time,
when the misty sun descends at half past three.

Mysterious dusk, pink sky and dark lace trees
put me in mind of fairy places,
and a richness beyond the everyday.

I stand and watch in stillness,
while the busy world careers along,
oblivious of this time, this solstice, my magic.   ¤ *Rosa Davis 1998*

Calistos   © *S. J. Hugdahl 1989*

Winter Solstice

Winter Solstice is the midpoint of winter stillness and is a celebration of faith and hope. Though the wheel has turned with the days starting to get longer, much of winter's cold and darkness is still ahead. Festivals of light abound worldwide to honor this turning point. In the quiet dark of winter's womb, new ideas and creations start to gestate. Their existence is fragile, not fully manifest. Their vitality must stand the test of winter's darkness. Mid-winter is a time of sharing resources and supporting each other.

Our challenge physically is keeping up our reserves of health against colds and flus. Our bodies slow down in the winter. Dandelion root (a liver tonic and mild laxative) helps with nutrient assimilation and keeps the digestive system moving. Add it to chai tea for a warming winter drink. Garlic is a warming antiviral, anti-fungal and antibacterial herb. It helps lower cholesterol and discourages parasites.

Our challenge emotionally and spiritually is to sit still in the silence, and accept who we are. Conceive new goals. Cultivate trust and hope. Lemon Balm is an antidepressant and helps bring the sun's energy into our lives. Blue Vervain is a nerve calmer. Use the dried leaves and flowers as incense to reconnect to the Goddess or take 5–15 drops of tincture when you have lost faith in your growth process.

© *Colette Gardiner 1999*

December

Decembro

Monday
18

☽△♃	5:13 am
⚷ApG	5:31 am
☽△♆	7:39 am
☉⚹♂	9:08 am
☽△♀	9:23 pm
☽⚹♀	10:42 pm

□ Raggy Chris L. 1994

Callanish

Tuesday
19

☽△♅	7:22 am
♀⚹♀	1:07 pm
☿⚼♄	5:15 pm
☽⚹♅	8:48 pm

Wednesday
20

☽♂♂	1:41 am	
☉⚹☽	3:07 am	v/c
☽→♏	5:12 am	
☽□♆	2:24 pm	

Thursday
21

☉→♑	5:37 am
☽□♀	10:09 am
☽□♅	3:19 pm

Solstice

♑

Sun in Capricorn 5:37 am PST

Friday
22

☽☍♄	4:28 am	v/c
☿ApG	4:51 am	
☿⚹♂	10:31 am	
☽→♐	1:57 pm	
☿→♑	6:03 pm	
☽☍♃	7:46 pm	
☽⚹♆	11:42 pm	

All aspects in Pacific Standard Time; add 3 hours for EST; add 8 hours for GMT

Year at a Glance for ♑ CAPRICORN (Dec. 21–Jan. 20)

This year it pays to develop an acute sense of timing and capitalize upon windfalls of opportunities. This is a great time for you to gamble, take some chances. You have just left or will soon be leaving a job that no longer feels meaningful in order to pursue new skills and interests. A job change may be scary, as Capricorn so depends on career and financial security for a sense of safety and self-worth. However, in 2000 you can tap into a sense of adventure as your values undergo a profound revolution.

You hunger to break barriers with innovations or insights. You will be most successful if you present them in a careful, well-timed and deliberate manner. New career opportunities will emerge from the pursuit of more play and fun in your life. Find ways to let out the playful child self, live out unfulfilled dreams. Consider taking a part in a local play production, coaching a sport or working with kids. Even if it doesn't directly land you a job, it will definitely improve your style and attitude.

If you have children, the extra time and attention you gave them last year should begin to show results. A child discovers a passion or a gift and blossoms in its pursuit. Encourage a realistic plan. If your own inner child is blossoming, your greatest satisfaction will come from being an idealist with well-planted feet. Staying grounded will keep you clear of any deception, confusion or muddle in money matters. Most auspicious for you are artistic fields or providing a service to your community. © *Gretchen Lawlor 1999*

Berridraun: Stone Teller
© *Carolyn Hillyer 1997*

ħħħ   sabato

♐   ● Saturday
23

♂→♏   6:37 am
☽♂♀   4:11 pm
♀♂♅   9:52 pm

☉☉☉   dimanĉo

♐   ● Sunday
24

☉⊼♃   1:31 am
☽⚹♅   1:40 am
☽⚹♀   2:03 am   v/c
☿⊼♃   12:58 pm

So We Gonna Have a Party

So we gonna have a party   You want to come?
Think a high rise
pointing out the flat dark sky
sun   goes   down
every little square bursts into electric light
bang yell fire! or money! at every door
just trying to get folks to fall out file down the hall
down   down   down to Mama ground
yeh like they say dance in the streets to this and that beat
let it be night free flight
hoping on the chance of a better dawn
oh so anyway
we gonna have this party and there's gonna be some changes
cuz the way it's been going it ain't flowing
the way night excitement sexy and everything
got all mixed up with violence and killing
this time round a woman ain't gonna have to wonder
if she's in danger of going down   just for getting up
if she moves her hips will she get ripped
if she lets it flow   will she live to crow
with that brilliant blaze of tomorrow
So get it   when I say party   I mean in the ancient sense of the word
as when women danced free

                              it ain't history
                              it's the way it's gonna be
we are gonna dance this living open   leave the squares of electric light
                              and split round ripe
                              life flowers in the night
we are gonna outlive   a thousand years of rape
                    hate
                    slavery on the take
the concrete under our barefeet is gonna wear away
and we'll feel mud slide between brightly painted toes
and Goddess knows
pleasure will realign with the divine and honey on my lips
we gonna have a party
                    revolution
                    it's heart beat
                    bass line   'bout time.

□ *Ellen Marie Hinchcliffe 1998*

Nicole's Wild Side
© Angie Coffin 1998

December
Desemba

♐
♑

Monday
25

))→♑	12:54 am
)✶♂	3:05 am
)♂♅	9:15 am
⊙♂)	9:22 am
⊙♂♅	11:23 am

New Moon in ♑ Capricorn 9:22 am PST
Partial Solar Eclipse 9:35 am PST (0.723 mag.)
Eclipse visible from North and Central America

♑

Tuesday
26

♑
♒

Wednesday
27

)△♄	2:52 am v/c
♀✶♇	5:42 am
)→♒	1:25 pm
♂⊼♃	2:00 pm
)△♃	6:34 pm
)□♂	6:50 pm

♒

Thursday
28

)♂♆	12:00 am
)ApG	7:05 am
)✶♀	5:15 pm

♒

Friday
29

)♂♅	3:09 am
♀□♄	2:35 pm
)□♄	3:40 pm
)♂♀	3:47 pm v/c

All aspects in Pacific Standard Time; add 3 hours for EST; add 8 hours for GMT

Maiden/Mother/Crone

© Ulla Anobile 1997

Net Work

We have a part in building each other's bridges
over this next river. Our words feeling out
these shaky structures, their delicacy and strength,
the naked places where we need a spar to shore us up,
a warm touch to earth us through these uncertain months
of storm and fire. Gifts we give go soul to soul,
make us real, even in these new unwieldy bags of aging skin.

excerpt © Rose Flint 1998

ħħħ Jumamosi

≈
 H

Saturday
30

☽→H   2:27 am
☽□♃   7:07 am
☽△♂   11:00 am
☉⚹☽   10:23 pm

☉☉☉ Jumapili

H

Sunday
31

☽⚹♀   5:47 am
☽□♀   6:08 am

January
Januar

2001

♓
♈

Monday
1

☽⚹♄	3:36 am	v/c
♂□♆	9:01 am	
☽→♈	2:14 pm	
☽⚹♃	6:20 pm	

───── ♂♂♂　Dienstag ─────────────────

♈

Tuesday
2

☽⚹♆	12:40 am
☉□☽	2:32 pm
☽△♀	4:52 pm

───── ☿☿☿　Mittwoch ─────　Waxing Half Moon in ♈ Aries 2:32 pm PST

♈
♉

Wednesday
3

☽□☿	12:58 am	
☽⚹♅	2:09 am	v/c
♀→♓	10:14 am	
☽→♉	10:57 pm	

───── ♃♃♃　Donnerstag ─────────────────

♉

Thursday
4

☽⚹♀	12:06 am
☽□♆	8:51 am
☽☍♂	11:55 am

───── ♀♀♀　Freitag ─────────────────

♉

Friday
5

☉△☽	2:04 am	
♀□♃	3:14 am	
☽□♅	8:37 am	
☽△☿	2:38 pm	
☽♂♄	6:09 pm	v/c

All aspects in Pacific Standard Time; add 3 hours for EST; add 8 hours for GMT

© *Anne Dreyer 1998*

♉
♊

Saturday

6

☽→♊	3:44 am
☽☌♃	6:45 am
☽□♀	9:10 am
☽△♆	1:04 pm
☿△ħ	7:46 pm

♊

Sunday

7

☽☍♀	3:07 am	
☽△♅	11:19 am	v/c

January
‘Ianuali

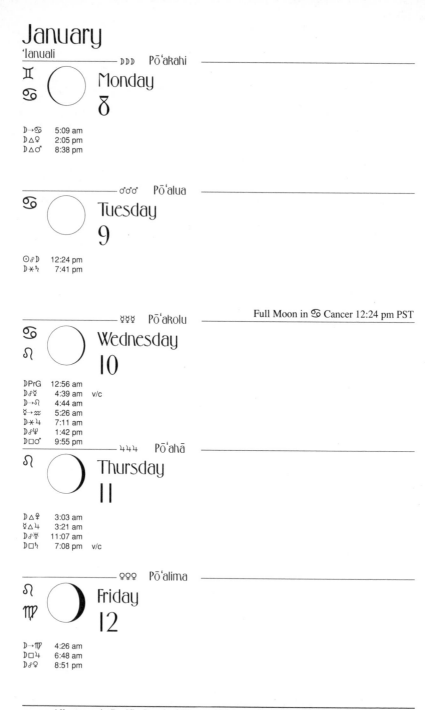

————))) Pō‘akahi ————

♊︎
♋︎ Monday
8

☽→♋︎ 5:09 am
☽△♀ 2:05 pm
☽△♂ 8:38 pm

———— ♂♂♂ Pō‘alua ————

♋︎ Tuesday
9

☉☍☽ 12:24 pm
☽⚹♄ 7:41 pm

———— ☿☿☿ Pō‘akolu ————   Full Moon in ♋︎ Cancer 12:24 pm PST

♋︎
♌︎ Wednesday
10

☽PrG 12:56 am
☽☍♅ 4:39 am   v/c
☽→♌︎ 4:44 am
☿→♒︎ 5:26 am
☽⚹♃ 7:11 am
☽☍♆ 1:42 pm
☽□♂ 9:55 pm

———— ♃♃♃ Pō‘ahā ————

♌︎ Thursday
11

☽△♀ 3:03 am
☿△♃ 3:21 am
☽☍♅ 11:07 am
☽□♄ 7:08 pm   v/c

———— ♀♀♀ Pō‘alima ————

♌︎
♍︎ Friday
12

☽→♍︎ 4:26 am
☽□♃ 6:48 am
☽☍♀ 8:51 pm

———————————————————————————————
All aspects in Pacific Standard Time; add 3 hours for EST; add 8 hours for GMT

The Future is Female

© Schar Cbear Freeman 1998

Ceremonial Attire for a New Millennium

© Wendy Ponca 1999

How to Become a We'Moon Contributor

We'Moon is an exploration of a world created in Her image. We welcome artwork by, for and about womyn. Our focus on womyn is an affirmation of the range and richness of a world where womyn are whole unto themselves. Many earth-based cultures traditionally have womyn-only spaces and times, which, through deepening the female experience, are seen to enhance womyn's contributions to the whole of society. **We'Moon** invites all womyn who love and honor womyn to join us in this spirit, and we offer what we create from such a space for the benefit of all beings.

Currently creating WE'MOON '01: MAGIC
Now accepting contributions for WE'MOON '02

If you are interested in being a **We'Moon** contributor contact us—send a business-sized SASE (self-addressed stamped #10 envelope) or an SAE and 2 international postal coupons. By July 2000, we will send you a Call for Contributions (which includes information about the theme and how to submit your art and writing) and a Release Form to return with your work. *Please do not send in any work without first receiving a Call for Contributions . . . thanks.*

How to Order WE'MOON and Mother Tongue Ink Products

Call or write to request our catalog or order direct—

•**We'Moon '00** (with lay-flat binding) and **We'Moon Unbound '00** (a loose-leaf edition for customized use) $17.95 each ($14.95 plus $3.00 surface p/h). Postage free for orders of 3 or more to the same address.

•Also available—**Lunar Power Packet '99 and Lunar Power Packet '00!** Each Lunar Power Packet (LPP) includes a mix of 13 beautiful, full-color, 4"x 6" postcards of 8 original art pieces that have been published in either **We'Moon '99** or **We'Moon '00** and a "LUNAR POWER" bumpersticker, woman-made, black on white, 2" x 10". Call for prices.

• Inquire about additional charges for 1st class or air mail. When ordering please include the following: a check or money order in U.S. funds made out to Mother Tongue Ink *and* a note listing your name, address, phone number, and product and quantity ordered.

Mother Tongue Ink write: P.O. Box 1395-A Estacada, OR 97023 or call: 503-630-7848 or toll free 877-693-6666 (877-0 WE-MOON) or email: wemoon@teleport.com

ACKNOWLEDGEMENTS

Production on this **We'Moon** has been full of much flux on the homefront. As we go to press there are many unknowns and I'm being asked to stay open to what the universe offers—the theme always comes home!

I want to thank Nell and Rebecca who enthusiastically helped create **We'Moon '00** and run the business this last year. The Creatrix team—Musawa, Nell, Bethroot and me (Beth)—did an awesome job editing/weaving this edition. I am deeply grateful to the contributions of our guest editor, Bethroot, who was a dream to work with as well as being thorough and thoughtful. Additional thanks to all who were involved: Musawa for your wisdom as crone consultant and for tending the sacred space so that the spirit of **We'Moon** can come through; We'Moon Land sisters for your support; Nell, Eagle, Shell, Lori and Amy for your copy editing and proofing; all fifty-five we'moon who diligently sat in weaving circles sharing responses to art and writing; and Weaving Circle hosts: Full Circle Temple, Katya, Fly Away Home and We'Moon Land; and Gisela and Rosemary who spin the web for the German edition—translating, typesetting, networking and marketing. Lastly, thank you all who are part of the living worldwide web of we'Moon, by and for whom it is created.

◻ *Beth Freewomon, We'moonager 1999*

ADDENDUM

Apologies to Ivie Manuel because we published "Mali's Sacred Passage" drawing in **We'Moon '99** without her explicit permission to do so independent of its companion piece of writing.

Also there continues to be some controversy about the origins of the song "We All Come from the Goddess." We credited it in **We'Moon '98**, as a neo-traditional Circle Song. In **We'Moon '99**, Z. Budapest wrote about her experience of birthing the song during a women's ritual in 1972 and copyrighting it in 1986, after hearing a recording of the song which credited it to a man.

Now Kris Ohman has written us with her belief that the song is a revised version of a Zen Buddhist chant current in the '70s. She credits her friend Maddie with revising the original "God" language at a women's circle in 1978. Another woman writes of hearing a version of the song at a full moon sweat with the Bear Community some thirty years ago.

It is not our job as editors to make judgments about these different stories-of-origin. Songs are mysterious—they shift and change among us. This dispute highlights the importance, and the difficulty sometimes, of passing on the oral tradition about a song's origin. Sacred circle songs are a precious part of the culture we are making. When we pass along our songs, let's do our best to pass along their herstories, complex as they may sometimes be.

◻ *We'Moon Matrix 1999*

DEDICATION

We lovingly dedicate **We'Moon '00** to Marsha A. Gomez, 46, sculptor, activist and Executive Director of Alma de Mujer Center for Social Change in Austin, Texas. She was an innovative teacher, using cultural arts and history as a vehicle for social change. She worked mostly with women and youth of color. She was co-founder of Artistas Indigenas National and founding mother of the National Indigenous Women's Network. She was named 1997 Bannerman Fellow for her work as an educator, organizer and artist. She has been a **We'Moon** contributor since 1995.

Prayer to the Moon
© *Marsha A. Gomez 1994*

Marsha died Sept. 27, 1998. Her 25-year-old son, Mekaya, is accused of murdering her during a lapse in his schizophrenia medication. The work she left behind—both her art and her advocacy for Native American women—is monumental. Her beautiful spirit touches us all. For more information please contact: The Marsha A. Gomez Foundation, 227 Congress Ave. # 203, Austin, TX 78701.

COVER NOTES

Front cover art, "Shakti" by Lynn Dewart. Shakti is the Hindu Mother of the World. She is the embodiment of the Divine Feminine and the source of all energy. Sprinkling stars across the heavens, she dances the universe into being, creating all beginnings and endings, initiating the cyclic flow. Shakti breathes life into our bodies, her enchanting beauty enters us and awakens our senses. Her energy encompasses the universe and she invites us to join in her ecstatic dance towards wholeness. Shakti came to me in a dream/vision and this soft sculpture of Her is the image I saw.

Back cover art, "Leap of Faith" by Linda Sweatt. This painting which pictures the Taos Gorge, came from looking at myself and my life. I began to heal through Harmonics and saw how big my mission is and how far I have to fly to be what I want to create. The crane represents my highest self. As I leap and fly over my fears, I soar into my own power. All the images I draw on paper first and then transfer them to silk. I paint exclusively on silk with Japanese brushes, a process very similar to painting with watercolors.

© Copyrights ¤ and Contacting Contributors

Copyrights of individual works in **We'Moon '00** belong to each contributor. Please honor the copyrights: © means <u>do not reproduce without the express permission of the artist or author</u>. Some we'moon prefer to free the copyright on their work. ¤ means <u>this work may be passed on among women who wish to reprint it "in the spirit of We'Moon", with credit given (to them and **We'Moon**) and a copy sent to the author/artist</u>. Contributors can be contacted directly when their addresses are given in the bylines, or by sending us a letter with an envelope with sufficient postage plus $1 handling fee for each contributor to be contacted.

Contributor Bylines and Index*

* Each page number at the end of a byline indicates on which page you will find the contributor's work.

Barb Ryman (Minneapolis, MN), a performing songwriter, has produced three recordings, *Winds of Good Fortune, Lay Me Open* and *Like a Tree*. Her CDs have aired on radio folk programs in the U.S. and abroad. She performs throughout the Midwest at coffeehouses, festivals and concerts. p. 53

Becky Bee (Murphy, OR) teaches women how to hand-sculpt cob (earthen) homes—inexpensive, earth-friendly and beautiful. PO Box 381, Murphy, OR 97533; www.cpros.com/~sequoia; 541-471-3470. pp. 128, 140

Berta R. Freistadt (London, England) is a poet, performer, teacher and mother of Dracula, her cat. She still enjoys living and working in London. Shame about the asthma! Her work: catching words and images, sewing quilts. Hobbies: laughing, noshing, gossiping and purr-therapy. p. 158

Beth Freewomon (We'Moon Land, Estacada, OR): Blue Serpent, Capricorn, land dyke, we'moonager and ex-New Yorker learning how *not* to choose stress and how to choose flow. I'm loving my martial arts practice and my first bike—Dancing Queen, a 1983 Kawasaki 250 cc motorcycle. pp. 8–10, 24

Bethroot Gwynn (Fly Away Home, OR) has been living on wimmin's land for 24 years, growing food, art, ritual. She loves working with the **We'Moon** art and writing! FFI about work exchange visits or spiritual gatherings on the land, send SASE to Fly Away Home, PO Box 593, Myrtle Creek, OR 97457. p. 11–14

beth milander (Seaside, OR): I am a 33-year-old single mom/artist who teaches Women's Studies at a community college on the coast. I did most of my work when I was pregnant with my daughter. I dedicate my art to Claire! p. 117

Betty LaDuke (Ashland, OR) is an artist, writer and art educator. Africa has been the focus of her work and annual travels since 1986. Her recent publications: *Africa, Women's Art, Women's Lives* and *Women Against Hunger, a Sketchbook Journey*. Her art appears at galleries in California and Oregon. p. 37

Brenna Jael Nies (Eastsound, WA) enjoys running through a dripping mossy forest island, gardening and living life, rebelling against the system positively, weaving my part of the web of womyn . . . lunatic fringe unite! p. 45

Bridget Benton (Portland, OR) is a painter, fiber artist, writer, and performance artist living in the Pacific Northwest. She believes it is all part of the journey, and that the journey is fueled largely by coffee. pp. 88, 142

C. Tall Mountain (Oakland, CA): I am an ecofeminist who paints, writes and does astrology. I have an ongoing love affair with nature. pp. 40, 96

Candida Sea Blyth (Ashburton, S. Devon, U.K): I live on the side of Dartmoor by the River Dart, the current passion of my life! I paint solely with earth pigments, celebrating the colours and contours of the planet Gaia's body. p. 165

Carol Sawyer (San Francisco, CA) is a much-traveled and multi-lingual teacher, gardener, crone and agent for change. A poet since early childhood and finishing her PhD, she is seeking out a congenial rural community in the Northwest. Contact her at 415-775-2881 or at csawyer@well.com. p. 163

Carolyn Hillyer (Dartmoor, Devon, U.K.) is an artist, composer, musician and writer. She paints large bold images of the pre-Celtic foremothers of the ancient moorland where she lives. She performs, exhibits and holds workshops. Contact her at Postbridge, Dartmoor, Devon PL20 6TJ U.K. pp. 33, 48, 155, 177

Christina Baldwin (Langley, WA) and her partner Ann Linnea have a vision for community they call PeerSpirit. Basing their work on Christina's book *Calling the Circle*, they teach PeerSpirit Circles throughout the U.S. and Canada. PO Box 550, Langley, WA 98260. www.peerspirit.com   pp. 72, 83

Christine Fox (Boulder, CO) is a loving woman who expresses her femininity and spirituality though her poetry. She is building a beautiful existence with her partner Emily and hopes to one day write for a living.   p. 153

Claire Serpell (Exeter, Devon, England): I am a gentle dreamer who seeks deep peace through meditation. I walk the earth and talk to her. I love animals dearly. I am a lover of simplicity. I write with heart, create art with magic, light my candles and cook a good broth. I am alive! Hello!   p. 130

Colette Gardiner (Eugene, OR) is a green witch and plant lover who has been working with herbs for 20 years. She teaches apprenticeships and offers herb walks out of Eugene.   pp. 47,67,85,103,121,139,157,175

Colleen Redman (Floyd, VA): My love of language and word play have roots in my Irish Celtic background. I break words down, expand on them, read them in ways other than left to "write," always looking for information on letter sound properties. Please write.   p. 77

Cora Greenhill (Peak District, England) is still living among the sacred stones here, dancing, facilitating "Thirteenth Moon" workshops and Rhythm Dance, writing, connecting, seeking publisher for my novel *The Arms of Artemis*. Love receiving email: cora@thirteenthmoon.demon.co.uk.   pp. 57. 82

DebRA Sawers (Grande Prairie, AB, Canada) is a generalist, artist, ceremonialist, mother, and founder of Full Circle workshops, circles and retreats devoted to enhancing journeys and returns to connectedness to Earth.   pp. 143, 159

Demetra George (Eugene, OR) is author of *Asteroid Goddess, Astrology for Yourself, Mysteries of the Dark Moon,* and *Finding Our Way through the Dark.* She incorporates archetypes, transpersonal healing and astrology in her lecturing, writing and counseling. She teaches internationally.   pp. 28–29, 199–200

Diana Bryer (Santa Cruz, NM): Her imagery is based on the celebration of life, our relationship to each other, the animal kingdom, the seasons and Mother Earth. Each painting is a prayer for peace, the earth and for balance within the heart.   p. 167

Diane Goldsmith (Nelson, BC, Canada): My home is in the country in the beautiful Kootenanys of southern BC. I am an elementary school teacher and counselor, and like to spend time writing, gardening, walking and being close to the Earth in all her wisdom.   pp. 189, 123

Donna Goodwin (Santa Fe, NM): I am a native New Mexican artist. Within swirling clouds, twisted wood and red clay, I behold the essence of my existence. I derive sustenance from the powerful and ever-changing manifestations of nature. Vision is my purpose. Call 505-473-3627.   p. 1

Durga Bernhard (Red Hook, NY) is a painter, printmaker, illustrator for more than 15 children's books, teacher of West African dance and drum, and mother of two children. Her images of spirit and earth have long been inspired by ancient and tribal cultures from all over the world.   pp. 95, 145

Eleanor Carolan (Felton, CA): An artist since childhood, I explore dreams and the divine feminine in my paintings and poetry. I commune with and heal Mother Earth by building gardens and healing environments. Letters welcome, c/o Living Patterns, PO Box 1403, Felton, CA 95018. p. 162

Elena I. Rego (Whittier, CA) is an artist, writer, massage therapist, magickal green thumb, workshop facilitator for Spiral Musings, a partnership dedicated to creating art and sacred circles that promote sweet sisterhood. If interested in our trips, write to 14908 Dunton Dr., Whittier, CA 90604. p. 32

Elizabeth Rosefield (Twain Hart, CA): After doing self-taught acrylic painting for 10 years focusing on Baja botanicals and landscapes, I progressed to oils which reflect my love of the Goddess in nature, mother and child, and mythological goddesses in tune with my own spiritual development. p. 111

Ellen Jaffe (Woodstock, ON, Canada) is a writer, shamanic healer, play therapist, mother, (sometimes lover), who finds peace in water and music and is exploring women's communities. E-mail me: ejaffe@netcom.ca or write me at 473 Drew St., Woodstock, ON N45 4V4, Canada. p. 142

Ellen Marie Hinchcliffe (Olympia, WA): I want Leonard Peltier out of prison now! The year 00 finds me resisting, creating, loving and dancing my ass off. So boogie down sisters, cuz we are still here! My poetry zine is $2 at PO Box 12781 Olympia, WA 98508. Peace. p. 178

Erin Dragonsong (Denman Island, BC, Canada) still lives on her adored island with her beloved and many animal friends. She has been published here and there and is currently birthing a career in counseling. She looks forward with idealistic optimism to the grand adventure of our next century. p. 144

Erin Kenny (Seattle, WA): I live in the ancient forests of the western Washington Cascades practicing the wise-woman ways of healing. I can be reached through my web page at: nwherbs.org. Blessed be. p. 73

Fay Leta (San Ramon, CA): I am an artist, teacher, a seeker, a journeywoman, and the creator of the Multi-Cultural Women's Wisdom Cards. p. 91

Ghermaine Knight (Dorset, England): I awakened to the Goddess while my daughter blossomed in my womb and I now feel her spirit in all that I create: art, poetry, dreamcatchers, textiles, laughter, tears, love, fears and ultimately self-healing. Blessings be. p. 73

Greta Undersun (Bisbee, AZ) is an herbalist, dancer and dreamer. She and her dog Jack are currently going crazy in Bisbee, Arizona. p. 75

Gretchen Lawlor (Whidbey Island,WA) is an astrologess and naturopathic practitioner. I write, love to teach (invite me—I'm into traveling) and do astrological consultations in person, by mail and phone. POB 753, Langley, WA 98260 (360)221-4341, e-mail: light@whidbey.com. pp. 15–16 and Moon I–XII

Hannah 19 Hatfield (Montville, ME) is a servant of the universe working at manifesting her feral tendencies, living, breathing and paying attention to the raw earthling part of herself and beyond. p. 76

Hazel Collins (Brooklyn, NY) is an artist living in Brooklyn. pp. 15, 116

Helen C. Castonguay (Halifx, NS, Canada): I am an open, loving, playful

Aquarian visionary who loves to stand in the fire of change. I be and become through art, teaching, acting for social justice and my relationships with womyn. Thanks to my guide, may we be at peace. pp. 80, 84

Hope Harris (Sacramento, CA) is a photographer whose love of humanity, strong sense of diversity and appreciation of eclectic design distinguish her work. Her interest in photography was sparked while living in Turkey. Her greeting cards are distributed nationally by Marcel Shurman Paper Co. p. 122

Ingrid Kiehl-Krau (Braunfels, Germany): A chronic disease destroyed my first life. I am now struggling to mend the pieces. Letters and mail welcome. Kiehl-Krau@t-online.de. p. 81

J. Davis Wilson (Eugene, OR) is an eco-poet teaching toddlers words, love and faeries. p. 150

Janine Canan (Sonoma, CA) is a psychiatrist and the author of ten books of poetry, including *Love, Enter* and *Changing Woman.* She translated *Star in My Forehead: Selected Poems by Else Lasker-Schuler,* and edited *She Rises Like the Sun.* p. 108

Jennet Inglis (Santa Fe, NM): I am a guru-free visionary, a scientist, an artist and a lunatic. I live in the core of the Earth, in the stars and on the fragile shifting plates of the Great Mother. p. 63

Jenny Yates (Quito, Ecuador): I'm a roving lesbian astrologer with one book out there in the world, *Your Horoscope: A Guide to Interpretation.* I live with my girlfriend in a city ringed by volcanoes and spend the summers traveling, teaching and consulting in the U.S. pp. 17–19, 20–21

Jill Smith (Glastonbury, Somerset, England) is an artist, writer, performer. She is inspired by the sacred landscape of the British Isles and has lived ten years in the wondrous Western Isles of Scotland. She now resides in ancient Avalon, England. I have work for sale. Call 01458-831953 when in Glastonbury. p. 38

Jodi Reeb-Myers (Richfield, MN) is a teacher, artist, printmaker and mother of two living near Minneapolis. She uses natural materials as voice for her work. pp. 74, 79, 124

Joell Lanfrank (South Royalton, VT) I am a 25-year-old weemoon living in the beautiful green hills of Vermont with my boyfriend and the sweetest pit bull. I love to blow glass, snowboard, hike and enjoy the change of seasons. p. 135

Joey Garcia (El Dorado Hills, CA) is a writer, poet and artist who serves as a companion to people who are on the spiritual path. p. 52

Jude Woods (Pecos, NM) is a British artist currently living in New Mexico. p. 137

Julia Butterfly Hill (Luna Tree, CA) is the activist who climbed into a 1,000 year-old Redwood tree (now known as Luna) on Dec. 10, 1997 to protect it from the saws and make the world aware of the plight of our planet's forests. She was still living in the tree as of May 1999. PO Box 388, Garberville, CA 95542. p. 97

Julie Weber (Ashland, OR) celebrates the seasons, loves gardening and poetry and lives with her lunarworks lover in a small town surrounded by strong women and womyn's lands. p. 161

Karuna Greenberg (Forks of Salmon, CA): I am a photographer, writer, ecological land management planner, and general lover of life struggling to preserve community, find peace within, and keep expression flowing in the mountains of northern California. p. 90

Katelyn Mariah (St. Paul, MN) is a visionary artist and creator of the *Awaken the Goddess Meditation* deck, does soul portraits and conducts workshops on discovering the Goddess within. p. 12

Kathleen Sweeney (Lahaina, HI) is a Wiccan solo sailor wanderlusting around Mother Oceans, in and out of her lands, connecting with her children and lore; writing poems, articles and a book. Anyone want to play? koleakate@hotmail.com
p. 49

Keely Meagan (West Wind, NM) is a witch and natural builder happily based in the Santa Fe area. I teach earth plastering and cob workshops and have founded Artisan Earth, a women's plaster crew finishing strawbale homes in the Southwest. 505-438-6651; PO Box 304, Ribera, NM 87560. pp. 67, 133, 142

Laura Hershey (Denver, CO) is a poet, writer, artist and activist who works to create both a vision and reality of freedom, justice and self-realization. Her work has appeared in *MS, Sojourner, Sinister Wisdom, Disability Rag, The Mouth, Progressive* and elsewhere. p. 132

Laura Weaver (Boulder, CO): I am a mother, poet, activist and massage therapist living with my family. I am always looking to collaborate with other musicians, visual artists, writers, dancers to create performance art. Interested? 970 North St. #101, Boulder, CO 80304 pp. 87, 94

Lavonne Marie (Hailey, ID) is a wise woemyn of water coming into cronehood joyfully. Come visit and play in our hot spring and find healing there with me! Blessed be. p. 173

Lea Moore (New York, NY) is a creative artist, lover, friend, daughter, sister and 2nd mommie, concerned with bringing out the best in myself and others. p. 35

Lilian de Mello (Kapaa, HI): Inspired by Hawaii's nature and believing that art is essential to the human soul, I try to live from my fine art (nature/landscape/ wimmin in nature), color, black and white and experimental photography. Contact me at: ldmphoto@gte.net p. 61

Liliuda (Paia, Maui, HI) is a Canadian artist, writer, Tantra teacher/student, and lover, currently enjoying island life. p. 47

Linda S. Smith (Drury, MO) lives at Hawk Hill Community Land Trust in the Ozarks Mountains. She is Director of the Aradia Project and leads workshops utilizing a labyrinth to help women find their own sacred path. Contact her: HC 73, Box 172, Drury, MO 65538 or aradia@goin.missouri.org p. 30

Linda Sweatt (Cundiyo, NM): My mission as a goddess/artist is to capture the essence of powerful women and to show their joy, beauty and strength. I create paintings and wearable art and live outside Sante Fe in a tiny village in the mountains on a gorgeous river, my inspiration. back cover

Lisa de St. Croix (Ramah, NM): Painting in a ritualistic way, I weave layers of my prophetic dreams, Goddesses, sacred places I have visited and the magical beauty where I live between Navaho and Zuni reservations telling my story.   p. 87

Lisa L. Beebe (Camden, ME): I am a struggling woman, daughter, mother, wife, R.N., photographer creating my life as it creates me. I am curious, adventurous, a survivor.   p. 47

Lynn Dewart (San Diego, CA): Artist, teacher, costume-maker, engineer, I'm fascinated with detail and symbology, truth and depth of the inner world, exploration, integration, tarot, yoga and leading a simple, mindful life of integrity.
Cover, p.174

Mara Friedman (Lorane, OR) lives and creates in the nourishing green womb of the Pacific Northwest. Her paintings honor the beautiful spirit of the Sacred Feminine. For a catalog of cards and prints, write her at PO Box 23, Lorane, Or 97451.   pp. 101, 139, 149

Mari Susan Selby (Santa Fe, NM) is a poet of the Earth, a Dakini of strong laughter, and an astrologer of individual and planetary evolution.   pp. 25, 63

Marja de Vries (Oldenzaal, the Netherlands): My work focusses on where the physical and non-physical worlds meet. As a fabric artist I make wall-hangings depicting the essence of someone's personal symbols. I also teach spiritual training. Contact: Lindestraat 30, 7572 TV Oldenzaal, the Netherlands.   p. 105

Marlene Permar (Casper, CA): I recently moved to Casper by the sea and I'm having a wonderful time in this very strong female energy area. I'm a needle artist and play in several dimensions—fairy realm and all.   p. 85

Marna (Seattle, WA) frolics with spirit, magic and mud through permaculture, earthen building, and temple with systers of creation.   pp. 50, 93

Marsha A. Gomez (Austin, TX) was a clay sculptor, environmental/human rights activist for 22 years and director of Alma de Mujer Retreat Center for Social Change. She died Sept. 27, 1998. (see Dedication p. 188)   pp. 57, 163

Martina Hoffman (Boulder, CO) is a painter and sculptress who explores the realms of spirit and the unknown in colorful visions of light and energy. As a magical realist, she projects her own gnosis onto the canvas.   pp. 31, 43

Martine Palmiter (Rockville, MD) is a hip mama, massage therapist, artist, writer and life enthusiast.   pp. 4, 141

Mary Billy (Squamish, BC, Canada) will soon have her book of poems, *Over the Falls,* released. She dedicates her life to women. She was recently one of 20 women from around the world awarded the first International Helen Prize, given to ordinary women who make a difference in their community.   p. 104

May Trillium (Portland, OR): I am a five-year-old vegetarian. I love to do art, play dress-up, run around naked and experience magic.   p. 171

Maya Fulan Yue (Estacada, OR) is a four-year-old artist born in China who enjoys life with her two moms on the West Coast, for now, and wants to be a pirate when she grows up.   pp. 27, 70

Michèle A. Belluomini (Philadelphia, PA) is a poet and storyteller, a librarian, and has long been interested in and studied the history of matriarchy and the tarot.
p. 71

Mimi Baczewska (Ava, MO) shaved her head in solidarity with a friend who was to lose her hair from chemo treatments. Her friend passed with a full head of hair and in the process, Mimi was born anew. **Dolfin**, photographer, is honored to document the wild life both human and otherly in the Ozarks.   p. 83

Monica Sjöö (Bristol, Avon, England) is a Swedish-born artist and writer. She is co-author of *The Great Cosmic Mother* and sole author of *New Age and Armageddon*. Based in Britain for many years, she is involved in Goddess Earth Mysteries and is rediscovering ancient Sweden.   p. 168

Musawa (We'Moon Land/ARF) I am enjoying living part-time in a high desert wimmin's community in New Mexico and part-time in the rain forest of We'moon community in Oregyn, migrating seasonally through the a-mazing lands that lay in between.   pp. 5–14, 22, 24, 26, 55, 151

Nancy Bareis (Queens, NY) is a photographer and dedicated NEWMR festival planner.   p. 134

Nell Stone (Estacada, OR) is a woman in transition. She is a writer, artist, musician and mom who recently moved to the West Coast with her mamily from Michigan trying to find a home. She is learning about life in general through the eyes of her four-year-old daughter.   pp. 26, 62, 147

Pamela Moore (San Pedro, CA) is a feminist dianic and an illustrator. She lives next to the ocean with her partner, baby and three ill-tempered cats. Reach her at PO Box 2583, San Pedro, CA 90731 or pam@surfmusic.net   p. 119

Patricia Dines (Sebastopol, CA): What an honor to be on the Earth, seeking ever to feel, receive and serve Spirit!   p. 127

Patricia Worth (Las Vegas, NM) is a Celtic poet, prairie witch and pot stirrer. She is one of the reclaiming mothers of the shamanic art of Bone Dancing. For classes and consultations, call 505-427-0008 or write PO Box 1844, Las Vegas, NM 87701.   pp. 39, 166

Prinny Alaví (New York, NY) is a Persian-American artist who received her BSA from Parsons School of Design. She is a creative art director in advertising and computer graphics and loves being in nature near water.   p. 46

Raggy Chris L. (Tofino, BC, Canada): I am the author of *A Cabin in Clayoquat* and *New Power* and live with a green man in a floathouse, gardening on the water, learning self-esteem. We must save the earth.   pp. 17, 142, 176

Renna Shesso (Denver, CO) writes, teaches, makes art, edits, watches the birds and clouds, enjoys train travel and shamanic journeying. Her *(S)*heroes are Susan Weed, Emma Peel, warrior princesses. PO Box 201475, Denver, CO 80220. p. 169

Rosa Davis (Stroud, Gloucestershire, U.K.): My images and words are an outward expression of my inner process, refined over many years. I also work as a trainer of couple counselors.   pp. 157, 174

Rose Flint (Bath, Avon, England) is a poet and artist. She teaches creative writing and is training as an art therapist. She is the resident poet at the Goddess Conference held at Lammas in Glastonbury.   p. 181

S. J. Hugdahl (Forks of Salmon, CA): I live on the Salmon River in Siskiyou County with my family and the garden, mountains, trees, deer, bluejays, otter, horse, two dogs, lizards, bear, wrens, squirrels, swallowtails, chinook and steelhead, the ferns and everyone else that I couldn't fit. p. 175

Sabrina Vourvoulias (Earlville, NY) is an artist and writer of Guatemalan and Greek ancestry. She lives off-the-grid in a log cabin with her partner, her daughter Morgan Sophia, the cat Taliessin and other wild beings. p. 47

Sandra Pastorius (Santa Cruz, CA): I published the *Lunar Muse–a Monthly Moon Guide* for ten years, gaining a reputation as a poet and astrologer. I now teach groups The Zodiac as a Path to Wellness course and offer spiritual guidance as a ceremonialist and mentor. POB 2344, Santa Cruz, CA 95063 p. 25

Sandra Stanton (Farmington, ME) is a painter whose work is dedicated to the many faces of the Goddess, her creatures and our beautiful Mother Earth. Prints are available at RR #2, Box 2564-B, Farmington, ME 04938. p. 109

Sara-Lou Klein (Denver, CO) is an artist and student of Wicca, and is happily blessed with inspiration. p. 142

Schar Cbear Freeman (Portland, OR) is a mother, artist, poet of the Pacific Northwest whose poetry and paintings have been published and exhibited throughout the planet and cyberspace. They may be viewed at http://www.womenfolk.com/poetsite/cbear pp. 72, 113, 120, 121, 185

Selina di Girolamo (Wendover, Bucks, England) is a womb-in artist, priestess to the dark Goddess, poet, mother of sons, witch, reclaiming endarkenment and celebrating wombscape, honoring my ancestors and the spirits of the land with rich mud, wise blood and wild ritual. p. 69

Selka D. Kind (Russel, ON, Canada): I'm working in a multitude of arts and exploration, publishing a zine, searching and philosophizing—laugh! p. 170

Shae Irving (Berkeley, CA) is a lover of ripe fruit and raw words. Her poetry has appeared in several literary journals including *Fireweed* (Toronto) and *In the Grove* (California). p. 122

Shelley Stefan (Portland, OR): Greetings. I love art and self-portraits are a way for me to connect with the journey of my intense art spirit. I feel blessed and I pray to keep honoring and tending to the creative fire within. p. 65

Shiloh McCloud (Port Townsed, WA): I am an artist, feminist and Christian dedicated to women's healing. I create my work for and about women. My art illustrates women in positions of power, strength and wisdom. pp. 2, 107, 148

Sierra Lonepine Briano (Gaston, OR) is a dyke artist approaching cronehood at ArtSprings, a retreat for women artists. She also grows gardens, makes paper and tends to her ducks. p. 130

Singing Tree (Snohomish, WA): I am a wild weedy witch waxing wordy in the woods of Washington. Currently, I am birthing a tape of healing songs and eating well. pp. 58, 152

Sioux Patullo (Victoria, Australia) is teaching performing arts and dancing under a vast, vast sky, floating, dabbing, swinging, changing, rearranging, being and listening to the ravens. pp. 99, 107, 113

Soma (Biggar, SK, Canada) finds her poems in the Bear Hills under stones and long grasses. Heartfelt apologies to Jane. There are angels everywhere. p. 154

Sudie Rakusin (Hillsborough, NC) is an artist and an ecofeminist. Her love and concern for the Earth and her creatures influences all her choices and permeate her work. She lives in the woods with her dog companions and her ever-expanding gardens.   pp. 6, 81, 92, 115

Sue Silvermarie (Ontario, WI) holds an MSW and is a poet/performer/presenter and author of *Tales from My Teachers on the Alzheimer's Unit*. The other side of 50 finds her surprisingly hopeful about our small planet and her earthlings. Write to sue@silvermarie.com; http://www.silvermarie.com   pp. 36, 41, 118, 138

Susan Levitt (San Francisco, CA), author of *Taoist Astrology*, is a fey mermaid priestess, tarot reader, astrologer and feng shui consultant in the Bay Area. 415-642-8019 or e-mail: susanlevitt@slip.net or visit www.taoism-astrology-tarot.com
                                                    pp. 22–23, 24

Suzanne Harding (Santa Cruz, CA): I am a life-loving artist deeply connected to nature and all its beings. I surround myself with animals, flowers, pencils and paint, yearning to express the magic of life and death through my process of creating.   p. 143

Tamara Leibfarth (Ridgefield, WA) has been a chef for 20 years. She loves to nourish people, photograph through heart's eye, travel, be in nature and have life-altering adventures like her encounter with a Grizzly while working in Denali National Park in 1995.   p. 103

Tracey Schavone (Jacksonville, FL): I am a woman deeply inspired by the divine feminine in all her forms and through her graces.   p. 159

Tracy Harrison (Acton, ON, Canada) is an artist and art therapist. Her work is of a highly spiritual nature often reflecting her reverence of the earth, the Goddess and ancient stories.   pp. 19, 143

Ulla Anobile (Los Angeles, CA): Her mixed media masks and sculpture explore the world and soul of women and nature spirits. She was born in Finland and her work has been shown nationally in galleries and museums.   p. 181

Veronica M. Murphy (Toledo, OH) is a performing poet, lawyer and teacher with 56 years of experience in dancing on my limitations and ever-increasing capacity for joy.   p. 56

Viviane Gordon Voa (Santa Fe, NM)   p. 102

Wendy Ponca (El Rito, NM) I am the mother of four children, two boys and two girls. We are members of the Osage Nation. I feel that art and love are the two most important aspects of life. These things allow for the communication that transforms our existance into a positive dream.   p. 185

Willow Fox (Corvallis, OR): I am a young artist becoming my Goddess-self with the help of Mama, Papa, animal, plant and people friends and the uni-verse. Blessings to all of us changing the world through our visions and love. May the strength of our spirits unite us all.   p. 45

Zella Bardsley (Boise, ID) is a steel artist, writer and illustrator of feminist and spiritual themes. She loves drumming under a full moon with way-cool women and always invites comments on her work.   p. 59

ASTEROIDS

The asteroids, a belt of planetary bodies orbiting in the solar system mostly between Mars and Jupiter, were discovered in the early 1800's. Since the sighting of new planets in the solar system corresponds to the activation of new centers of consciousness in the human psyche, the discovery of these planetary bodies, carrying the names of hundreds of goddesses, points to an awakening of a feminine-defined principle.

Because traditional astrology uses a ten-planet system (and only two of these symbols, the Moon and Venus, represent feminine archetypes), astrology by default has not had a set of symbols by which to describe other avenues of feminine expression. It has tried to fit all other women's experiences into masculine-defined archetypes.

The asteroids signify new archetypal symbols in the astrological language and they specifically address the current psychological and social issues that are arising in today's world due to the activation of the feminine principle. Synchronistic with the publication of the asteroid goddess ephemeris, the forefront of the women's movement emerged into society. At this time new aspects of feminine expression began to enter into human consciousness. Women became imbued with the possibilities of feminine creativity and intelligence that expanded and transcended the traditional roles of wife and mother (Venus and the Moon). This also marked a time of the rediscovery of women's ancient history, the growth of women's culture and sexuality independent of men, and the rebirth of the Goddess in women's spirituality.

On the following page the mandala of asteriod goddesses can help us to better understand the meaning of Ceres, Pallas, Juno and Vesta (the first four asteroids discovered). The large circle in the mandala represents the Moon, which is the foundation of the feminine principle and contains potential expressions of the feminine nature. Behind the Moon resides the Sun. The union of these two energies gives rise to what mystics define as "oneness." In the center of the mandala resides Venus, the core essence of the feminine nature in her activated form, who embodies the well-spring of feminine creative, magnetic, sexual, reproductive vital life force. Venus is surrounded by Ceres, Pallas, Vesta and Juno who represent the primary relationships of a woman's life, that of mother, daughter, sister and partner, respectively. Each asteroid utilizes the creative sexual energy of Venus at the center of the circle in her own unique way, as she expresses various functions and activities of the feminine principle. They are placed at the four cardinal directions of the mandala. In the horoscope this fourfold division is designated by the four angles: the Ascendent and Descendent, which define the line of the horizon, and the Midheaven and Nadir, which mark the meridian line.

Ceres, as the Great Mother and Goddess of agriculture, gives birth to the world of physical form; she births children and provides food for their survival. As the Nadir (IC) she represents a point of foundation, roots, and family.

Pallas Athene, as the daughter and the Goddess of Wisdom, generates mental and artistic creations from her mind. At the Midheaven (MC), where visible and socially useful accomplishments are realized, she represents the principle of creative intelligence.

Vesta, as the Sister, is the Temple Priestess and is a virgin in the original sense of being whole and complete in oneself. As the Ascendant (ASC.), Vesta corresponds to the Self. She signifies the principle of spiritual focus and devotion to following one's calling.

Juno, as the Goddess of Marriage, fosters and sustains union with a partner. Placed at the Descendant (DESC.), the point of one-to-one relationships, Juno symbolizes the principle of relatedness and commitment to the other.

© *Demetra George 1996 excerpted and reprinted from* Asteroid Goddesses Natal Report *(a software program published by Astrolabe)*

SOUTH

Goddess of Wisdom & Warrior Queen
Courage and Will
MC
air
Pallas Athene
daughter

Temple Priestess
Goddess of Marriage

fire

water

EAST

ASC.
Vesta
sister
Clarity and Insight

DESC.
Juno
partner
Compassion and Healing

WEST

earth
Ceres
mother
IC

The Mandala of the Asteroid Goddesses

© *Demetra George 1995*

Great Mother
Silence and Strenth

NORTH

2000 ASTEROID EPHEMERIS

2000	Ceres 1	Pallas 2	Juno 3	Vesta 4
JAN 1	04≏20.7	14 R 08.3	07♍48.6	05♐42.7
11	06 18.6	11 ♌43.4	11 32.5	10 53.1
21	07 42.6	08 33.2	15 16.8	15 58.9
31	08 28.3	05 10.2	19 00.6	20 59.3
FEB 10	08 R 31.6	02 08.7	22 42.9	25 52.8
20	07 51.3	29♋56.1	26 22.5	00♑37.8
MAR 1	06 30.0	28 44.0	29 58.3	05 12.9
11	04 35.3	28 D 33.3	03≏29.1	09 36.1
21	02 21.2	29 18.1	06 53.4	13 44.8
31	00 04.9	00♌49.3	10 09.8	17 36.5
APR 10	28♍03.8	02 58.0	13 16.5	21 08.0
20	26 32.3	05 36.6	16 11.4	24 15.4
30	25 38.8	08 38.7	18 52.3	26 54.6
MAY 10	25 D 26.6	11 59.6	21 16.1	29 00.0
20	25 54.9	15 35.0	23 16.3	00♒26.6
30	27 00.2	19 21.6	24 59.6	01 09.4
JUN 9	28 38.3	23 17.7	26 13.3	01 R04.1
19	00≏44.6	27 21.0	26 50.8	00 10.4
29	03 14.7	01♍30.1	26 R54.2	28♑32.6
JUL 9	06 05.0	05 44.0	26 18.6	26 22.0
19	09 12.2	10 01.8	25 24.1	23 57.1
29	12 33.3	14 22.7	23 14.5	21 38.4
AUG 8	16 06.4	18 46.3	20 50.0	19 45.5
18	19 49.2	23 11.7	18 32.1	18 32.3
28	23 40.1	27 38.9	16 33.6	18 D05.2
SEP 7	27 37.9	02≏07.4	14 11.0	18 25.3
17	01♏41.3	06 36.5	12 46.8	19 29.5
27	05 49.1	11 06.1	12 04.5	21 12.5
OCT 7	10 00.6	15 35.7	12 D07.6	23 29.5
17	14 14.6	20 04.7	12 54.4	26 15.1
27	18 30.6	24 32.6	14 21.8	29 24.5
NOV 6	22 47.6	28 58.8	16 25.8	02♒53.9
16	27 04.8	03♏22.5	19 01.0	06 39.9
26	01♐21.5	07 43.0	22 05.8	10 39.5
DEC 6	05 36.8	11 59.2	25 34.1	14 50.4
16	09 49.8	16 09.9	29 23.6	19 10.4
26	13 59.6	20 14.0	03♏31.3	23 37.9
JAN 5	18♐05.2	24♏09.8	07♏55.1	28♒11.5

2000	Sappho 80	Amor 1221	Pandora 55	Icarus 1566
JAN 1	07♌45.9	17♓23.5	12♏47.7	12♏48.9
11	12 12.8	20 18.3	17 09.6	17 35.5
21	16 37.7	23 25.5	21 33.0	22 12.3
31	20 59.6	26 42.6	25 57.3	26 40.9
FEB 10	25 17.5	00♈08.1	00♒21.6	01♒02.5
20	29 30.0	03 40.1	04 45.0	05 17.5
MAR 1	03♍35.9	07 17.4	09 06.6	09 26.5
11	07 33.2	10 58.9	13 25.6	13 29.8
21	11 19.8	14 43.5	17 40.9	17 27.5
31	14 53.6	18 30.4	21 51.4	21 19.8
APR 10	18 11.3	22 18.8	25 56.0	25 06.3
20	21 09.4	26 08.1	29 53.2	28 46.8
30	23 43.6	29 57.6	03♓41.5	02♓21.1
MAY 10	25 48.5	03♉46.7	07 19.0	05 48.3
20	27 18.6	07 34.9	10 43.5	09 07.5
30	28 07.7	11 21.5	13 52.6	12 17.7
JUN 9	28♍10.2	15 06.1	16 43.0	15 16.9
19	27 23.6	18 47.6	19 11.1	18 02.4
29	25 50.0	22 25.6	21 13.1	20 30.6
JUL 9	23 38.9	25 58.9	22 44.1	22 34.4
19	21 09.2	29 26.4	23 39.7	24 02.3
29	18 44.4	02♊46.9	23 R55.9	24 R28.8
AUG 8	16 48.2	05 58.3	23 29.9	22 37.8
18	15 38.5	08 58.6	22 23.1	11 55.5
28	15 D23.8	11 45.3	20 41.2	00♐53.4
SEP 7	16 06.0	14 14.4	18 35.8	19≏21.1
17	17 41.5	16 21.9	16 24.0	11 52.3
27	20 04.4	18 02.4	14 23.6	07 47.1
OCT 7	23 08.4	19 08.9	12 51.0	05♍44.5
17	26 47.2	19 34.1	11 57.6	15 29.9
27	00♎55.1	19 R09.9	11 D47.9	06♌46.4
NOV 6	05 27.6	17 49.1	12 22.8	22 03.7
16	10 20.3	15 29.6	13 39.2	03♊37.6
26	15 29.8	12 16.9	15 32.7	12 58.5
DEC 6	20 53.3	08 29.1	17 58.5	20 53.4
16	26 27.8	04 35.6	20 51.7	27 49.4
26	02♏11.4	01 08.5	24 07.9	04♋03.5
JAN 5	08♏02.1	28♉34.9	27♍43.5	09♋46.3

2000	Psyche 16	Eros 433	Lilith 1181	Toro 1685
JAN 1	00♓07.9	25♏54.1	17♏58.4	03♏31.9
11	04 16.0	03♐13.0	22 11.4	19 33.7
21	08 32.4	10 15.5	26 38.8	10♈47.8
31	13 55.6	17 01.4	01♐18.3	06♉17.0
FEB 10	17 24.4	23 30.4	06 08.1	00♊21.2
20	21 57.6	29 41.4	11 06.3	18 48.6
MAR 1	26 33.9	05♑34.1	16 11.6	02♋08.7
11	01♈12.8	11 07.1	21 12.1	12 11.0
21	05 53.0	16 18.9	26 38.5	20 15.9
31	10 34.0	21 07.6	01♑57.8	27 10.2
APR 10	15 14.9	25 30.4	07 20.0	03♌21.8
20	19 54.9	29 23.4	12 44.0	09 06.7
30	24 33.5	02♒42.3	18 09.2	14 34.0
MAY 10	29 09.9	05 20.5	23 35.1	19 49.9
20	03♉43.3	07 10.5	29 00.7	24 58.1
30	08 13.0	08 03.5	04♒25.6	00♍00.8
JUN 9	12 38.2	07 R49.6	09 49.2	05 00.0
19	16 57.8	06 22.4	15 10.9	09 56.6
29	21 11.1	03 41.5	20 30.1	14 51.5
JUL 9	25 16.5	29♑59.2	25 46.4	19 45.5
19	29 12.9	25 44.5	00♓58.8	24 39.0
29	02♊58.5	21 35.7	06 08.4	29 32.5
AUG 8	06 31.3	18 09.3	11 09.7	04♎26.4
18	09 48.9	15 49.0	16 06.4	09 21.1
28	12 48.7	14 41.8	20 56.1	14 16.7
SEP 7	15 27.2	14 D45.2	25 37.5	19 13.9
17	17 40.7	15 50.7	00♈09.1	24 12.5
27	19 25.2	17 48.5	04 29.5	29 13.2
OCT 7	20 35.7	20 30.3	08 36.4	04♏16.2
17	21 08.6	23 48.5	12 27.5	09 21.6
27	21 R00.5	27 37.2	16 00.1	14 30.0
NOV 6	20 11.0	01♓52.2	19 10.4	19 41.5
16	18 43.8	06 29.6	21 54.7	24 56.5
26	16 47.3	11 26.8	24 08.3	00♐15.5
DEC 6	14 35.5	16 42.1	25 45.9	05 39.0
16	12 25.3	22 13.6	26 42.8	11 07.4
26	10 32.7	28 00.3	26 R54.7	16 41.5
JAN 5	09♊10.6	04♓01.7	26♈19.2	22♐22.3

2000	Diana 78	Hidalgo 944	Urania 30	Chiron 2060
JAN 1	27♐08.4	27♐06.1	22♏49.6	11♐33.9
11	00♑57.7	28 33.1	27 42.3	12 40.6
21	04 42.0	29 57.0	02♒38.3	13 42.2
31	08 20.3	01♑16.3	07 36.9	14 37.8
FEB 10	11 51.5	02 29.4	12 37.7	15 26.3
20	15 13.9	03 34.9	17 39.9	16 06.7
MAR 1	18 26.3	04 31.3	22 42.9	16 38.2
11	21 26.8	05 17.0	27 46.3	17 00.2
21	24 13.4	05 50.6	02♓49.2	17 12.2
31	26 44.1	06 10.9	07 51.2	17 R14.1
APR 10	28 56.3	06 R16.7	12 51.7	17 06.1
20	00♒47.0	06 07.4	17 49.8	16 48.8
30	02 13.6	05 42.7	22 45.0	16 23.2
MAY 10	03 12.5	05 02.8	27 36.4	15 50.5
20	03 40.8	04 09.1	02♈22.8	15 12.5
30	03 R36.2	03 03.5	07 03.4	14 31.3
JUN 9	02 57.4	01 48.7	11 36.5	13 48.9
19	01 45.4	00 28.4	16 00.6	13 07.8
29	00 04.3	29♐06.5	20 13.8	12 29.8
JUL 9	28♑01.4	27 47.2	24 13.4	11 57.1
19	25 47.7	26 34.5	27 56.4	11 31.2
29	23 35.6	25 31.9	01♉19.5	11 13.2
AUG 8	21 37.1	24 41.9	04 17.7	11 04.2
18	20 02.5	24 06.5	06 46.0	11 D04.5
28	18 58.0	23 46.7	08 38.5	11 14.2
SEP 7	18 27.0	23 D42.7	09 48.4	11 33.3
17	18 D29.7	23 54.2	10 10.3	12 01.3
27	19 04.4	24 20.5	09 R40.7	12 37.7
OCT 7	20 08.6	25 00.5	08 20.8	13 21.6
17	21 38.9	25 52.9	06 20.3	14 12.3
27	23 32.0	26 56.5	-03 56.4	15 08.8
NOV 6	25 45.2	28 09.7	01 33.0	16 10.1
16	28 15.5	29 31.0	29♈34.2	17 15.2
26	01♒00.3	00♑59.1	28 17.3	18 22.9
DEC 6	03 57.5	02 32.4	27 D52.0	19 32.3
16	07 05.1	04 09.4	28 19.7	20 42.2
26	10 21.3	05 48.8	29 36.5	21 51.4
JAN 5	13♒44.6	07♑29.0	01♉36.9	22♐58.8

© *Astro Communications Services, Inc. 1986, reprinted with permission from* Asteroid Goddesses

Giving the positions of asteroids every
ten days in LONGITUDE at 00:00 GMT

NOON PLANETARY EPHEMERIS: GMT*

JANUARY 2000

Day	Sid.Time	☉	0 hr ☽	Noon☽	True☊	☿	♀	♂	♃	♄	♅	♆	♇
1 Sa	18 41 50	10♑22 5	7♏17 4	13♏18 54	3♌57.0	1♑53.3	1♐33.9	27♒57.8	25♈15.2	10♉23.7	14♒48.6	3♒11.6	11♐27.2
2 Su	18 45 46	11 23 16	19 18 30	25 16 20	3R53.4	3 26.8	2 46.5	28 44.3	25 17.7	10R22.6	14 51.6	3 13.7	11 29.3
3 M	18 49 43	12 24 26	1♐12 47	7♐ 8 16	3 49.5	5 0.7	3 59.1	29 30.8	25 20.5	10 21.6	14 54.6	3 15.9	11 31.4
4 Tu	18 53 39	13 25 37	13 3 6	18 57 38	3 45.8	6 34.9	5 11.8	0♓17.4	25 23.4	10 20.6	14 57.7	3 18.1	11 33.5
5 W	18 57 36	14 26 47	24 52 8	0♑46 55	3 42.7	8 9.4	6 24.6	1 3.9	25 26.6	10 19.8	15 0.8	3 20.2	11 35.5
6 Th	19 1 32	15 27 58	6♑42 11	12 38 13	3 40.5	9 44.3	7 37.4	1 50.5	25 29.9	10 19.1	15 4.0	3 22.4	11 37.6
7 F	19 5 29	16 29 9	18 35 14	24 33 28	3 39.2	11 19.6	8 50.3	2 37.0	25 33.5	10 18.6	15 7.1	3 24.6	11 39.6
8 Sa	19 9 26	17 30 19	0♒33 8	6♒34 29	3D39.0	12 55.3	10 3.2	3 23.5	25 37.2	10 18.1	15 10.3	3 26.8	11 41.6
9 Su	19 13 22	18 31 29	12 37 46	18 43 14	3 39.6	14 31.4	11 16.2	4 10.0	25 41.1	10 17.7	15 13.5	3 29.0	11 43.6
10 M	19 17 19	19 32 39	24 51 10	1♓ 1 53	3 40.7	16 7.9	12 29.2	4 56.6	25 45.3	10 17.5	15 16.7	3 31.2	11 45.5
11 Tu	19 21 15	20 33 48	7♓15 42	13 32 55	3 42.0	17 44.8	13 42.3	5 43.1	25 49.6	10 17.3	15 20.0	3 33.5	11 47.5
12 W	19 25 12	21 34 57	19 53 55	26 19 2	3 43.1	19 22.2	14 55.4	6 29.5	25 54.1	10D17.3	15 23.2	3 35.7	11 49.4
13 Th	19 29 8	22 36 5	2♈48 37	9♈22 59	3 43.9	21 0.0	16 8.5	7 16.0	25 58.8	10 17.4	15 26.5	3 38.0	11 51.3
14 F	19 33 5	23 37 13	16 2 27	22 47 17	3R44.2	22 38.4	17 21.7	8 2.5	26 3.6	10 17.6	15 29.8	3 40.2	11 53.2
15 Sa	19 37 1	24 38 19	29 37 40	6♉33 43	3 44.0	24 17.2	18 35.0	8 48.9	26 8.7	10 17.9	15 33.1	3 42.5	11 55.0
16 Su	19 40 58	25 39 26	13♉35 26	20 42 43	3 43.4	25 56.5	19 48.3	9 35.4	26 13.9	10 18.4	15 36.4	3 44.7	11 56.8
17 M	19 44 55	26 40 31	27 55 19	5♊12 50	3 42.6	27 36.3	21 1.6	10 21.8	26 19.3	10 18.9	15 39.7	3 47.0	11 58.7
18 Tu	19 48 51	27 41 36	12♊34 45	20 0 21	3 41.9	29 16.6	22 14.9	11 8.2	26 24.9	10 19.6	15 43.1	3 49.2	12 0.4
19 W	19 52 48	28 42 40	27 28 48	4♋59 9	3 41.3	0♒57.4	23 28.3	11 54.6	26 30.7	10 20.3	15 46.5	3 51.5	12 2.2
20 Th	19 56 44	29 43 43	12♋30 22	20 1 21	3 41.0	2 38.8	24 41.7	12 40.9	26 36.7	10 21.2	15 49.8	3 53.8	12 4.0
21 F	20 0 41	0♒44 46	27 30 59	4♌58 11	3D40.9	4 20.6	25 55.2	13 27.3	26 42.8	10 22.2	15 53.2	3 56.1	12 5.7
22 Sa	20 4 37	1 45 47	12♌21 58	19 41 24	3 41.0	6 3.0	27 8.7	14 13.6	26 49.1	10 23.3	15 56.6	3 58.3	12 7.4
23 Su	20 8 34	2 46 49	26 55 43	4♍ 4 18	3 41.1	7 45.8	28 22.2	14 59.9	26 55.5	10 24.5	16 0.1	4 0.6	12 9.0
24 M	20 12 30	3 47 49	11♍ 6 41	18 2 33	3R41.1	9 29.1	29 35.8	15 46.1	27 2.1	10 25.8	16 3.5	4 2.9	12 10.7
25 Tu	20 16 27	4 48 49	24 51 46	1♎34 21	3 41.0	11 12.8	0♑49.4	16 32.4	27 8.9	10 27.3	16 6.9	4 5.2	12 12.3
26 W	20 20 24	5 49 49	8♎10 25	14 40 15	3 40.9	12 56.9	2 3.0	17 18.6	27 15.8	10 28.8	16 10.4	4 7.4	12 13.9
27 Th	20 24 20	6 50 48	21 4 11	27 22 40	3 40.7	14 41.3	3 16.7	18 4.8	27 22.9	10 30.4	16 13.8	4 9.7	12 15.4
28 F	20 28 17	7 51 46	3♏36 10	9♏45 14	3D40.7	16 26.0	4 30.4	18 51.0	27 30.2	10 32.2	16 17.3	4 12.0	12 17.0
29 Sa	20 32 13	8 52 44	15 50 26	21 52 21	3 40.8	18 10.8	5 44.1	19 37.2	27 37.6	10 34.1	16 20.7	4 14.3	12 18.5
30 Su	20 36 10	9 53 41	27 51 34	3♐48 40	3 41.3	19 55.7	6 57.9	20 23.3	27 45.2	10 36.0	16 24.2	4 16.6	12 20.0
31 M	20 40 6	10 54 38	9♐44 13	15 38 47	3 42.0	21 40.5	8 11.6	21 9.5	27 52.9	10 38.1	16 27.7	4 18.8	12 21.4

LONGITUDE

FEBRUARY 2000

Day	Sid.Time	☉	0 hr ☽	Noon☽	True☊	☿	♀	♂	♃	♄	♅	♆	♇
1 Tu	20 44 3	11♒55 33	21♐32 52	27♐27 0	3♌42.9	23♒25.0	9♑25.4	21♓55.6	28♈ 0.8	10♉40.3	16♒31.2	4♒21.1	12♐22.9
2 W	20 47 59	12 56 28	3♑21 37	9♑17 9	3 43.8	25 9.1	10 39.3	22 41.6	28 8.8	10 42.6	16 34.7	4 23.4	12 24.3
3 Th	20 51 56	13 57 22	15 14 0	21 12 30	3 44.5	26 52.5	11 53.1	23 27.7	28 17.0	10 45.0	16 38.1	4 25.6	12 25.6
4 F	20 55 53	14 58 15	27 12 59	3♒15 43	3R44.8	28 34.9	13 7.0	24 13.7	28 25.3	10 47.5	16 41.6	4 27.9	12 27.0
5 Sa	20 59 49	15 59 7	9♒20 56	15 28 49	3 44.5	0♓16.1	14 20.8	24 59.7	28 33.8	10 50.2	16 45.1	4 30.1	12 28.3
6 Su	21 3 46	16 59 57	21 39 34	27 53 18	3 43.5	1 55.6	15 34.7	25 45.7	28 42.4	10 52.9	16 48.6	4 32.4	12 29.6
7 M	21 7 42	18 0 47	4♓10 7	10♓30 8	3 41.9	3 33.2	16 48.6	26 31.6	28 51.1	10 55.7	16 52.1	4 34.6	12 30.8
8 Tu	21 11 39	19 1 35	16 53 25	23 20 1	3 39.7	5 8.2	18 2.6	27 17.5	29 0.0	10 58.6	16 55.6	4 36.8	12 32.0
9 W	21 15 35	20 2 21	29 50 0	6♈23 24	3 37.2	6 40.1	19 16.5	28 3.4	29 9.0	11 1.6	16 59.1	4 39.0	12 33.2
10 Th	21 19 32	21 3 6	13♈ 0 15	19 40 35	3 35.0	8 8.5	20 30.4	28 49.2	29 18.2	11 4.8	17 2.6	4 41.2	12 34.4
11 F	21 23 28	22 3 50	26 24 26	3♉11 50	3 33.2	9 32.6	21 44.4	29 35.0	29 27.5	11 8.0	17 6.0	4 43.4	12 35.5
12 Sa	21 27 25	23 4 32	10♉ 2 45	16 57 13	3D32.3	10 51.8	22 58.4	0♈20.8	29 36.9	11 11.3	17 9.5	4 45.6	12 36.6
13 Su	21 31 22	24 5 12	23 55 9	0♊56 29	3 32.4	12 5.4	24 12.4	1 6.6	29 46.4	11 14.7	17 13.0	4 47.8	12 37.7
14 M	21 35 18	25 5 51	8♊ 1 6	15 8 47	3 33.2	13 12.6	25 26.3	1 52.3	29 56.1	11 18.3	17 16.5	4 50.0	12 38.7
15 Tu	21 39 15	26 6 28	22 19 17	29 32 16	3 34.6	14 12.8	26 40.3	2 37.9	0♉ 5.9	11 21.9	17 19.9	4 52.2	12 39.7
16 W	21 43 11	27 7 3	6♋47 20	14♋ 3 58	3 36.0	15 5.3	27 54.3	3 23.6	0 15.8	11 25.6	17 23.4	4 54.3	12 40.7
17 Th	21 47 8	28 7 36	21 21 35	28 39 32	3R36.9	15 49.3	29 8.4	4 9.2	0 25.8	11 29.4	17 26.8	4 56.5	12 41.6
18 F	21 51 4	29 8 8	5♌57 7	13♌13 35	3 36.6	16 24.3	0♒22.4	4 54.7	0 35.9	11 33.3	17 30.3	4 58.6	12 42.5
19 Sa	21 55 1	0♓ 8 38	20 28 10	27 40 6	3 35.1	16 49.7	1 36.4	5 40.2	0 46.2	11 37.3	17 33.7	5 0.7	12 43.4
20 Su	21 58 57	1 9 7	4♍48 39	11♍53 10	3 32.1	17 5.3	2 50.5	6 25.7	0 56.5	11 41.3	17 37.1	5 2.8	12 44.2
21 M	22 2 54	2 9 34	18 53 3	25 47 50	3 28.0	17R10.7	4 4.5	7 11.1	1 7.0	11 45.5	17 40.5	5 4.9	12 45.0
22 Tu	22 6 51	3 9 59	2♎37 9	9♎20 45	3 23.2	17 6.0	5 18.6	7 56.5	1 17.6	11 49.8	17 43.9	5 6.9	12 45.8
23 W	22 10 47	4 10 23	15 58 31	22 30 29	3 18.3	16 51.2	6 32.7	8 41.9	1 28.3	11 54.1	17 47.3	5 9.0	12 46.5
24 Th	22 14 44	5 10 46	28 56 46	5♏17 37	3 14.1	16 26.9	7 46.8	9 27.2	1 39.1	11 58.5	17 50.7	5 11.0	12 47.2
25 F	22 18 40	6 11 7	11♏33 21	17 44 25	3 10.9	15 53.5	9 0.9	10 12.5	1 50.0	12 3.0	17 54.1	5 13.1	12 47.9
26 Sa	22 22 37	7 11 27	23 51 17	29 54 30	3 9.2	15 12.0	10 15.0	10 57.7	2 1.0	12 7.6	17 57.4	5 15.1	12 48.5
27 Su	22 26 33	8 11 46	5♐54 40	11♐52 23	3D 9.0	14 23.5	11 29.1	11 43.0	2 12.1	12 12.3	18 0.8	5 17.1	12 49.1
28 M	22 30 30	9 12 3	17 48 18	23 43 3	3 10.0	13 29.1	12 43.2	12 28.1	2 23.3	12 17.1	18 4.1	5 19.1	12 49.7
29 Tu	22 34 26	10 12 18	29 37 17	5♑31 39	3 11.6	12 30.4	13 57.3	13 13.3	2 34.6	12 21.9	18 7.4	5 21.0	12 50.2

Ephemeris reprinted with permission from Astro Communications Services, Inc.

Each planet's retrograde period is shaded gray.

*Giving the positions of planets daily at noon, in LONGITUDE Greenwich Mean Time

NOON EPHEMERIS: GMT*

MARCH 2000

Day	Sid.Time	☉	0 hr ☽	Noon ☽	True ☊	☿	♀	♂	♃	♄	♅	♆	♇
1 W	22 38 23	11♓12 32	11♑26 44	17♑23 9	3♌13.4	11♓28.9	15♒11.5	13♈58.4	2♉46.0	12♉26.9	18♒10.7	5♒23.0	12♐50.7
2 Th	22 42 20	12 12 45	23 21 26	29 22 6	3R 14.4	10R 26.0	16 25.6	14 43.4	2 57.5	12 31.9	18 13.9	5 24.9	12 51.2
3 F	22 46 16	13 12 56	5♒25 38	11♒32 24	3 14.1	9 23.3	17 39.8	15 28.4	3 9.1	12 37.0	18 17.2	5 26.8	12 51.6
4 Sa	22 50 13	14 13 5	17 42 46	23 57 0	3 12.0	8 22.2	18 53.9	16 13.4	3 20.8	12 42.1	18 20.4	5 28.7	12 52.0
5 Su	22 54 9	15 13 12	0♓15 18	6♓37 47	3 7.8	7 24.0	20 8.0	16 58.3	3 32.5	12 47.4	18 23.6	5 30.6	12 52.4
6 M	22 58 6	16 13 18	13 4 30	19 35 24	3 1.8	6 29.7	21 22.2	17 43.2	3 44.4	12 52.7	18 26.8	5 32.4	12 52.7
7 Tu	23 2 2	17 13 21	26 10 25	2♈49 20	2 54.4	5 40.3	22 36.3	18 28.1	3 56.3	12 58.1	18 30.0	5 34.2	12 53.0
8 W	23 5 59	18 13 23	9♈31 56	16 17 57	2 46.4	4 56.5	23 50.5	19 12.9	4 8.3	13 3.6	18 33.2	5 36.0	12 53.2
9 Th	23 9 55	19 13 23	23 7 3	29 58 56	2 38.8	4 18.7	25 4.6	19 57.6	4 20.4	13 9.1	18 36.3	5 37.8	12 53.5
10 F	23 13 52	20 13 20	6♉53 15	13♉49 40	2 32.4	3 47.3	26 18.8	20 42.3	4 32.6	13 14.7	18 39.4	5 39.6	12 53.6
11 Sa	23 17 48	21 13 16	20 47 52	27 47 36	2 27.9	3 22.4	27 32.9	21 27.0	4 44.9	13 20.4	18 42.5	5 41.3	12 53.8
12 Su	23 21 45	22 13 9	4♊48 36	11♊50 39	2 25.6	3 4.2	28 47.0	22 11.6	4 57.2	13 26.1	18 45.5	5 43.0	12 53.9
13 M	23 25 42	23 13 0	18 53 34	25 57 11	2D 25.1	2 52.5	0♓ 1.2	22 56.2	5 9.6	13 31.9	18 48.6	5 44.7	12 54.0
14 Tu	23 29 38	24 12 49	3♋ 1 20	10♋ 5 52	2 25.8	2D 47.1	1 15.3	23 40.8	5 22.1	13 37.8	18 51.6	5 46.4	12 54.0
15 W	23 33 35	25 12 35	17 10 38	24 15 27	2 26.8	2 48.0	2 29.4	24 25.2	5 34.6	13 43.8	18 54.6	5 48.1	12R 54.1
16 Th	23 37 31	26 12 20	1♌20 6	8♌24 19	2R 26.9	2 54.7	3 43.6	25 9.7	5 47.3	13 49.8	18 57.5	5 49.7	12 54.0
17 F	23 41 28	27 12 2	15 27 48	22 30 13	2 25.1	3 7.1	4 57.7	25 54.1	5 59.9	13 55.8	19 0.4	5 51.3	12 54.0
18 Sa	23 45 24	28 11 41	29 31 8	6♍30 9	2 20.9	3 24.9	6 11.8	26 38.4	6 12.7	14 1.9	19 3.3	5 52.9	12 53.9
19 Su	23 49 21	29 11 19	13♍26 48	20 20 37	2 14.2	3 47.8	7 25.9	27 22.7	6 25.5	14 8.1	19 6.2	5 54.4	12 53.8
20 M	23 53 17	0♈10 55	27 11 11	3♎58 3	2 5.3	4 15.5	8 40.0	28 6.9	6 38.4	14 14.4	19 9.1	5 55.9	12 53.6
21 Tu	23 57 14	1 10 28	10♎40 51	17 19 18	1 55.0	4 47.7	9 54.1	28 51.1	6 51.3	14 20.7	19 11.9	5 57.4	12 53.4
22 W	0 1 11	2 10 0	23 53 10	0♏22 19	1 44.4	5 24.2	11 8.2	29 35.3	7 4.3	14 27.0	19 14.7	5 58.9	12 53.2
23 Th	0 5 7	3 9 30	6♏46 43	13 6 26	1 34.5	6 4.6	12 22.3	0♉19.4	7 17.4	14 33.4	19 17.4	6 0.3	12 53.0
24 F	0 9 4	4 8 58	19 21 38	25 32 34	1 26.2	6 48.9	13 36.4	1 3.5	7 30.5	14 39.9	19 20.1	6 1.8	12 52.7
25 Sa	0 13 0	5 8 24	1♐39 35	7♐43 6	1 20.1	7 36.7	14 50.5	1 47.5	7 43.6	14 46.4	19 22.8	6 3.2	12 52.4
26 Su	0 16 57	6 7 48	13 43 36	19 41 38	1 16.4	8 27.8	16 4.6	2 31.4	7 56.9	14 53.0	19 25.5	6 4.5	12 52.0
27 M	0 20 53	7 7 11	25 37 48	1♑32 43	1 14.9	9 22.0	17 18.7	3 15.4	8 10.1	14 59.6	19 28.1	6 5.9	12 51.6
28 Tu	0 24 50	8 6 32	7♑27 4	13 21 31	1D 14.8	10 19.3	18 32.8	3 59.2	8 23.5	15 6.3	19 30.7	6 7.2	12 51.2
29 W	0 28 46	9 5 51	19 16 45	25 13 27	1 15.3	11 19.3	19 46.9	4 43.1	8 36.8	15 13.0	19 33.3	6 8.5	12 50.8
30 Th	0 32 43	10 5 8	1♒12 18	7♒13 56	1R 15.3	12 22.0	21 1.0	5 26.9	8 50.3	15 19.8	19 35.8	6 9.7	12 50.3
31 F	0 36 40	11 4 24	13 18 57	19 27 55	1 13.7	13 27.2	22 15.1	6 10.6	9 3.7	15 26.6	19 38.3	6 10.9	12 49.8

LONGITUDE

APRIL 2000

Day	Sid.Time	☉	0 hr ☽	Noon ☽	True ☊	☿	♀	♂	♃	♄	♅	♆	♇
1 Sa	0 40 36	12♈ 3 37	25♒41 21	1♓59 38	1♌ 9.9	14♓34.9	23♓29.2	6♉54.3	9♉17.3	15♉33.5	19♒40.7	6♒12.1	12♐49.2
2 Su	0 44 33	13 2 49	8♓23 6	14 52 0	1R 3.4	15 44.8	24 43.3	7 37.9	9 30.8	15 40.4	19 43.1	6 13.3	12R 48.7
3 M	0 48 29	14 1 59	21 26 24	28 6 19	0 54.4	16 56.9	25 57.3	8 21.5	9 44.4	15 47.3	19 45.5	6 14.4	12 48.0
4 Tu	0 52 26	15 1 6	4♈51 35	11♈41 56	0 43.5	18 11.2	27 11.4	9 5.1	9 58.1	15 54.3	19 47.9	6 15.6	12 47.4
5 W	0 56 22	16 0 12	18 36 57	25 36 9	0 31.6	19 27.5	28 25.5	9 48.6	10 11.8	16 1.3	19 50.2	6 16.6	12 46.7
6 Th	1 0 19	16 59 16	2♉38 55	9♉44 36	0 20.1	20 45.7	29 39.5	10 32.1	10 25.5	16 8.4	19 52.4	6 17.7	12 46.0
7 F	1 4 15	17 58 18	16 52 30	24 1 55	0 10.2	22 5.9	0♈53.6	11 15.5	10 39.3	16 15.5	19 54.7	6 18.7	12 45.3
8 Sa	1 8 12	18 57 17	1♊12 10	8♊22 36	0 2.7	23 27.9	2 7.6	11 58.8	10 53.1	16 22.6	19 56.9	6 19.7	12 44.6
9 Su	1 12 8	19 56 14	15 32 42	22 41 57	29♋58.1	24 51.8	3 21.6	12 42.2	11 6.9	16 29.8	19 59.0	6 20.6	12 43.8
10 M	1 16 5	20 55 10	29 49 59	6♋56 30	29 55.9	26 17.3	4 35.6	13 25.4	11 20.8	16 37.0	20 1.1	6 21.6	12 43.0
11 Tu	1 20 2	21 54 2	14♋ 1 18	21 4 13	29D 55.4	27 44.7	5 49.6	14 8.6	11 34.7	16 44.3	20 3.2	6 22.5	12 42.1
12 W	1 23 58	22 52 53	28 5 11	5♌ 4 9	29R 55.4	29 13.7	7 3.6	14 51.8	11 48.6	16 51.6	20 5.2	6 23.3	12 41.3
13 Th	1 27 55	23 51 41	12♌ 1 6	18 56 1	29 54.5	0♈44.4	8 17.6	15 34.9	12 2.6	16 58.9	20 7.2	6 24.2	12 40.4
14 F	1 31 51	24 50 26	25 48 53	2♍39 38	29 51.6	2 16.8	9 31.6	16 18.0	12 16.5	17 6.2	20 9.2	6 25.0	12 39.4
15 Sa	1 35 48	25 49 10	9♍28 12	16 14 29	29 46.0	3 50.8	10 45.6	17 1.0	12 30.5	17 13.6	20 11.1	6 25.7	12 38.5
16 Su	1 39 44	26 47 51	22 58 21	29 39 38	29 37.4	5 26.5	11 59.5	17 44.0	12 44.6	17 21.0	20 12.9	6 26.5	12 37.5
17 M	1 43 41	27 46 30	6♎18 9	12♎53 42	29 26.3	7 3.8	13 13.5	18 26.9	12 58.6	17 28.4	20 14.7	6 27.2	12 36.5
18 Tu	1 47 37	28 45 7	19 26 6	25 55 9	29 13.5	8 42.8	14 27.4	19 9.7	13 12.7	17 35.8	20 16.5	6 27.8	12 35.5
19 W	1 51 34	29 43 42	2♏20 45	8♏42 45	29 0.2	10 23.4	15 41.4	19 52.6	13 26.8	17 43.3	20 18.2	6 28.5	12 34.4
20 Th	1 55 31	0♉42 16	15 1 7	21 15 52	28 47.5	12 5.7	16 55.3	20 35.3	13 40.9	17 50.8	20 19.9	6 29.1	12 33.3
21 F	1 59 27	1 40 47	27 27 4	3♐34 52	28 36.6	13 49.6	18 9.2	21 18.1	13 55.1	17 58.3	20 21.6	6 29.7	12 32.2
22 Sa	2 3 24	2 39 17	9♐39 29	15 41 13	28 28.2	15 35.2	19 23.1	22 0.7	14 9.2	18 5.8	20 23.2	6 30.2	12 31.1
23 Su	2 7 20	3 37 46	21 40 26	27 37 33	28 22.5	17 22.4	20 37.1	22 43.4	14 23.4	18 13.4	20 24.7	6 30.7	12 30.0
24 M	2 11 17	4 36 12	3♑33 4	9♑27 30	28 19.4	19 11.4	21 51.0	23 25.9	14 37.6	18 21.0	20 26.3	6 31.2	12 28.8
25 Tu	2 15 13	5 34 37	15 21 28	21 15 35	28 18.3	21 2.0	23 4.9	24 8.5	14 51.8	18 28.6	20 27.7	6 31.6	12 27.6
26 W	2 19 10	6 33 0	27 10 31	3♒ 6 55	28 18.2	22 54.3	24 18.8	24 51.0	15 6.0	18 36.2	20 29.1	6 32.0	12 26.4
27 Th	2 23 6	7 31 22	9♒ 5 30	15 6 57	28 18.1	24 48.3	25 32.7	25 33.4	15 20.3	18 43.8	20 30.5	6 32.4	12 25.2
28 F	2 27 3	8 29 42	21 11 56	27 21 8	28 16.8	26 44.0	26 46.6	26 15.8	15 34.5	18 51.4	20 31.8	6 32.8	12 23.9
29 Sa	2 31 0	9 28 1	3♓35 8	9♓54 30	28 13.5	28 41.3	28 0.5	26 58.2	15 48.8	18 59.1	20 33.1	6 33.1	12 22.6
30 Su	2 34 56	10 26 18	16 19 43	22 51 8	28 7.8	0♉40.3	29 14.3	27 40.5	16 3.0	19 6.8	20 34.4	6 33.4	12 21.3

*Giving the positions of planets daily at noon,
in LONGITUDE Greenwich Mean Time

NOON EPHEMERIS: GMT* — MAY 2000

Day	Sid.Time	☉	0 hr ☽	Noon☽	True☊	☿	♀	♂	♃	♄	♅	♆	♇
1 M	2 38 53	11♉24 33	29♓29 0	6♈13 28	27♋59.6	2♉40.9	0♉28.2	28♉22.7	16♉17.3	19♉14.4	20♒35.5	6♒33.6	12♐20.0
2 Tu	2 42 49	12 22 47	13♈ 4 27	20 1 46	27R49.5	4 43.1	1 42.1	29 5.0	16 31.6	19 22.1	20 36.7	6 33.8	12R18.7
3 W	2 46 46	13 20 59	27 5 1	4♉13 40	27 38.3	6 46.8	2 55.9	29 47.1	16 45.8	19 29.8	20 37.8	6 34.0	12 17.3
4 Th	2 50 42	14 19 10	11♉27 0	18 44 11	27 27.4	8 51.9	4 9.8	0♊29.3	17 0.1	19 37.5	20 38.8	6 34.1	12 16.0
5 F	2 54 39	15 17 19	26 4 16	3♊26 17	27 17.9	10 58.3	5 23.7	1 11.4	17 14.4	19 45.2	20 39.8	6 34.3	12 14.6
6 Sa	2 58 35	16 15 26	10♊49 13	18 12 5	27 10.7	13 5.9	6 37.5	1 53.4	17 28.7	19 53.0	20 40.8	6 34.3	12 13.2
7 Su	3 2 32	17 13 31	25 33 59	2♋54 7	27 6.2	15 14.6	7 51.3	2 35.4	17 43.0	20 0.7	20 41.7	6 34.4	12 11.7
8 M	3 6 29	18 11 35	10♋11 47	17 26 27	27 4.3	17 24.0	9 5.2	3 17.3	17 57.3	20 8.4	20 42.5	6R34.4	12 10.3
9 Tu	3 10 25	19 9 37	24 37 41	1♌45 12	27D 4.0	19 34.2	10 19.0	3 59.2	18 11.6	20 16.1	20 43.3	6 34.4	12 8.9
10 W	3 14 22	20 7 36	8♌48 50	15 48 30	27R 4.4	21 44.7	11 32.8	4 41.1	18 25.8	20 23.9	20 44.1	6 34.3	12 7.4
11 Th	3 18 18	21 5 34	22 44 14	29 36 4	27 4.1	23 55.5	12 46.6	5 22.9	18 40.1	20 31.6	20 44.8	6 34.3	12 5.9
12 F	3 22 15	22 3 30	6♍24 7	13♍ 8 32	27 2.3	26 6.1	14 0.4	6 4.6	18 54.4	20 39.3	20 45.4	6 34.1	12 4.4
13 Sa	3 26 11	23 1 24	19 49 26	26 26 57	26 58.1	28 16.3	15 14.2	6 46.3	19 8.6	20 47.0	20 46.0	6 34.0	12 2.9
14 Su	3 30 8	23 59 16	3♎ 1 12	9♎32 18	26 51.4	0♊25.9	16 27.9	7 28.0	19 22.9	20 54.8	20 46.6	6 33.8	12 1.4
15 M	3 34 4	24 57 7	16 0 20	22 25 20	26 42.5	2 34.5	17 41.7	8 9.6	19 37.1	21 2.5	20 47.1	6 33.6	11 59.9
16 Tu	3 38 1	25 54 56	28 47 23	5♏ 6 31	26 32.1	4 41.9	18 55.5	8 51.2	19 51.4	21 10.2	20 47.5	6 33.4	11 58.3
17 W	3 41 58	26 52 43	11♏22 46	17 36 11	26 21.3	6 47.8	20 9.2	9 32.7	20 5.6	21 17.9	20 48.0	6 33.1	11 56.8
18 Th	3 45 54	27 50 29	23 46 48	29 54 44	26 11.0	8 51.9	21 23.0	10 14.2	20 19.8	21 25.6	20 48.3	6 32.8	11 55.2
19 F	3 49 51	28 48 14	6♐ 0 4	12♐ 2 57	26 2.1	10 54.1	22 36.7	10 55.6	20 34.0	21 33.3	20 48.6	6 32.4	11 53.7
20 Sa	3 53 47	29 45 57	18 3 34	24 2 9	25 55.3	12 54.2	23 50.5	11 37.0	20 48.1	21 41.0	20 48.9	6 32.1	11 52.1
21 Su	3 57 44	0♊43 39	29 58 58	5♑54 22	25 50.9	14 51.9	25 4.2	12 18.4	21 2.3	21 48.6	20 49.1	6 31.7	11 50.5
22 M	4 1 40	1 41 20	11♑48 41	17 42 23	25 48.7	16 47.1	26 18.0	12 59.7	21 16.5	21 56.3	20 49.3	6 31.2	11 48.9
23 Tu	4 5 37	2 39 0	23 35 56	29 29 49	25D48.4	18 39.7	27 31.7	13 40.9	21 30.6	22 4.0	20 49.4	6 30.8	11 47.3
24 W	4 9 33	3 36 39	5♒24 38	11♒20 56	25 49.3	20 29.6	28 45.4	14 22.2	21 44.7	22 11.6	20 49.5	6 30.3	11 45.7
25 Th	4 13 30	4 34 17	17 19 21	23 20 32	25 50.4	22 16.8	29 59.2	15 3.4	21 58.8	22 19.2	20R49.5	6 29.8	11 44.1
26 F	4 17 27	5 31 54	29 25 7	5♓33 45	25R51.0	24 1.0	1♊12.9	15 44.5	22 12.8	22 26.8	20 49.4	6 29.2	11 42.5
27 Sa	4 21 23	6 29 29	11♓47 4	18 5 39	25 50.2	25 42.4	2 26.6	16 25.6	22 26.9	22 34.4	20 49.4	6 28.6	11 40.9
28 Su	4 25 20	7 27 4	24 30 4	1♈ 0 47	25 47.7	27 20.8	3 40.4	17 6.6	22 40.9	22 42.0	20 49.2	6 28.0	11 39.3
29 M	4 29 16	8 24 38	7♈38 11	14 22 33	25 43.3	28 56.3	4 54.1	17 47.7	22 54.9	22 49.6	20 49.0	6 27.4	11 37.7
30 Tu	4 33 13	9 22 12	21 13 59	28 12 27	25 37.4	0♋28.7	6 7.8	18 28.6	23 8.9	22 57.1	20 48.8	6 26.7	11 36.0
31 W	4 37 9	10 19 44	5♉17 45	12♉29 28	25 30.6	1 58.0	7 21.6	19 9.6	23 22.8	23 4.6	20 48.5	6 26.0	11 34.4

LONGITUDE — JUNE 2000

Day	Sid.Time	☉	0 hr ☽	Noon☽	True☊	☿	♀	♂	♃	♄	♅	♆	♇
1 Th	4 41 6	11♊17 15	19♉47 0	27♉ 9 34	25♋23.8	3♋24.2	8♊35.3	19♊50.5	23♉36.7	23♉12.1	20♒48.2	6♒25.3	11♐32.8
2 F	4 45 2	12 14 46	4♊36 15	12♊ 5 58	25R17.9	4 47.4	9 49.1	20 31.4	23 50.6	23 19.6	20R47.8	6R24.5	11R31.2
3 Sa	4 48 59	13 12 16	19 37 35	27 9 55	25 13.5	6 7.3	11 2.8	21 12.2	24 4.5	23 27.0	20 47.4	6 23.7	11 29.5
4 Su	4 52 56	14 9 44	4♋41 48	12♋12 9	25 11.1	7 24.1	12 16.5	21 53.0	24 18.3	23 34.5	20 47.0	6 22.9	11 27.9
5 M	4 56 52	15 7 12	19 39 57	27 4 19	25D10.5	8 37.5	13 30.2	22 33.7	24 32.1	23 41.9	20 46.4	6 22.1	11 26.3
6 Tu	5 0 49	16 4 38	4♌24 33	11♌40 6	25 11.2	9 47.7	14 44.0	23 14.4	24 45.8	23 49.2	20 45.9	6 21.2	11 24.7
7 W	5 4 45	17 2 3	18 50 32	25 55 37	25 12.6	10 54.5	15 57.7	23 55.1	24 59.5	23 56.6	20 45.3	6 20.3	11 23.0
8 Th	5 8 42	17 59 27	2♍55 14	9♍49 23	25 13.7	11 57.9	17 11.4	24 35.7	25 13.2	24 3.9	20 44.6	6 19.4	11 21.4
9 F	5 12 38	18 56 50	16 38 8	23 21 41	25R13.8	12 57.7	18 25.1	25 16.2	25 26.9	24 11.2	20 43.9	6 18.5	11 19.8
10 Sa	5 16 35	19 54 12	0♎ 0 14	6♎34 2	25 12.6	13 54.0	19 38.8	25 56.8	25 40.5	24 18.4	20 43.2	6 17.5	11 18.2
11 Su	5 20 31	20 51 32	13 3 23	19 28 35	25 9.8	14 46.6	20 52.5	26 37.3	25 54.0	24 25.6	20 42.4	6 16.5	11 16.6
12 M	5 24 28	21 48 52	25 49 55	2♏ 7 39	25 5.7	15 35.4	22 6.3	27 17.7	26 7.5	24 32.8	20 41.5	6 15.5	11 15.0
13 Tu	5 28 25	22 46 11	8♏22 6	14 33 31	25 0.6	16 20.4	23 20.0	27 58.1	26 21.0	24 40.0	20 40.6	6 14.4	11 13.4
14 W	5 32 21	23 43 28	20 42 9	26 48 15	24 55.2	17 1.4	24 33.7	28 38.5	26 34.4	24 47.1	20 39.7	6 13.3	11 11.9
15 Th	5 36 18	24 40 46	2♐52 1	8♐53 43	24 50.1	17 38.3	25 47.4	29 18.8	26 47.8	24 54.2	20 38.8	6 12.2	11 10.3
16 F	5 40 14	25 38 2	14 53 32	20 51 43	24 45.8	18 11.2	27 1.1	29 59.1	27 1.1	25 1.2	20 37.7	6 11.1	11 8.7
17 Sa	5 44 11	26 35 18	26 48 29	2♑44 4	24 42.7	18 39.7	28 14.8	0♋39.4	27 14.4	25 8.2	20 36.7	6 10.0	11 7.2
18 Su	5 48 7	27 32 34	8♑38 45	14 32 47	24 40.9	19 3.9	29 28.5	1 19.6	27 27.7	25 15.2	20 35.6	6 8.8	11 5.6
19 M	5 52 4	28 29 49	20 26 30	26 20 13	24D40.5	19 23.7	0♋42.2	1 59.8	27 40.9	25 22.1	20 34.4	6 7.7	11 4.1
20 Tu	5 56 0	29 27 3	2♒14 17	8♒ 9 6	24 41.2	19 39.1	1 55.9	2 40.0	27 54.0	25 29.0	20 33.3	6 6.5	11 2.6
21 W	5 59 57	0♋24 18	14 5 6	20 2 43	24 42.5	19 49.8	3 9.6	3 20.1	28 7.1	25 35.8	20 32.0	6 5.2	11 1.1
22 Th	6 3 54	1 21 32	26 2 27	2♓ 4 47	24 44.2	19 56.0	4 23.3	4 0.2	28 20.1	25 42.6	20 30.8	6 4.0	10 59.6
23 F	6 7 50	2 18 46	8♓10 15	14 19 24	24 45.6	19R57.7	5 37.0	4 40.2	28 33.1	25 49.4	20 29.5	6 2.7	10 58.1
24 Sa	6 11 47	3 15 59	20 32 46	26 50 52	24 46.5	19 54.7	6 50.8	5 20.2	28 46.0	25 56.1	20 28.1	6 1.4	10 56.6
25 Su	6 15 43	4 13 13	3♈14 14	9♈43 19	24R46.5	19 47.3	8 4.5	6 0.2	28 58.9	26 2.8	20 26.7	6 0.1	10 55.1
26 M	6 19 40	5 10 27	16 18 34	23 0 17	24 45.7	19 35.6	9 18.2	6 40.1	29 11.7	26 9.4	20 25.3	5 58.8	10 53.7
27 Tu	6 23 36	6 7 40	29 48 45	6♉44 4	24 44.1	19 19.6	10 32.0	7 20.1	29 24.4	26 15.9	20 23.8	5 57.5	10 52.2
28 W	6 27 33	7 4 54	13♉46 12	20 54 59	24 42.0	18 59.6	11 45.7	7 59.9	29 37.1	26 22.5	20 22.3	5 56.1	10 50.8
29 Th	6 31 29	8 2 8	28 10 3	5♊30 52	24 39.9	18 36.0	12 59.5	8 39.8	29 49.7	26 28.9	20 20.8	5 54.7	10 49.4
30 F	6 35 26	8 59 22	12♊56 42	20 26 41	24 38.0	18 8.9	14 13.2	9 19.6	0♊ 2.3	26 35.3	20 19.2	5 53.3	10 48.0

*Giving the positions of planets daily at noon, in LONGITUDE Greenwich Mean Time

JULY 2000

Day	Sid.Time	☉	0 hr ☽	Noon ☽	True ☊	☿	♀	♂	♃	♄	♅	♆	♇
1 Sa	6 39 23	9♋56 36	27♊59 48	5♋34 54	24♋36.8	17♋38.8	15♋27.0	9♋59.4	0♊14.8	26♉41.7	20♒17.6	5♒51.9	10♐46.7
2 Su	6 43 19	10 53 50	13♋10 49	20 46 19	24D 36.3	17R 6.2	16 40.7	10 39.2	0 27.2	26 48.0	20R 16.0	5R 50.5	10R 45.3
3 M	6 47 16	11 51 3	28 20 13	5♌51 25	24 36.4	16 31.6	17 54.5	11 18.9	0 39.6	26 54.3	20 14.3	5 49.1	10 44.0
4 Tu	6 51 12	12 48 17	13♌18 54	20 41 50	24 37.1	15 55.4	19 8.3	11 58.6	0 51.9	27 0.5	20 12.6	5 47.6	10 42.7
5 W	6 55 9	13 45 30	27 59 28	5♍11 18	24 37.9	15 18.4	20 22.0	12 38.2	1 4.1	27 6.6	20 10.8	5 46.1	10 41.4
6 Th	6 59 5	14 42 43	12♍16 57	19 16 14	24 38.8	14 41.1	21 35.8	13 17.8	1 16.2	27 12.7	20 9.0	5 44.7	10 40.1
7 F	7 3 2	15 39 56	26 9 3	2♎55 29	24 39.3	14 4.2	22 49.6	13 57.4	1 28.3	27 18.7	20 7.2	5 43.2	10 38.8
8 Sa	7 6 59	16 37 8	9♎35 43	16 10 1	24R 39.5	13 28.3	24 3.3	14 37.0	1 40.3	27 24.7	20 5.4	5 41.6	10 37.6
9 Su	7 10 55	17 34 20	22 38 43	29 2 11	24 39.4	12 54.1	25 17.1	15 16.5	1 52.2	27 30.6	20 3.5	5 40.1	10 36.4
10 M	7 14 52	18 31 33	5♏20 52	11♏35 12	24 38.9	12 22.1	26 30.8	15 55.9	2 4.0	27 36.4	20 1.6	5 38.6	10 35.2
11 Tu	7 18 48	19 28 45	17 45 38	23 52 38	24 38.3	11 52.9	27 44.6	16 35.4	2 15.8	27 42.2	19 59.7	5 37.1	10 34.0
12 W	7 22 45	20 25 57	29 56 37	5♐58 1	24 37.8	11 27.1	28 58.4	17 14.8	2 27.4	27 47.9	19 57.7	5 35.5	10 32.9
13 Th	7 26 41	21 23 9	11♐57 16	17 54 46	24 37.3	11 5.1	0♌12.1	17 54.2	2 39.0	27 53.6	19 55.7	5 33.9	10 31.7
14 F	7 30 38	22 20 22	23 50 51	29 45 55	24 37.0	10 47.4	1 25.9	18 33.6	2 50.5	27 59.2	19 53.7	5 32.4	10 30.6
15 Sa	7 34 34	23 17 35	5♑40 16	11♑34 13	24 36.9	10 34.3	2 39.7	19 12.9	3 1.9	28 4.7	19 51.7	5 30.8	10 29.5
16 Su	7 38 31	24 14 48	17 28 6	23 22 11	24D 36.8	10 26.2	3 53.4	19 52.2	3 13.3	28 10.1	19 49.6	5 29.2	10 28.5
17 M	7 42 28	25 12 1	29 16 46	5♒12 8	24R 36.8	10D 23.2	5 7.2	20 31.4	3 24.5	28 15.5	19 47.5	5 27.6	10 27.5
18 Tu	7 46 24	26 9 15	11♒ 8 33	17 6 19	24 36.8	10 25.6	6 21.0	21 10.7	3 35.7	28 20.8	19 45.4	5 26.0	10 26.4
19 W	7 50 21	27 6 29	23 5 43	29 7 4	24 36.6	10 33.6	7 34.7	21 49.9	3 46.7	28 26.0	19 43.3	5 24.4	10 25.5
20 Th	7 54 17	28 3 44	5♓10 41	11♓16 54	24 36.2	10 47.2	8 48.5	22 29.1	3 57.7	28 31.2	19 41.1	5 22.8	10 24.5
21 F	7 58 14	29 0 59	17 26 2	23 38 28	24 35.7	11 6.5	10 2.3	23 8.2	4 8.6	28 36.3	19 38.9	5 21.2	10 23.6
22 Sa	8 2 10	29 58 16	29 54 33	6♈14 39	24 35.2	11 31.6	11 16.0	23 47.3	4 19.3	28 41.3	19 36.7	5 19.6	10 22.7
23 Su	8 6 7	0♌55 33	12♈39 9	19 8 23	24 34.8	12 2.5	12 29.8	24 26.4	4 30.0	28 46.3	19 34.5	5 18.0	10 21.8
24 M	8 10 3	1 52 51	25 42 41	2♉22 21	24D 34.7	12 39.1	13 43.6	25 5.5	4 40.6	28 51.1	19 32.3	5 16.3	10 20.9
25 Tu	8 14 0	2 50 10	9♉ 7 38	15 58 43	24 34.9	13 21.4	14 57.4	25 44.6	4 51.1	28 55.9	19 30.1	5 14.7	10 20.1
26 W	8 17 57	3 47 29	22 55 40	29 58 30	24 35.4	14 9.5	16 11.2	26 23.6	5 1.5	29 0.6	19 27.8	5 13.1	10 19.3
27 Th	8 21 53	4 44 50	7♊ 7 4	14♊21 6	24 36.2	15 3.2	17 25.0	27 2.6	5 11.8	29 5.3	19 25.5	5 11.5	10 18.5
28 F	8 25 50	5 42 12	21 40 12	29 3 47	24 37.0	16 2.4	18 38.8	27 41.6	5 21.9	29 9.8	19 23.2	5 9.8	10 17.8
29 Sa	8 29 46	6 39 35	6♋31 9	14♋ 1 26	24 37.6	17 7.0	19 52.6	28 20.5	5 32.0	29 14.3	19 20.9	5 8.2	10 17.1
30 Su	8 33 43	7 36 59	21 33 40	29 6 48	24R 37.7	18 17.0	21 6.4	28 59.5	5 42.0	29 18.7	19 18.6	5 6.6	10 16.4
31 M	8 37 39	8 34 24	6♌39 41	14♌11 12	24 37.2	19 32.2	22 20.2	29 38.4	5 51.8	29 23.0	19 16.3	5 5.0	10 15.7

LONGITUDE

AUGUST 2000

Day	Sid.Time	☉	0 hr ☽	Noon ☽	True ☊	☿	♀	♂	♃	♄	♅	♆	♇
1 Tu	8 41 36	9♌31 49	21♌40 15	29♌ 5 47	24♋35.9	20♋52.4	23♌34.0	0♌17.2	6♊ 1.5	29♉27.3	19♒13.9	5♒ 3.3	10♐15.1
2 W	8 45 32	10 29 15	6♍26 53	13♍42 44	24R 34.1	22 17.5	24 47.8	0 56.1	6 11.1	29 31.4	19R 11.6	5R 1.7	10R 14.5
3 Th	8 49 29	11 26 42	20 52 43	27 56 21	24 32.0	23 47.2	26 1.6	1 34.9	6 20.6	29 35.4	19 9.2	5 0.1	10 13.9
4 F	8 53 26	12 24 10	4♎53 19	11♎43 31	24 30.0	25 21.4	27 15.3	2 13.7	6 30.0	29 39.4	19 6.8	4 58.5	10 13.4
5 Sa	8 57 22	13 21 38	18 26 56	25 3 44	24 28.4	26 59.8	28 29.1	2 52.4	6 39.3	29 43.3	19 4.4	4 56.9	10 12.9
6 Su	9 1 19	14 19 7	1♏34 11	7♏58 40	24 27.5	28 42.1	29 42.9	3 31.2	6 48.4	29 47.1	19 2.1	4 55.3	10 12.4
7 M	9 5 15	15 16 37	14 17 36	20 31 31	24D 27.4	0♌28.0	0♍56.7	4 9.9	6 57.4	29 50.8	18 59.7	4 53.7	10 12.0
8 Tu	9 9 12	16 14 7	26 40 56	2♐46 26	24 28.2	2 17.2	2 10.5	4 48.6	7 6.3	29 54.4	18 57.3	4 52.1	10 11.6
9 W	9 13 8	17 11 38	8♐48 34	14 47 57	24 29.6	4 9.3	3 24.2	5 27.2	7 15.1	29 57.9	18 54.9	4 50.5	10 11.2
10 Th	9 17 5	18 9 11	20 45 8	26 40 39	24 31.3	6 3.8	4 38.0	6 5.9	7 23.7	0♊ 1.4	18 52.5	4 48.9	10 10.8
11 F	9 21 1	19 6 44	2♑35 4	8♑28 51	24 32.8	8 0.6	5 51.7	6 44.5	7 32.2	0 4.7	18 50.1	4 47.3	10 10.5
12 Sa	9 24 58	20 4 18	14 22 30	20 16 25	24R 33.6	9 59.0	7 5.5	7 23.1	7 40.6	0 7.9	18 47.7	4 45.8	10 10.2
13 Su	9 28 55	21 1 53	26 11 1	2♒ 6 41	24 33.5	11 58.9	8 19.2	8 1.6	7 48.8	0 11.1	18 45.3	4 44.2	10 10.0
14 M	9 32 51	21 59 30	8♒ 3 43	14 2 25	24 32.0	13 59.8	9 33.0	8 40.2	7 56.9	0 14.2	18 42.9	4 42.7	10 9.7
15 Tu	9 36 48	22 57 7	20 3 4	26 5 52	24 29.2	16 1.4	10 46.7	9 18.7	8 4.9	0 17.1	18 40.6	4 41.2	10 9.6
16 W	9 40 44	23 54 46	2♓11 1	8♓18 44	24 25.2	18 3.3	12 0.4	9 57.2	8 12.7	0 20.0	18 38.2	4 39.6	10 9.4
17 Th	9 44 41	24 52 26	14 29 9	20 42 26	24 20.4	20 5.3	13 14.2	10 35.7	8 20.4	0 22.8	18 35.8	4 38.1	10 9.3
18 F	9 48 37	25 50 7	26 58 41	3♈18 5	24 15.2	22 7.2	14 27.9	11 14.1	8 27.9	0 25.4	18 33.4	4 36.6	10 9.2
19 Sa	9 52 34	26 47 50	9♈40 44	16 6 46	24 10.3	24 8.6	15 41.6	11 52.5	8 35.3	0 28.0	18 31.1	4 35.1	10 9.1
20 Su	9 56 30	27 45 35	22 36 19	29 9 32	24 6.3	26 9.5	16 55.3	12 30.9	8 42.6	0 30.5	18 28.7	4 33.7	10D 9.1
21 M	10 0 27	28 43 21	5♉46 34	12♉27 31	24 3.6	28 9.6	18 9.0	13 9.3	8 49.7	0 32.8	18 26.4	4 32.2	10 9.1
22 Tu	10 4 23	29 41 9	19 12 33	26 1 45	24D 2.5	0♍ 8.9	19 22.7	13 47.7	8 56.7	0 35.1	18 24.0	4 30.8	10 9.1
23 W	10 8 20	0♍38 58	2♊55 14	9♊53 0	24 2.8	2 7.2	20 36.4	14 26.1	9 3.5	0 37.3	18 21.7	4 29.3	10 9.2
24 Th	10 12 17	1 36 50	16 55 4	24 1 20	24 3.9	4 4.4	21 50.1	15 4.4	9 10.2	0 39.4	18 19.4	4 27.9	10 9.3
25 F	10 16 13	2 34 43	1♋11 37	8♋25 41	24 5.2	6 0.5	23 3.8	15 42.7	9 16.7	0 41.3	18 17.1	4 26.5	10 9.4
26 Sa	10 20 10	3 32 38	15 43 6	23 3 24	24R 5.9	7 55.4	24 17.4	16 21.0	9 23.0	0 43.2	18 14.8	4 25.2	10 9.6
27 Su	10 24 6	4 30 35	0♌25 56	7♌49 58	24 5.2	9 49.1	25 31.1	16 59.3	9 29.2	0 45.0	18 12.5	4 23.8	10 9.8
28 M	10 28 3	5 28 34	15 14 40	22 39 8	24 2.7	11 41.6	26 44.8	17 37.6	9 35.2	0 46.6	18 10.3	4 22.5	10 10.0
29 Tu	10 31 59	6 26 34	0♍ 2 22	7♍23 25	23 58.2	13 32.7	27 58.4	18 15.8	9 41.1	0 48.2	18 8.0	4 21.1	10 10.3
30 W	10 35 56	7 24 35	14 41 21	21 55 16	23 52.0	15 22.7	29 12.1	18 54.0	9 46.8	0 49.6	18 5.8	4 19.8	10 10.6
31 Th	10 39 52	8 22 39	29 4 23	6♎ 8 4	23 45.0	17 11.3	0♎25.8	19 32.2	9 52.3	0 51.0	18 3.6	4 18.5	10 10.9

*Giving the positions of planets daily at noon, in LONGITUDE Greenwich Mean Time

Day	Sid.Time	☉	0 hr ☽	Noon ☽	True ☊	☿	♀	♂	♃	♄	♅	♆	♇
1 F	10 43 49	9♏20 43	13≏ 5 48	19≏57 13	23≏37.9	18♏58.7	1≏39.4	20♌10.4	9♏57.7	0♉52.2	18♒ 1.4	4♒17.3	10♐11.3
2 Sa	10 47 46	10 18 49	26 42 10	3♏20 35	23R31.7	20 44.8	2 53.0	20 48.5	10 2.9	0 53.3	17R59.2	4R16.0	10 11.7
3 Su	10 51 42	11 16 57	9♏52 36	16 18 27	23 26.9	22 29.7	4 6.6	21 26.7	10 7.9	0 54.4	17 57.1	4 14.8	10 12.1
4 M	10 55 39	12 15 6	22 38 31	28 53 13	23 24.0	24 13.3	5 20.2	22 4.8	10 12.8	0 55.3	17 55.0	4 13.6	10 12.6
5 Tu	10 59 35	13 13 16	5♐ 3 7	11♐ 8 45	23D23.0	25 55.8	6 33.8	22 42.9	10 17.5	0 56.1	17 52.9	4 12.4	10 13.1
6 W	11 3 32	14 11 28	17 10 47	23 9 51	23 23.3	27 7.4	7 47.4	23 20.9	10 22.0	0 56.8	17 50.8	4 11.3	10 13.6
7 Th	11 7 28	15 9 42	29 6 36	5♑ 1 43	23 24.5	29 17.0	9 1.0	23 59.0	10 26.3	0 57.4	17 48.8	4 10.1	10 14.2
8 F	11 11 25	16 7 57	10♑55 49	16 49 33	23 25.5	0≏55.9	10 14.5	24 37.0	10 30.5	0 57.9	17 46.7	4 9.0	10 14.8
9 Sa	11 15 21	17 6 13	22 43 31	28 37 17	23R25.5	2 33.7	11 28.1	25 15.0	10 34.4	0 58.2	17 44.7	4 7.9	10 15.4
10 Su	11 19 18	18 4 32	4♒34 22	10♒32 16	23 23.9	4 10.3	12 41.6	25 53.0	10 38.2	0 58.5	17 42.8	4 6.9	10 16.1
11 M	11 23 15	19 2 51	16 32 24	22 35 9	23 20.0	5 45.7	13 55.1	26 31.0	10 41.8	0 58.7	17 40.8	4 5.8	10 16.8
12 Tu	11 27 11	20 1 13	28 40 48	4♓49 38	23 13.7	-7 20.1	15 8.6	27 9.0	10 45.2	0R58.7	17 38.9	4 4.8	10 17.5
13 W	11 31 8	20 59 36	11♓ 1 48	17 17 26	23 5.3	8 53.3	16 22.1	27 46.8	10 48.5	0 58.7	17 37.0	4 3.8	10 18.3
14 Th	11 35 4	21 58 1	23 36 37	29 59 19	22 55.3	10 25.4	17 35.5	28 24.8	10 51.5	0 58.5	17 35.2	4 2.8	10 19.1
15 F	11 39 1	22 56 28	6♈25 31	12♈55 7	22 44.8	11 56.5	18 49.0	29 2.7	10 54.4	0 58.2	17 33.4	4 1.9	10 19.9
16 Sa	11 42 57	23 54 57	19 28 1	26 4 5	22 34.6	13 26.4	20 2.4	29 40.5	10 57.1	0 57.8	17 31.6	4 1.0	10 20.7
17 Su	11 46 54	24 53 28	2♉43 9	9♉25 5	22 25.9	14 55.3	21 15.8	0♍18.4	10 59.6	0 57.4	17 29.8	4 0.1	10 21.6
18 M	11 50 50	25 52 1	16 9 44	22 57 1	22 19.3	16 23.2	22 29.2	0 56.2	11 1.8	0 56.8	17 28.1	3 59.2	10 22.5
19 Tu	11 54 47	26 50 36	29 46 49	6♊39 3	22 15.3	17 49.7	23 42.6	1 34.1	11 3.9	0 56.1	17 26.4	3 58.4	10 23.5
20 W	11 58 44	27 49 14	13♊33 41	20 30 40	22 13.6	19 15.2	24 56.0	2 11.9	11 5.9	0 55.3	17 24.8	3 57.6	10 24.5
21 Th	12 2 40	28 47 54	27 29 58	4♋31 32	22D13.5	20 39.6	26 9.4	2 49.7	11 7.6	0 54.3	17 23.2	3 56.8	10 25.5
22 F	12 6 37	29 46 36	11♋35 19	18 41 12	22R13.9	22 2.8	27 22.8	3 27.5	11 9.1	0 53.3	17 21.6	3 56.1	10 26.5
23 Sa	12 10 33	0≏45 20	25 49 1	2♌58 34	22 13.5	23 24.8	28 36.1	4 5.3	11 10.4	0 52.2	17 20.1	3 55.4	10 27.6
24 Su	12 14 30	1 44 7	10♌ 9 30	17 21 28	22 11.3	24 45.6	29 49.5	4 43.0	11 11.5	0 51.0	17 18.6	3 54.7	10 28.7
25 M	12 18 26	2 42 56	24 33 56	1♍46 21	22 6.5	26 5.1	1♏ 2.9	5 20.8	11 12.4	0 49.6	17 17.1	3 54.0	10 29.9
26 Tu	12 22 23	3 41 47	8♍58 5	16 8 24	21 58.9	27 23.3	2 16.1	5 58.5	11 13.2	0 48.2	17 15.7	3 53.4	10 31.0
27 W	12 26 19	4 40 40	23 16 35	0≏21 56	21 48.8	28 40.1	3 29.4	6 36.2	11 13.7	0 46.6	17 14.3	3 52.8	10 32.2
28 Th	12 30 16	5 39 35	7≏23 42	14 21 18	21 37.3	29 55.4	4 42.7	7 13.9	11 14.0	0 44.9	17 12.9	3 52.2	10 33.4
29 F	12 34 13	6 38 32	21 14 9	28 1 49	21 25.5	1♍ 9.2	5 56.0	7 51.5	11R14.1	0 43.2	17 11.6	3 51.7	10 34.7
30 Sa	12 38 9	7 37 31	4♏44 0	11♏20 31	21 14.5	2 21.4	7 9.2	8 29.2	11 14.0	0 41.3	17 10.4	3 51.2	10 36.0

Longitude October 2000

Day	Sid.Time	☉	0 hr ☽	Noon ☽	True ☊	☿	♀	♂	♃	♄	♅	♆	♇
1 Su	12 42 6	8≏36 31	17♏51 19	24♏16 29	21≏ 5.5	3♍31.9	8♏22.5	9♍ 6.8	11♏13.7	0♉39.3	17♒ 9.1	3♒50.7	10♐37.3
2 M	12 46 2	9 35 34	0♐36 14	6♐50 52	20R59.0	4 40.5	9 35.7	9 44.4	11R13.2	0R37.3	17R 8.0	3R50.3	10 38.6
3 Tu	12 49 59	10 34 39	13 0 50	19 6 37	20 55.1	5 47.?							
4 W	12 53 55	11 33 45	25 8 46	1♑ 7 55	20 53.3	6 51.?							
5 Th	12 57 52	12 32 53	7♑ 4 43	12 59 51	20D53.0	7 54.0	13 15.3	11 37.1	11 10.5	0 30.5	17 4.7	3 49.1	10 44.3
6 F	13 1 48	13 32 3	18 54 0	24 47 10	20R53.0	8 53.7	14 28.4	12 14.6	11 9.2	0 28.0	17 3.7	3 48.8	10 44.8
7 Sa	13 5 45	14 31 15	0♒42 12	6♒37 35	20 52.2	9 50.8	15 41.5	12 52.2	11 7.7	0 25.5	17 2.8	3 48.5	10 45.7
8 Su	13 9 41	15 30 28	12 34 42	18 34 9	20 49.7	10 44.9	16 54.6	13 29.7	11 6.0	0 22.8	17 1.9	3 48.3	10 47.2
9 M	13 13 38	16 29 43	24 36 30	0♓42 14	20 44.7	11 35.8	18 7.7	14 7.1	11 4.1	0 20.1	17 1.0	3 48.0	10 48.8
10 Tu	13 17 35	17 29 0	6♓51 48	13 5 31	20 36.9	12 23.2	19 20.8	14 44.6	11 2.0	0 17.3	17 0.2	3 47.9	10 50.3
11 W	13 21 31	18 28 19	19 23,40	25 46 20	20 26.6	13 6.7	20 33.8	15 22.0	10 59.7	0 14.3	16 59.4	3 47.7	10 51.9
12 Th	13 25 28	19 27 40	2♈13 50	8♈45 54	20 14.3	13 46.0	21 46.8	15 59.4	10 57.2	0 11.3	16 58.7	3 47.6	10 53.5
13 F	13 29 24	20 27 3	15 22 27	22 3 18	20 1.3	14 20.6	22 59.8	16 36.9	10 54.5	0 8.2	16 58.0	3 47.5	10 55.1
14 Sa	13 33 21	21 26 28	28 48 9	5♉36 36	19 48.7	14 50.2	24 12.8	17 14.2	10 51.6	0 5.0	16 57.4	3 47.4	10 56.8
15 Su	13 37 17	22 25 55	12♉28 15	19 22 40	19 37.8	15 14.3	25 25.7	17 51.6	10 48.5	0 1.8	16 56.8	3D47.4	10 58.5
16 M	13 41 14	23 25 24	26 19 22	3♊11 57	19 29.3	15 32.2	26 38.6	18 29.0	10 45.2	29♈58.4	16 56.3	3 47.4	11 0.2
17 Tu	13 45 10	24 24 56	10♊17 58	17 19 5	19 23.9	15 43.6	27 51.5	19 6.3	10 41.8	29 55.0	16 55.8	3 47.5	11 1.9
18 W	13 49 7	25 24 30	24 20 58	1♋23 22	19 21.2	15R47.9	29 4.4	19 43.6	10 38.1	29 51.5	16 55.4	3 47.6	11 3.6
19 Th	13 53 4	26 24 6	8♋26 16	15 28 55	19D20.4	15 44.6	0♐17.2	20 21.0	10 34.3	29 47.9	16 55.0	3 47.7	11 5.4
20 F	13 57 0	27 23 44	22 31 49	29 34 39	19R20.4	15 33.1	1 30.1	20 58.3	10 30.2	29 44.2	16 54.7	3 47.8	11 7.2
21 Sa	14 0 57	28 23 25	6♌37 20	13♌39 47	19 19.8	15 13.0	2 42.9	21 35.5	10 26.0	29 40.5	16 54.4	3 48.0	11 9.0
22 Su	14 4 53	29 23 8	20 41 52	27 43 12	19 17.3	14 44.2	3 55.7	22 12.8	10 21.6	29 36.7	16 54.1	3 48.2	11 10.9
23 M	14 8 50	0♏22 53	4♍44 18	11♍44 12	19 12.2	14 6.4	5 8.4	22 50.0	10 17.1	29 32.8	16 53.9	3 48.5	11 12.7
24 Tu	14 12 46	1 22 41	18 42 51	25 39 52	19 4.3	13 19.8	6 21.2	23 27.3	10 12.3	29 28.8	16 53.8	3 48.8	11 14.6
25 W	14 16 43	2 22 30	2≏34 52	9≏27 27	18 53.7	12 24.7	7 33.9	24 4.5	10 7.4	29 24.8	16 53.7	3 49.2	11 16.5
26 Th	14 20 39	3 22 22	16 17 10	23 3 37	18 41.6	11 22.4	8 46.6	24 41.6	10 2.3	29 20.7	16D53.7	3 49.6	11 18.4
27 F	14 24 36	4 22 16	29 47 13	6♏25 50	18 29.0	10 13.4	9 59.2	25 18.8	9 57.0	29 16.6	16 53.7	3 49.8	11 20.4
28 Sa	14 28 33	5 22 11	12♏59 45	19 29 50	18 17.2	8 59.7	11 11.9	25 56.0	9 51.5	29 12.4	16 53.8	3 50.2	11 22.3
29 Su	14 32 29	6 22 9	25 55 22	2♐16 20	18 7.3	7 43.2	12 24.5	26 33.1	9 46.0	29 8.1	16 53.9	3 50.7	11 24.3
30 M	14 36 26	7 22 8	8♐32 49	14 45 1	17 60.0	6 26.0	13 37.1	27 10.2	9 40.2	29 3.8	16 54.1	3 51.2	11 26.3
31 Tu	14 40 22	8 22 9	20 53 11	26 57 42	17 55.4	5 10.6	14 49.6	27 47.3	9 34.3	28 59.4	16 54.3	3 51.7	11 28.3

*Giving the positions of planets daily at noon,
in LONGITUDE Greenwich Mean Time

NOON EPHEMERIS: GMT* — NOVEMBER 2000

Day	Sid.Time	☉	0 hr ☽	Noon ☽	True ☊	☿	♀	♂	♃	♄	♅	♆	♇
1 W	14 44 19	9♏22 12	2♑59 0	8♑57 34	17♋53.2	3♏59.4	16♐ 2.2	28♍24.3	9♊28.2	28♉55.0	16♒54.6	3♒52.3	11♐30.4
2 Th	14 48 15	10 22 16	14 53 57	20 48 46	17D 52.9	2R 54.6	17 14.6	29 1.4	9R 22.0	28R 50.5	16 54.9	3 52.8	11 32.4
3 F	14 52 12	11 22 23	26 42 40	2♒36 18	17 53.4	1 58.0	18 27.1	29 38.4	9 15.7	28 46.0	16 55.3	3 53.5	11 34.5
4 Sa	14 56 8	12 22 30	8♒30 22	14 25 32	17R 53.6	1 11.3	19 39.5	0♎15.4	9 9.2	28 41.4	16 55.7	3 54.1	11 36.5
5 Su	15 0 5	13 22 39	20 22 32	26 22 1	17 52.6	0 35.5	20 51.9	0 52.3	9 2.6	28 36.8	16 56.2	3 54.8	11 38.6
6 M	15 4 2	14 22 50	2♓24 38	8♓31 1	17 49.6	0 11.2	22 4.2	1 29.3	8 55.8	28 32.2	16 56.7	3 55.5	11 40.7
7 Tu	15 7 58	15 23 2	14 41 43	20 57 13	17 44.3	29♎58.5	23 16.5	2 6.2	8 49.0	28 27.5	16 57.3	3 56.3	11 42.9
8 W	15 11 55	16 23 16	27 17 57	3♈44 14	17 36.6	29D 57.3	24 28.7	2 43.1	8 42.0	28 22.8	16 58.0	3 57.1	11 45.0
9 Th	15 15 51	17 23 31	10♈16 16	16 54 7	17 27.2	0♏ 7.1	25 40.9	3 20.0	8 34.9	28 18.0	16 58.6	3 57.9	11 47.2
10 F	15 19 48	18 23 48	23 37 45	0♉26 59	17 16.9	0 27.3	26 53.1	3 56.9	8 27.7	28 13.3	16 59.4	3 58.7	11 49.3
11 Sa	15 23 44	19 24 6	7♉21 29	14 20 48	17 6.9	0 57.0	28 5.2	4 33.7	8 20.4	28 8.5	17 0.2	3 59.6	11 51.5
12 Su	15 27 41	20 24 26	21 24 24	28 31 36	16 58.1	1 35.4	29 17.2	5 10.5	8 13.0	28 3.7	17 1.0	4 0.5	11 53.7
13 M	15 31 37	21 24 48	5♊41 42	12♊53 57	16 51.6	2 21.5	0♑29.2	5 47.3	8 5.5	27 58.8	17 1.9	4 1.5	11 55.9
14 Tu	15 35 34	22 25 12	20 7 36	27 21 55	16 47.5	3 14.5	1 41.2	6 24.1	7 57.9	27 54.0	17 2.8	4 2.5	11 58.1
15 W	15 39 31	23 25 38	4♋36 13	11♋49 54	16D 45.9	4 13.6	2 53.1	7 0.8	7 50.2	27 49.1	17 3.8	4 3.5	12 0.3
16 Th	15 43 27	24 26 5	19 2 27	26 13 25	16 46.1	5 17.9	4 4.9	7 37.6	7 42.5	27 44.2	17 4.8	4 4.5	12 2.6
17 F	15 47 24	25 26 35	3♌22 28	10♌29 19	16 47.1	6 26.8	5 16.8	8 14.3	7 34.7	27 39.4	17 5.9	4 5.6	12 4.8
18 Sa	15 51 20	26 27 6	17 33 47	24 35 45	16R 47.8	7 39.6	6 28.5	8 51.0	7 26.8	27 34.5	17 7.1	4 6.7	12 7.1
19 Su	15 55 17	27 27 39	1♍35 8	8♍31 51	16 47.2	8 55.8	7 40.2	9 27.6	7 18.9	27 29.6	17 8.3	4 7.8	12 9.3
20 M	15 59 13	28 28 13	15 25 53	22 17 12	16 44.7	10 14.9	8 51.9	10 4.3	7 10.9	27 24.7	17 9.5	4 9.0	12 11.6
21 Tu	16 3 10	29 28 50	29 5 46	5♎51 32	16 40.0	11 36.4	10 3.4	10 40.9	7 2.8	27 19.8	17 10.8	4 10.2	12 13.9
22 W	16 7 6	0♐29 28	12♎34 26	19 14 24	16 33.3	12 59.9	11 15.0	11 17.5	6 54.7	27 14.9	17 12.1	4 11.4	12 16.1
23 Th	16 11 3	1 30 7	25 51 21	2♏25 10	16 25.4	14 25.2	12 26.4	11 54.1	6 46.6	27 10.0	17 13.5	4 12.6	12 18.4
24 F	16 15 0	2 30 49	8♏55 47	15 23 6	16 17.1	15 51.9	13 37.8	12 30.6	6 38.5	27 5.1	17 14.9	4 13.9	12 20.7
25 Sa	16 18 56	3 31 32	21 47 3	28 7 36	16 9.3	17 19.8	14 49.2	13 7.1	6 30.3	27 0.3	17 16.4	4 15.2	12 23.0
26 Su	16 22 53	4 32 16	4♐24 44	10♐38 28	16 2.8	18 48.7	16 0.5	13 43.6	6 22.1	26 55.4	17 17.9	4 16.6	12 25.3
27 M	16 26 49	5 33 1	16 48 55	22 56 11	15 58.2	20 18.4	17 11.7	14 20.0	6 13.9	26 50.6	17 19.5	4 17.9	12 27.6
28 Tu	16 30 46	6 33 48	29 0 28	5♑ 2 0	15 55.6	21 48.8	18 22.8	14 56.5	6 5.7	26 45.8	17 21.1	4 19.3	12 30.0
29 W	16 34 42	7 34 36	11♑ 1 6	16 58 7	15D 54.9	23 19.8	19 33.9	15 32.8	5 57.5	26 41.1	17 22.7	4 20.8	12 32.3
30 Th	16 38 39	8 35 25	22 53 27	28 47 34	15 55.7	24 51.2	20 44.8	16 9.2	5 49.3	26 36.3	17 24.5	4 22.2	12 34.6

LONGITUDE — DECEMBER 2000

Day	Sid.Time	☉	0 hr ☽	Noon ☽	True ☊	☿	♀	♂	♃	♄	♅	♆	♇
1 F	16 42 35	9♐36 15	4♒40 58	10♒34 12	15♋57.3	26♏23.0	21♑55.7	16♎45.5	5♊41.2	26♉31.6	17♒26.2	4♒23.7	12♐36.9
2 Sa	16 46 32	10 37 6	16 27 50	22 22 29	15 59.2	27 55.1	23 6.5	17 21.8	5R 33.1	26R 26.9	17 28.0	4 25.2	12 39.2
3 Su	16 50 29	11 37 58	28 18 47	4♓17 23	16 0.4	29 27.4	24 17.2	17 58.1	5 24.9	26 22.3	17 29.9	4 26.7	12 41.6
4 M	16 54 25	12 38 50	10♓18 55	16 24 2	16R 0.6	0♐60.0	25 27.9	18 34.3	5 16.9	26 17.7	17 31.7	4 28.3	12 43.9
5 Tu	16 58 22	13 39 43	22 33 21	28 47 28	15 59.4	2 32.7	26 38.4	19 10.5	5 8.9	26 13.1	17 33.7	4 29.9	12 46.2
6 W	17 2 18	14 40 37	5♈ 6 55	11♈32 11	15 56.8	4 5.5	27 48.8	19 46.7	5 0.9	26 8.6	17 35.6	4 31.5	12 48.5
7 Th	17 6 15	15 41 32	18 3 39	24 41 35	15 52.9	5 38.4	28 59.1	20 22.8	4 53.0	26 4.1	17 37.7	4 33.1	12 50.9
8 F	17 10 11	16 42 28	1♉26 11	8♉17 26	15 48.4	7 11.5	0♒ 9.3	20 58.9	4 45.1	25 59.7	17 39.7	4 34.8	12 53.2
9 Sa	17 14 8	17 43 24	15 15 14	22 19 16	15 43.9	8 44.6	1 19.4	21 34.9	4 37.3	25 55.4	17 41.8	4 36.4	12 55.5
10 Su	17 18 4	18 44 21	29 29 6	6♊44 6	15 39.9	10 17.8	2 29.3	22 11.0	4 29.6	25 51.0	17 44.0	4 38.1	12 57.8
11 M	17 22 1	19 45 19	14♊ 3 32	21 26 30	15 37.1	11 51.1	3 39.2	22 47.0	4 22.0	25 46.8	17 46.1	4 39.9	13 0.1
12 Tu	17 25 58	20 46 18	28 52 4	6♋19 12	15 35.6	13 24.4	4 48.9	23 22.9	4 14.4	25 42.6	17 48.4	4 41.6	13 2.4
13 W	17 29 54	21 47 18	13♋46 53	21 14 7	15D 35.4	14 57.9	5 58.5	23 58.9	4 7.0	25 38.5	17 50.6	4 43.4	13 4.7
14 Th	17 33 51	22 48 19	28 39 57	6♌ 3 34	15 36.3	16 31.4	7 8.0	24 34.8	3 59.6	25 34.4	17 52.9	4 45.2	13 7.1
15 F	17 37 47	23 49 21	13♌24 11	20 41 12	15 37.7	18 5.1	8 17.3	25 10.6	3 52.3	25 30.4	17 55.3	4 47.0	13 9.3
16 Sa	17 41 44	24 50 23	27 54 9	5♍ 2 38	15 39.1	19 38.8	9 26.5	25 46.4	3 45.2	25 26.4	17 57.7	4 48.8	13 11.6
17 Su	17 45 40	25 51 27	12♍ 6 27	19 5 26	15 39.9	21 12.7	10 35.5	26 22.2	3 38.1	25 22.5	18 0.1	4 50.7	13 13.9
18 M	17 49 37	26 52 31	25 59 34	2♎48 52	15R 40.0	22 46.7	11 44.4	26 58.0	3 31.2	25 18.7	18 2.5	4 52.6	13 16.2
19 Tu	17 53 33	27 53 36	9♎33 28	16 13 31	15 39.1	24 20.9	12 53.2	27 33.7	3 24.4	25 15.0	18 5.0	4 54.5	13 18.5
20 W	17 57 30	28 54 42	22 49 10	29 20 39	15 37.4	25 55.2	14 1.8	28 9.3	3 17.7	25 11.4	18 7.5	4 56.4	13 20.7
21 Th	18 1 27	29 55 49	5♏48 11	12♏11 58	15 35.2	27 29.7	15 10.3	28 45.0	3 11.1	25 7.8	18 10.1	4 58.3	13 23.0
22 F	18 5 23	0♑56 57	18 32 14	24 49 12	15 32.8	29 4.4	16 18.5	29 20.6	3 4.7	25 4.3	18 12.7	5 0.3	13 25.2
23 Sa	18 9 20	1 58 5	1♐ 3 4	7♐14 2	15 30.7	0♑39.3	17 26.7	29 56.1	2 58.5	25 0.9	18 15.3	5 2.2	13 27.5
24 Su	18 13 16	2 59 14	13 22 17	19 28 2	15 29.0	2 14.4	18 34.6	0♏31.6	2 52.3	24 57.6	18 18.0	5 4.2	13 29.7
25 M	18 17 13	4 0 23	25 31 28	1♑32 47	15 27.9	3 49.8	19 42.4	1 7.0	2 46.3	24 54.3	18 20.7	5 6.2	13 31.9
26 Tu	18 21 9	5 1 33	7♑32 12	13 29 56	15D 27.5	5 25.4	20 50.0	1 42.4	2 40.5	24 51.2	18 23.4	5 8.2	13 34.1
27 W	18 25 6	6 2 43	19 26 12	25 21 18	15 27.7	7 1.3	21 57.3	2 17.8	2 34.9	24 48.1	18 26.2	5 10.3	13 36.3
28 Th	18 29 3	7 3 53	1♒15 31	7♒ 9 9	15 28.3	8 37.4	23 4.5	2 53.1	2 29.4	24 45.1	18 29.0	5 12.3	13 38.5
29 F	18 32 59	8 5 3	13 2 34	18 56 8	15 29.1	10 13.8	24 11.5	3 28.3	2 24.0	24 42.3	18 31.8	5 14.4	13 40.7
30 Sa	18 36 56	9 6 13	24 50 16	0♓45 24	15 29.9	11 50.6	25 18.3	4 3.5	2 18.8	24 39.5	18 34.7	5 16.5	13 42.8
31 Su	18 40 52	10 7 23	6♓42 2	12 40 40	15 30.6	13 27.6	26 24.8	4 38.7	2 13.8	24 36.8	18 37.6	5 18.6	13 45.0

*Giving the positions of planets daily at noon, in LONGITUDE Greenwich Mean Time

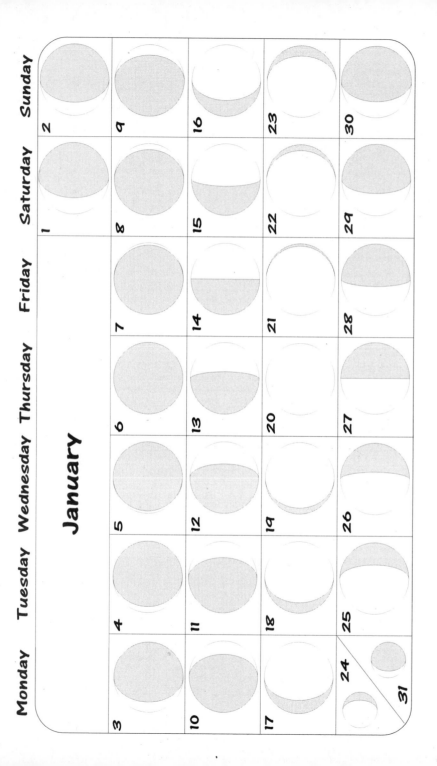

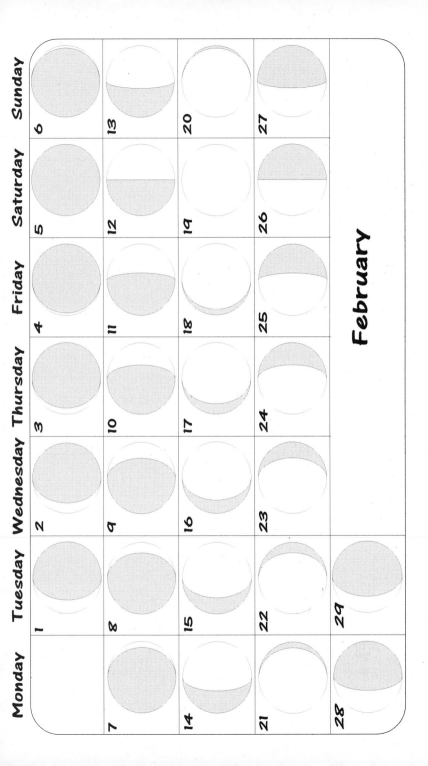

February

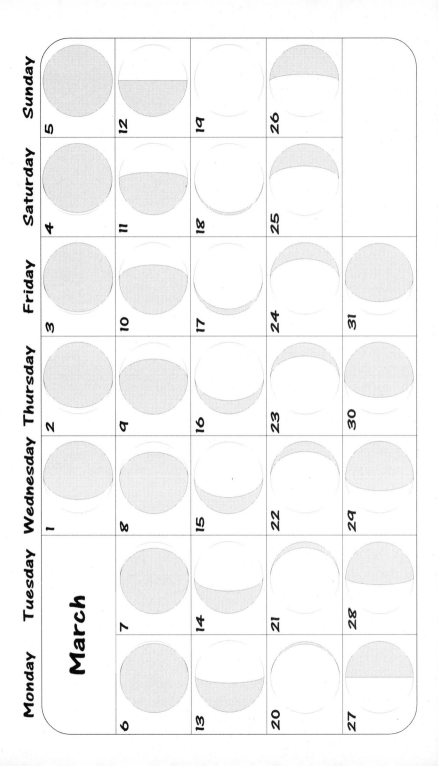

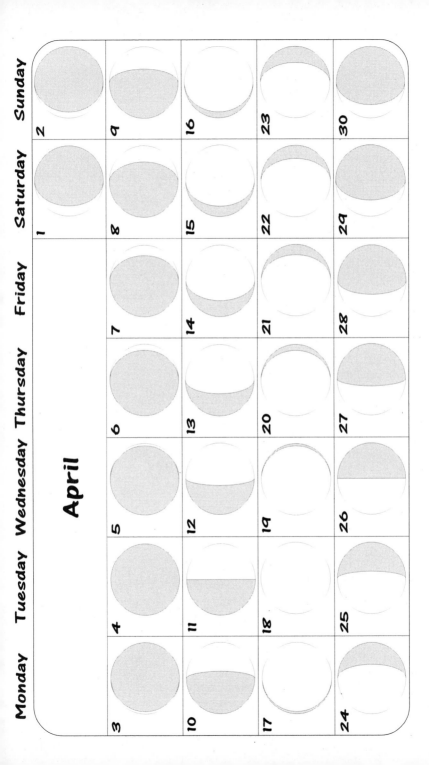

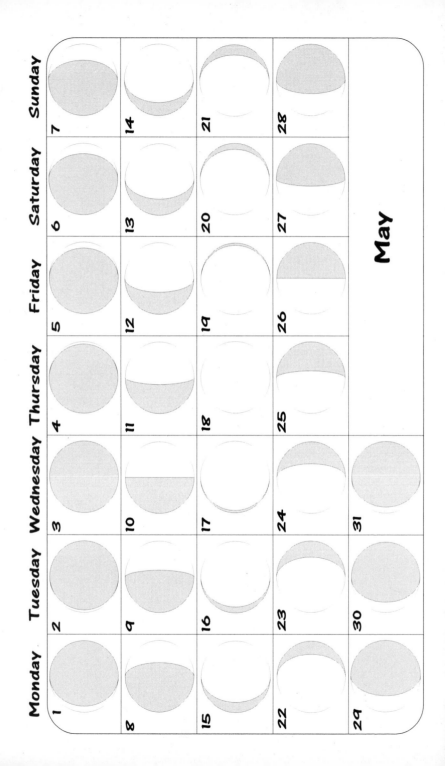

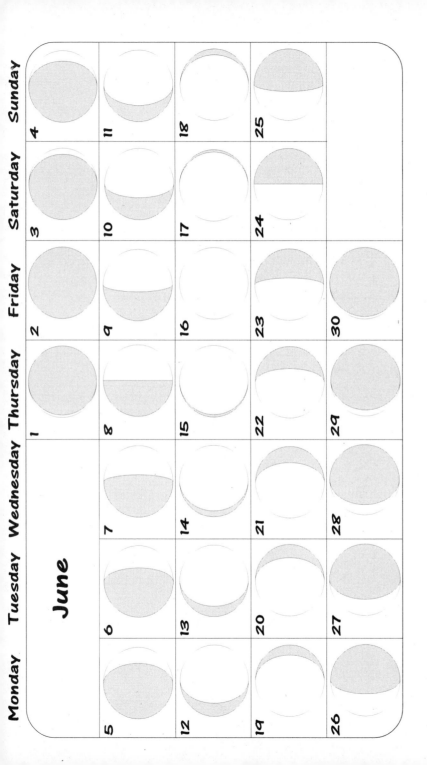

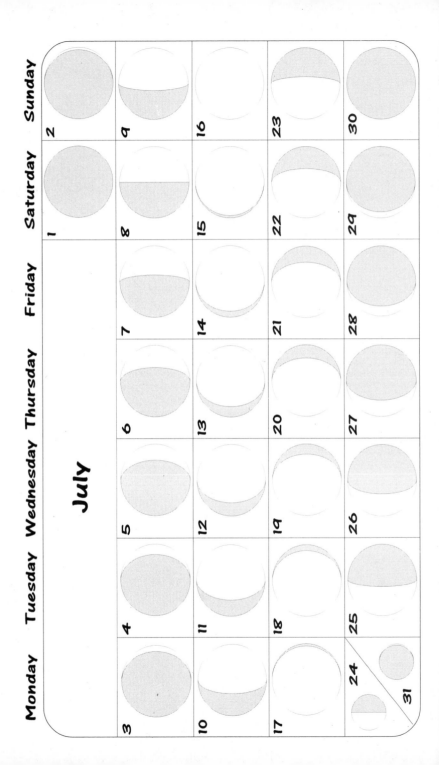

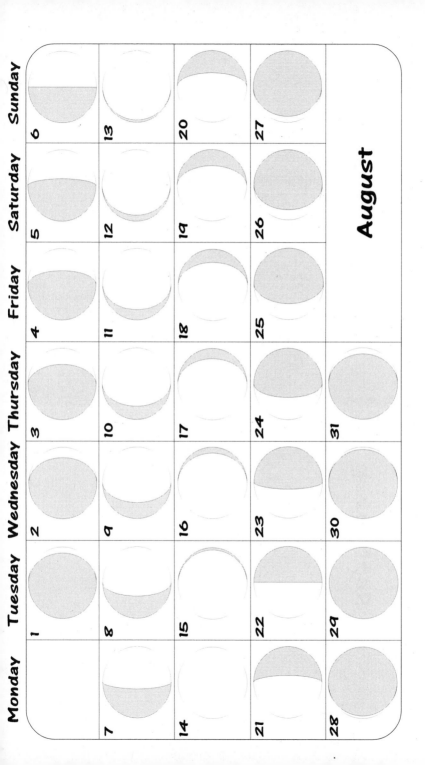

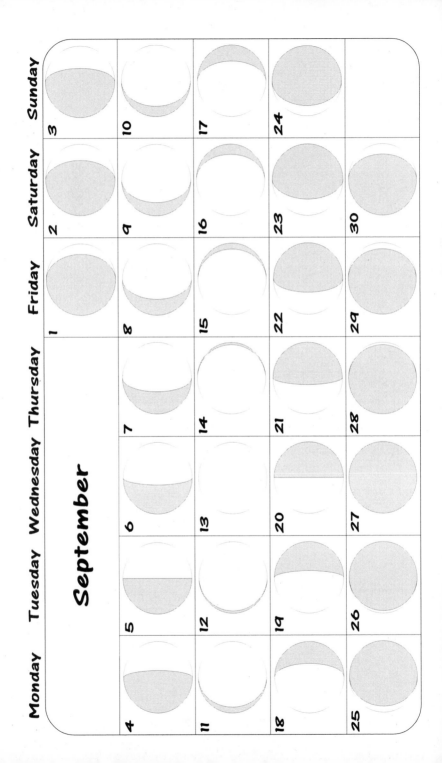

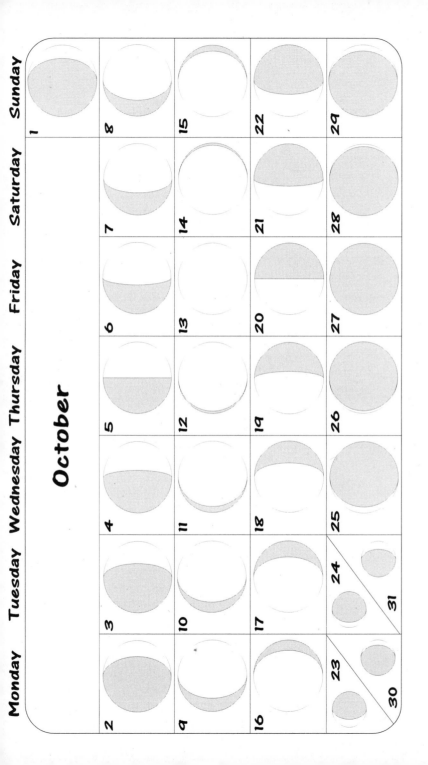

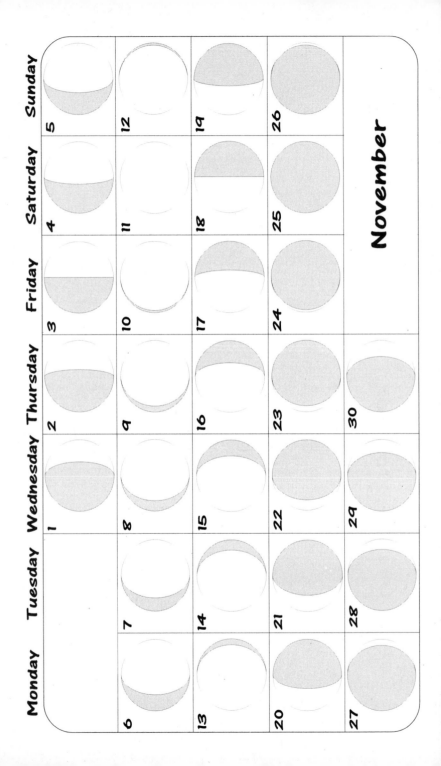

November

December

Monday	Tuesday	Wednesday	Thursday	Friday	Saturday	Sunday
				1	2	3
4	5	6	7	8	9	10
11	12	13	14	15	16	17
18	19	20	21	22	23	24
25	26	27	28	29	30	31

WORLD TIME ZONES

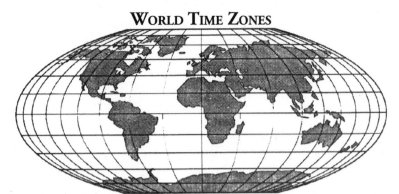

ID LW	NT BT	CA HT	YST	PST	MST	CST	EST	AST	BST	AT	WAT	GMT	CET	EET	BT	USSR Z3	USSR Z4	USSR Z5	SST	CCT	JST	GST	USSR Z10	ID LE
-12	-11	-10	-9	-8	-7	-6	-5	-4	-3	-2	-1	0	+1	+2	+3	+4	+5	+6	+7	+8	+9	+10	+11	+12
-4	-3	-2	-1	0	+1	+2	+3	+4	+5	+6	+7	+8	+9	+10	+11	+12	+13	+14	+15	+16	+17	+18	+19	+20

STANDARD TIME ZONES FROM WEST TO EAST CALCULATED FROM PST AS ZERO POINT:

IDLW:	International Date Line West	-4	**BT:**	Bagdhad Time	+11
NT/BT:	Nome Time/Bering Time	-3	**IT:**	Iran Time	+11 1/2
CA/HT:	Central Alaska & Hawaiian Time	-2	**USSR**	Zone 3	+12
YST:	Yukon Standard Time	-1	**USSR**	Zone 4	+13
PST:	Pacific Standard Time	0	**IST:**	Indian Standard Time	+13 1/2
MST:	Mountain Standard Time	+1	**USSR**	Zone 5	+14
CST:	Central Standard Time	+2	**NST:**	North Sumatra Time	+14 1/2
EST:	Eastern Standard Time	+3	**SST:**	South Sumatra Time & USSR Zone 6	+15
AST:	Atlantic Standard Time	+4	**JT:**	Java Time	+15 1/2
NFT:	Newfoundland Time	+4 1/2	**CCT:**	China Coast Time	+16
BST:	Brazil Standard Time	+5	**MT:**	Moluccas Time	+16 1/2
AT:	Azores Time	+6	**JST:**	Japanese Standard Time	+17
WAT:	West African Time	+7	**SAST:**	South Australian Standard Time	+17 1/2
GMT:	Greenwich Mean Time	+8	**GST:**	Guam Standard Time	+18
WET:	Western European Time (England)	+8	**USSR**	Zone 10	+19
CET:	Central European Time	+9	**IDLE:**	International Date Line East	+20
EET:	Eastern European Time	+10			

HOW TO CALCULATE TIME ZONE CORRECTIONS IN YOUR AREA:

ADD if you are **east** of PST (Pacific Standard Time); **SUBTRACT** if you are **west** of PST on this map (see right-hand column of chart above).

All times in this calendar are calculated from the West Coast of North America where it is made. Pacific Standard Time (PST Zone 8) is zero point for this calendar except during Daylight Savings Time (April 4–October 31, 1999 during which times are given for PDT Zone 7). If your time zone does not use Daylight Savings Time, add one hour to the standard correction during this time. At the bottom of each page EST/EDT (Eastern Standard or Daylight Time) and GMT (Greenwich Mean Time) times are also given. For all other time zones, calculate your time zone correction(s) from this map and write it on the inside cover for easy reference.

SIGNS AND SYMBOLS AT A GLANCE

PLANETS

Personal Planets are closest to Earth.

⊙ **Sun**: self radiating outward, character, ego
☽ **Moon**: inward sense of self, emotions, psyche
☿ **Mercury**: communication, travel, thought
♀ **Venus**: relationship, love, sense of beauty, empathy
♂ **Mars**: will to act, initiative, ambition

Asteroids are between Mars and Jupiter and reflect the awakening of feminine-defined energy centers in human consciousness. See "Asteroids" (p.199).

Social Planets are between personal and outer planets.

♃ **Jupiter**: expansion, opportunities, leadership
♄ **Saturn**: limits, structure, discipline
Note: the seven days of the week are named after the above seven heavenly bodies.

⚷ **Chiron**: is a small planetary body between Saturn and Uranus representing the wounded healer.

Transpersonal Planets are the outer planets.

♅ **Uranus**: cosmic consciousness, revolutionary change
♆ **Neptune**: spiritual awakening, cosmic love, all one
♇ **Pluto**: death and rebirth, deep, total change

ZODIAC SIGNS

♈	Aries
♉	Taurus
♊	Gemini
♋	Cancer
♌	Leo
♍	Virgo
♎	Libra
♏	Scorpio
♐	Sagittarius
♑	Capricorn
♒	Aquarius
♓	Pisces

ASPECTS

Aspects show the angle between planets; this informs how the planets influence each other and us. **We'Moon** lists only significant aspects:

♂ CONJUNCTION (planets are 0–5° apart)
   linked together, energy of aspected planets is mutually enhancing
⚹ SEXTILE (planets are 60° apart)
   cooperative, energies of this aspect blend well
□ SQUARE (planets are 90° apart)
   challenging, energies of this aspect are different from each other
△ TRINE (planets are 120° apart)
   harmonizing, energies of this aspect are in the same element
☍ OPPOSITION (planets are 180° apart)
   polarizing or complementing, energies are diametrically opposite
⚻ QUINCUNX (planets are 150° apart)
   variable, energies of this aspect combine contrary elements

OTHER SYMBOLS

☽ v/c: Moon is void of course from last lunar aspect till it enters new sign.
ApG–Apogee: Point in the orbit of a planet that's farthest from Earth.
PrG–Perigee: Point in the orbit of a planet that's nearest to Earth.
D or R–Direct or Retrograde: Describes when a planet moves forward (D) through the zodiac or appears to move backward (R).